FROM Baltimore TO Broadway

Joe, the Jets, and the
Super Bowl III Guarantee

FROM Baltimore TO Broadway

Joe, the Jets, and the Super Bowl III Guarantee

▼ ▼ ▼

Ed Gruver

TRIUMPH
BOOKS

Library of Congress Cataloging-in-Publication Data
Gruver, Ed, 1960-
  From Baltimore to Broadway : Joe, the Jets, and the Super Bowl III guarantee / Ed Gruver.
    p. cm.
  ISBN 978-1-60078-261-9
1. Namath, Joe Willie, 1943- 2. Baltimore Colts (Football Team)—History 3. New York Jets (Football team)—History 4. Super Bowl (3rd : 1969 : Miami, Fla.) 5. Football—History. I. Title.
  GV956.B3 G78 2009
  796.332'648—dc22

                                                                        2009018638

This book is available in quantity at special discounts for your group or organization. For further information, contact:

Triumph Books
542 South Dearborn Street
Suite 750
Chicago, Illinois 60605
(312) 939-3330
Fax (312) 663-3557
www.triumphbooks.com

Printed in U.S.A.
ISBN: 978-1-60078-261-9
Design by Sue Knopf
Photos courtesy of AP Images unless otherwise indicated

For Bobby Kane,
the Kipper

Contents

Foreword

By Don Maynard

I knew we were going to win Super Bowl III. I had played 10 years of pro football going into that game against the Baltimore Colts, and I was more confident than I had been for any game of my life. We had a great team in 1968, and we had a great team in 1967, too, but we had 15 knee operations that year and we still only got beat by a half-game for the AFL's Eastern Division title. Injuries can play a great part in any team's season. But in 1968 we only had one knee operation and that was to our backup fullback, Billy Joe.

The 1968 season was a great season for the Jets. It was a hard season, but we kept going until we got down to the two biggest games of the year—the AFL championship and the Super Bowl. To me, the biggest game of my career will always be that AFL Championship Game against the Oakland Raiders. That's the game you have to win to get to the Super Bowl. That's the pressure game. You've got to win, because if you lose, you go home and have to think about what you didn't do right.

I knew we would do okay against Baltimore if we didn't make any mistakes that could cost us. We had as good a running game as there was in football, and we had the No. 1 defense in the AFL. Our passing game, why, we had four receivers who had been All-Pro, and George Sauer, Pete Lammons, Joe Namath, and I all ended up going to the AFL All-Star Game that year. It was the first time in AFL history all three receivers from one team and their quarterback had gone to the same All-Star game.

We had good balance across the boards—offense, defense, special teams. And there were a lot of players on the Jets who knew about the ridicule and write-ups for the past nine years saying that the AFL wasn't as good as the NFL. We wanted to get even. We wanted to show we were as good as any team playing.

We had exchanged films with the Colts, and after we watched them, Pete Lammons, our tight end, told our coach, Weeb Ewbank, "Weeb, if you don't stop showing us these films, we're gonna get overconfident." Lammons said, "I guarantee ya, we're gonna beat these guys."

And that was our attitude in the team meetings the week before the Super Bowl. And then Joe Namath goes out that week to a banquet, and he makes the comment about guaranteeing a win, and naturally the writers play it up and put Joe on the spot for guaranteeing that we're going to win the game. Well, Lammons had been saying it all week long, so it wasn't anything new to us. It shook Weeb up (laughs), but us players, we just went about our business. Never even gave it a second thought.

We didn't have any doubts going into the Super Bowl. We knew we could play with anyone in the AFL or NFL. The Colts had won 10 in a row and were 15–1, but it really didn't matter to us. They were gonna run up against some ol' boys, and we were hungry.

Early in the game, I beat their zone coverage and beat it pretty bad. I was playing with a pulled hamstring, but that gave them some doubt about whether I was healthy or not. I knew they were going to be aware of me, so I lined up as wide as I could and forced Baltimore to show their coverage. When Joe came out of the huddle and walked up to the line of scrimmage, I was already lined up wide to his right. So Joe knew before he took the snap from our center, John Schmitt, that he was going to throw to his left to Sauer. Or he was going to throw the turn-in or hook pass to Lammons, or throw to one of the swinging backs, Matt Snell, Emerson Boozer, or Bill Mathis.

There were a lot of interesting things and some good strategy that worked out really well that day.

When John Unitas finally got into the game in the third quarter, the thing was, we knew he was comin'. I had played against him in the 1958 NFL Championship Game when Baltimore beat the New York Giants in the famous overtime game in Yankee Stadium. Having watched Unitas for years, you just hope the defense can stop him. But Unitas kept coming, and then the Colts scored, and then we were thinking about Johnny's track record and all the comebacks he'd made.

When I think back to it, the 1968 season was like a dream come true. To me, it took a while for everything to sink in. But when I look back, what the Jets did that season was to give hope to underdogs everywhere. People who were underdogs in their lives, they could look at the Jets season and the 1969 Super Bowl and think, *Hey, if the Jets can do the impossible, then so can I.*

It's what America is all about.

Introduction

The Age of Audacity

Preston Pearson would play in five Super Bowls, but he would never hear a sound such as this. It was a jarring, almost crushing noise, caused by a collision of anticipation and excitement from the 75,377 fans pushing their way through the turnstiles inside the Miami Orange Bowl in the early afternoon hours of January 12, 1969.

Most had come to Super Bowl III to see the Baltimore Colts, champions of the National Football League, stake their claim to being the greatest team in history. Others had come in the hope of bearing witness to a historic upset, to watch the 18-point underdogs from the Other League, the New York Jets, prove the worth of both the American Football League and the Super Bowl.

Along with his teammates, Pearson, the Colts' special teams star, ran through pregame drills in the west end of the sold-out Orange Bowl. Serving as backdrop were scudding, pewter-colored clouds and pale green palm trees that swayed from 18-mph winds. Winds of change, some said, in a decade marked by triumph and tragedy.

"It was an exciting time," Pearson said. "I was pretty aware that there were a lot of people interested in this game. Nineteen-sixty-eight had been a tumultuous year, and you were aware of what was going on in America."

What was going on was widespread unrest and a yearning for change. *Time* magazine called 1968 "the year that changed the world." The forces of social and political upheaval were everywhere and affected everyone. The assassination of civil rights leader Dr. Martin Luther

King Jr. on April 4 incited riots in 125 cities across the United States. Two days after King's death, members of the Colts watched Baltimore city become engulfed by the flames of more than a thousand fires that had been set in protest. Six people died, 700 were injured, and 4,500 were arrested amid rioting that left more than a thousand businesses burned and looted, many never to be reopened.

One of the most turbulent decades in American history reached its apex in 1968. The decade had begun with the promise of President John F. Kennedy's "New Frontier." But the torch that had been passed to a new generation of Americans was dropped in Dallas in November 1963 when America's young prince was felled by an assassin's bullets. Five years later, the brother of the young prince would fall; so, too, would a King. Camelot was over. Assassinations and riots tore the nation apart; Americans were further divided by an unpopular war in Vietnam. "Hell no, we won't let go!" became the chant of the disenchanted. Nineteen sixty-eight had become, in the words of NBC newsman Tom Brokaw, the "volcanic center of the Sixties."

Sports can, and often do, reflect the times. When Jack Johnson became the world's first black heavyweight champion in 1908, every defense of his title against a "Great White Hope" became a morality play set against the backdrop of turn-of-the-century America. The sight of the massive Johnson flashing his gold-toothed smile at ringsiders as he toyed with undersized and inferior white opponents—a black cat, it was said, playing with a white mouse—was too much for white America to endure. Each Johnson victory led to lynchings of black men and was enough to spur writer Jack London to publicly call upon white champion James J. Jeffries to come out of retirement: "Jeffries must now emerge from his alfalfa farm and remove that golden smile from Jack Johnson's face.... Jeff, it's up to you. The White Man must be rescued."

The idea of sports as symbolism soared in the Roaring Twenties, which provided the perfect setting for swashbuckling heroes Jack Dempsey, Babe Ruth, Red Grange, Knute Rockne, Bobby Jones, and Big Bill Tilden. In 1936, U.S. sprinter Jesse Owens' victories in the Berlin Olympics privately angered German chancellor Adolf Hiter.

Contrary to popular history, however, Hitler did not leave his seat in Olympic Stadium to avoid watching Owens' medal ceremonies. The Fuhrer did, however, confide to his architect, Albert Speer, that he was "highly annoyed" by the triumphs of a "primitive" over "civilized whites." Two years later, the dictator and U.S. president Franklin D. Roosevelt took intense interest in the showdown between another American black man, heavyweight champion Joe Louis, and German Max Schmeling, whom Hitler held up as personification of Aryan supremacy.

Amid the riotous summer of '68, U.S. Olympians Tommie Smith and John Carlos stood on the podium after winning the gold and bronze medals, respectively, in the 200-meter race and raised their black-gloved fists as a symbol of Black Power. In a show of solidarity, Australian Peter Norman, who had won the silver medal, wore an American civil rights badge to support Smith and Carlos.

Super Bowl III offered another such moment in time. The hippie Jets and hard-hat Colts were archetypes of their era, and the crowd, recognizing it, responded with cheers that rattled windows in a nearby neighborhood. Those with an understanding of the cultural revolution rocking America might have recalled the lyrics of Bob Dylan's 1964 protest song, "The Times They Are A-Changin'":

> *There's a battle outside*
> *And it is ragin'*
> *It'll soon shake your windows*
> *And rattle your walls*
> *For the times they are a-changin'*

Jets flanker Don Maynard believed that change was in the air. Maynard and his teammates were not social revolutionaries. But they read the newspapers, they watched the news broadcasts on television, and they knew about the issues that were dominating the day's headlines—Vietnam; LBJ and Nixon; civil rights marches and campus protests; drugs, free love and Flower Power; riots and racism; sit-ins and drop-outs. It was a different America. In retrospect, the only thing that seems stable about 1968 was the cost of living. The average price of a new home was $26,600. You could plunk down a nickel and get a first-class stamp. A gallon of gas was 34 cents; a gallon of milk was $1.07.

A former member of the New York Giants, Maynard played in the famous 1958 NFL championship against the Colts—an overtime classic that has been called the greatest pro football game ever played and is universally credited with creating the modern NFL. But Maynard was also an NFL castoff, as were several of his teammates, and they had joined the fledgling American Football League hoping for the opportunity to prove their worth as football players to the league that had cut them loose.

"We had lived in the shadow of the NFL for years," Maynard said in his Texas twang. "You don't think we were cranked up for Super Sunday? Shoot."

If the Jets were cranked up, the Colts were loose and confident. Losing was simply not in their lexicon. Dressed in bright blue nylon-durene jerseys that featured a white, UCLA-style shoulder loop popularized by Red Sanders' Bruins squads of the 1950s, the Colts carried themselves with an air of confidence that some thought bordered on arrogance. Marty Ralbovsky of the *New York Times* felt the champions of the National Football League were vainglorious in their smugness, pretending to be something more than mortal as they prepared to rout a Jets' squad listed as 18- to 22-point underdogs.

"We didn't think there was any way we could lose," Colts starting left guard Glenn Ressler said. "We had played AFL teams in the preseason and had beaten them pretty easily."

Colts All-Pro linebacker Mike Curtis believed the game was going to be as advertised—a mismatch. "We watched them on film and I thought, *Yeah, they look about like we thought they would,*" Curtis said. "We had just beaten Cleveland, and they were a very good team. So what's this AFL team? Our team was twice as good as the Jets. Twice as good. There just wasn't any comparison between the two teams."

Several members of the Jets could feel the contempt the Colts held for them. Place-kicker Jim Turner thought the Colts showed open disdain for the Jets during pregame warm-ups. Baltimore's gaudy 15-1 record in 1968 was the best in the 49-year history of its league. The Colts had lost just two games dating back to 1966 and compiled a

26–2–2 mark during the 1967–68 seasons. They outscored opponents by 258 points in 1968, and their margin of victory averaged more than 18 points per game.

"We won so easily," said quarterback Earl Morrall, the NFL's Most Valuable Player in 1968. "I thought we would win handily. We'd only lost twice in our last 30 games."

Baltimore's bulldog defense was its source of pride. The Colts were guided by a brain trust that included head coach Don Shula, who would go on to become pro football's winningest coach; defensive mastermind Bill Arnsparger, one of the game's more innovative minds and the man who would fashion the famed "53" defense that would help lead Miami to an undefeated season in 1972 and consecutive Super Bowl victories; and a young lieutenant named Chuck Noll, the future architect of Pittsburgh's "Steel Curtain" dynasty. Led by their All-Star coaching staff, the Colts tied a pro football record for fewest points allowed in a 14-game regular season with 144. They shut out four of their previous 10 opponents, including Cleveland, 34-0, in the NFL Championship Game, and surrendered just seven touchdowns in their last 10 games. They were considered by NFL experts to be a defensive unit without peer in the history of that league and were one victory away from being recognized as pro football's greatest team ever.

The frenzy surrounding the Colts' success was everywhere and thus not easy to resist. Linebacker Dennis Gaubatz graced the December 13 issue of *Life* magazine, and Baltimore poet Ogden Nash provided light verse for a seven-page color pictorial. In his writing, Nash noted the intense fan interest in the Colts:

> *"The cynic becomes a true believer*
> *When caught in the grip of that old Colts fever."*

The national media believed. In a poll taken on Super Saturday of 55 of the pro football writers who were in Miami to cover the game, 49 picked Baltimore to win. Estimated final scores for a Colts victory ranged from 27-0 to 38-0 to 47-0. Turner recalled hearing a prediction that the Jets would lose by more than 60 points. Tex Maule, who covered the NFL for *Sports Illustrated*, picked Baltimore, 43-0. All but five of the 55 who predicted a Colts win thought the final difference would be in double-digits.

Vince Lombardi, who coached the Green Bay Packers to one-sided victories over Kansas City and then Oakland in the first two AFL-NFL Championship Games, publicly dismissed the Jets' chances of victory as "infinitesimal." Privately, he had other thoughts. On the eve of the game, Lombardi encountered *Washington Star* columnist Mo Siegel at the media center in Super Bowl headquarters. The Jets, Lombardi confided, had a chance to win. The reason? Celebrated New York quarterback Joe Namath. "I've never seen," Lombardi said, "a quicker release from a passer than this kid's." And what of the point spread favoring Baltimore? Lombardi scoffed. Seventeen points, he said, is too much to give a guy like Namath.

Super Bowl III was still a half-hour away from its estimated 3:05 PM (EST) kickoff, but the crowd energy and noise level already surpassed that which accompanied the first two championship meetings between the warring leagues. This marked the first time the game was officially called the "Super Bowl," and although Miami was officially an AFL city—the expansion Dolphins joined the league in 1966—Sunshine State fans welcomed the Colts with a deafening crescendo.

Listeners to the NBC Radio broadcast strained to hear sportscasters Charlie Jones, who covered the AFL, and Pat Summerall, who covered the NFL on CBS and was on loan from the network known as the "Mighty Eye." Their pregame comments were almost drowned out at times by the noise from the huge crowd. Preston Pearson thought that if there had been a roof on the Orange Bowl, the noise would have lifted it sky-high. The young Colts player could feel his pulse racing; his adrenaline, he thought, must be pumping in gallon measures.

"I was living a dream," Pearson said. "Playing alongside a guy like Johnny Unitas and the other Colts? Wow. They already had a reputation for having played in the 1958 title game. And now we're playing the Jets, and they've got Joe Namath—brash, young whippersnapper, lady-chasin' Broadway Joe."

The object of the Colts' intensity and the crowd's attention stood in a stoop-shouldered stance at the 20-yard line at the closed end of the three-tiered stadium. Seeing Namath in person for the first time, the

Colts and NFL fans acknowledged that the AFL's Most Valuable Player in 1968 cut a charismatic figure. Baltimore special teams player Alex Hawkins found himself sneaking quick looks at Namath. Despite the fact that Namath had been playing professionally for four years, it was the first time the "Hawk" had seen Namath throw a football. Like many NFL players, Hawkins never deigned to watch an AFL game. "Not a down," he said. Without having ever seen him play, Hawkins was convinced that Namath was just another New York fabrication; "all glitter and no gold," Hawkins said. *Time* magazine would describe Namath as a "rocco rascal.... His hair was too long. His clothes were too loud. His lip was too loose."

Seeing Namath for the first time, however, the Hawk was impressed. The Jets quarterback had a nice shoulder motion, his footwork was excellent, and his feet were quick. He could, in fact, throw a football. Hawkins was impressed enough to point out Namath to Colts receiver Jimmy Orr. Because Orr was impressed as well, Hawkins figured that he had never seen Namath before, either.

One month earlier, Namath had accepted a then-hefty $10,000 payday to shave his famous Fu Manchu mustache in a live television commercial. The man glamorized as Broadway Joe would further shock football purists by appearing in a Hanes Beauty Mist pantyhose commercial in 1973 in which cameras panned a silken pair of long legs only to reveal a grinning Namath in his white Jets jersey.

"If Beauty Mist can make my legs look good," he said with a syrupy smile, "imagine what they can do for yours."

As he ran the Jets offense through its drills, Namath's skill at throwing a football was clearly evident. So, too, were the bulky steel braces that made his white uniform pants bulge at the knees. Namath's scarred legs, crystal-fragile as they were, had left him largely immobile in the pocket. But he compensated for his inability to scramble free of pressure put on by enemy defenders by developing the fastest backpedal in pro football history and matching it with a pass release as quick and accurate as a crossbow.

Cupping his hands under center John Schmitt in the warm-up prior to Super Bowl III, Namath shouted a series of signals and dropped back three steps. He moved so quickly on the sandy turf that his white uniform with the green trim seemed to be an illuminated blur; his low-cut white leather cleats flashed amid a sudden ray of sunlight. Two-inch-wide sweatbands had been pulled onto both wrists, and a streak of shoe-black was smeared beneath his eyes to cut the sun's glare. Holding the AFL's J5-V Spalding football, which was more streamlined than the NFL ball, "The Duke" (Lombardi thought the AFL ball looked "like a needle, a Long Island frankfurter"), Broadway Joe jammed his left heel into the spongy sod, straightened up, and fired in one smooth, seamless motion.

From his seat in the Orange Bowl, Lombardi studied Namath's movements on the decorated field below. The man regarded by many as "Invincible Vince" had retired as head coach of the Green Bay Packers the previous February, one month after his legendary champions had reasserted NFL dominance over the AFL by routing the Oakland Raiders, 33–14, in Super Bowl II. Lombardi had coached a future Hall of Fame quarterback in Bart Starr and had also coached against the NFL's top quarterbacks of the decade—Unitas, Y.A. Tittle, Norm Van Brocklin, Sonny Jurgensen, and Fran Tarkenton. Lombardi had seen Namath on film the previous year when the Packers were preparing for the Raiders, but watching him in person for the first time, Lombardi thought the AFL's MVP was equal to the NFL's best. "His arm, his release of the ball," Lombardi said, "are just perfect."

Namath's slick style offered a stark contrast to Colts quarterbacks Unitas and Morrall. If the 35-year-old Unitas, with his bristlebrush haircut and black hightop shoes, seemed to be a figure straight out of the conservative 1950s, the stylish, 25-year-old Namath symbolized the psychedelic 1960s. The contrast between the two seemed a perfect metaphor for an era when conservatives clashed with the counterculture.

Sociological lines were being drawn around a contest that saw the crewcut Colts challenged by the shaggy-haired Jets. The rebellious youths of the AFL were rising up against the established veterans of the NFL. Mike Curtis, nicknamed "Mad Dog" and "Animal" and said by a teammate to have political views just to the right of Attila the Hun, looked over at Namath. "Yeah," thought Curtis, a close-cropped graduate of Duke. "We've got to beat that longhair."

Super Sunday was a day for debate, and where one sat in the Orange Bowl that afternoon reflected not only if one was a fan of the AFL or NFL, but also a Democrat or Republican, hippie or a square. U.S. vice president–elect Spiro Agnew and comedian Bob Hope sat behind the Colts; Ted Kennedy and Jackie Gleason took seats behind the Jets.

There was a feeling among some that this game would be unlike any other in pro football history. Maury Allen of the *New York Post* felt the excitement surrounding Super Bowl III lifted it from the sports realm to a social event. The contrast between the AFL and NFL and the relative merits of the two leagues was discussed by Madison Avenue types and truck drivers, by wives and husbands, and by sons and fathers. Jim Simpson, an NBC sportscaster assigned to handle the halftime show, found himself debating the game with his 16-year-old son Bret.

"Check with Mr. DeRogatis or Mr. Rote," Simpson said, evoking the names of the two NBC sportscasters who would be doing color analysis of the game on TV. "You know they wouldn't say it if they didn't believe it. They think the Jets can win. They really do."

Bret Simpson, whose knowledge of the game was deepened by both his father's connections and Sunday afternoons spent at Washington Redskins games at RFK Stadium, was certain that Baltimore's ferocious blitzers would bury Broadway Joe and the Jets. Bret was a fan of the 6'7", 295-pound Colts defensive end Charles "Bubba" Smith, whose size and ferocity inspired Charm City fans to chant "Kill, Bubba, Kill!" When his father argued the Jets' cause, Bret countered with a three-word reply: "What about Bubba?"

Bubba's anger had been stirred earlier when he boarded one of the Colts' team buses bound for the Orange Bowl and saw the Jets' buses ahead of his. "Why are the Jets in front?" he asked. "The National League should be first. We're the senior league."

As game-time neared, there was hope, if not conviction, among some that the rogue Jets would topple the NFL establishment. Those wanting the status quo preserved cheered for the Colts. Fans traveling on Sunshine State Parkway to the Orange Bowl encountered a steady drizzle. By the time they reached Interstate 95, the concrete lip of the stadium was visible from its location at 1501 Northwest Third Street.

Built in the 1930s, the Orange Bowl was a college-style, bowl-shaped structure originally known as Roddy Burdine Stadium. The stadium's wooden stands were demolished in 1937 and replaced by the huge, concrete rim that became one of its trademarks. Until the Dolphins arrived in 1966, the stadium was used primarily for college football. It served as the home site of the University of Miami and as a neutral venue for the New Year's Day bowl game.

The Orange Bowl was distinctive for several reasons. Along with the pungent spray of sea air and the swaying palm trees, the stadium was known for the sudden and unpredictable winds that coursed through the open ends of the stands and played havoc with long passes and field goals. The stadium floor was a lush green at the west end, but sparse and sandy at the east end. The yard stripes, which provided a bright white-on-green contrast, were gullies.

Early arrivals saw a colorful field. A large portrait of the silver Tiffany Super Bowl Trophy to be awarded to the winner was painted against a blue rectangular background. Each end zone reflected the colors of the teams. The west end zone was bright blue and bore Baltimore's logo—a bucking Colt—with the red, white, and blue NFL shield framing the word "COLTS" painted in large white letters. The east end zone was a deep green, with "JETS" in white and framed by New York's logo—a football-shaped emblem—and the AFL logo of an eagle poised atop a football.

League loyalties were on vivid display, both inside and outside the stadium. AFL fans cheered and waved as the Jets' caravan of three team buses pulled inside the wire fence and onto stadium ground. Onlookers peered inside the windows of each bus. "Namath on this one?" As the Jets disembarked and headed for their locker room, AFL loyalists wearing $2 straw hats with a green band lifted Jets pennants high into the leaden sky. NFL fans grinned and gave thumbs-down signs.

In the press box high above the stadium floor, Howard Cosell looked up NBC sportscaster Curt Gowdy. "Cowboy," Cosell said, "the Colts are going to break Joe Namath's legs."

Norm Van Brocklin, an NFL icon, took a shot at the AFL when he announced in the press box, "Joe Namath is about to play his first pro football game."

By 2:30 PM, the sun had broken through the low ceiling of clouds, and the temperature stood at 72 degrees. The clear weather came on cue for NBC, whose cameras panned the colorful field as Gowdy opened the network's pregame show:

> *"The name of the game is defense. The offense sells the tickets, but defense wins the ballgame. And it will decide today's game between the Baltimore Colts, champions of the National Football League, and the New York Jets, champions of the American Football League, in pro football's family feud, the third annual Super Bowl game in Miami..."*

Dressed in a bright green blazer with the red interlocking NBC logo on the right breast pocket, Gowdy welcomed millions of viewers to a game that would join the 1958 Colts-Giants classic as the two most important contests in pro football history. Gowdy was gifted with a warm, distinctive voice and delivery. He had become NBC's top sports broadcaster after leaving ABC and joining the Peacock Network. He broadcast World Series games, Olympic events, and the NCAA Division I men's basketball championships. Known as the "the Cowboy"—he was born in Wyoming and was an avid outdoorsman—Gowdy was also known for his easy and informal manner behind the microphone. He avoided signature calls and catchphrases and made the occasional malapropism. To author John Updike, Gowdy sounded "like everybody's brother-in-law." To pro football fans, Gowdy was as much the voice of the AFL as Ray Scott was the NFL.

Studying the overflow crowd filling the Orange Bowl, Gowdy turned to broadcast partner and color analyst Al DeRogatis. "They could've sold 150,000 tickets to this one," Gowdy said.

NBC Sports president Carl Lindemann smiled. Two weeks before the game, Lindemann had been approached by Cosell. "I feel sorry for you," Cosell told him. "The AFL will be killed."

Lindemann was worried. He had an emotional stake in the game. Five years earlier, he had risked both his professional reputation and NBC's money when he persuaded the network's brass to pay a then-record $42 million over five years for exclusive television broadcast rights to AFL games. The contract represented five times what ABC had paid to carry the fledgling league in its formative years from 1960–63. Determined to gain a share of the booming pro football market at a time when CBS had an exclusive on the glamour package of sports, Lindemann and NBC gambled their future on what many considered to be a second-class league.

The risk paid off. NBC's money and television exposure saved the AFL, and the league's wide-open style of play on the field and the wide-open wallets of team owners lured blue-chip college athletes away from the staid NFL. By 1966, the league some had derided as a Mickey Mouse operation had forced the NFL into a merger agreement that would take place prior to the 1970 season. The AFL was the Other League no more; Mickey Mouse had become Mighty Mouse.

Still, Lindemann was concerned that Super Bowl III might be a ratings disaster for NBC. The AFL had yet to prove it was the equal of the NFL in championship play. Lombardi's Packers had forcefully stated the case for NFL superiority in the first two Super Bowls; the Green Bay strongman guided his team to victories over Kansas City and Oakland by a combined score of 68–24. The Packers' power and precision had convinced many that the Super Bowl lacked the drama and competitiveness of a true championship game. Don Weiss, the NFL's public relations director, agreed that the Super Bowl's credibility as a championship contest was in serious doubt. The NFL title games between Green Bay and Dallas in 1966 and '67 had been far more competitive than the two AFL-NFL World Championship Games that followed. The older league's dominance of its young rival was difficult to dispute. The morning after Green Bay overwhelmed Oakland in Super Bowl II, Robert Lipsyte of the *New York Times* wrote:

"It was an anticlimactic game in the sense that the millions spent to televise the game, the thousands to promote it, and the enormous emotion spent preparing for it, were not rewarded by either sustained drama or even moments of great excitement."

Lindemann knew the public's perception of the AFL as an inferior brand of football could hurt interest in Super Bowl III. Since NBC and CBS had agreed to alternate their coverage of the game on a yearly basis, he worried that NBC's ratings would pale in comparison to the numbers posted by CBS the previous year. When he saw the crowd surging into the stadium, Lindemann knew it was a good sign. Still, he tried not to look too long at the scene. *If this is a dream*, he thought, *I don't want it to blow up in my face.*

He looked instead at NBC's television monitors and saw Summerall doing taped interviews of various Colts players. Providing in-depth commentary on the NFL champions, Summerall was in the Baltimore locker room the eve of the game when he saw something that startled him. NBC technicians were applying long strips of white adhesive tape to the floor. Everyone, including the AFL's network, was so certain of a Colts victory that a rehearsal of the postgame trophy presentation was being held the day before the Super Bowl.

"This is where [Colts owner] Carroll Rosenbloom will stand," NBC techs told Summerall, who would be doing postgame interviews. "This is where Don Shula will stand."

Super Bowl III seemed more of a foregone conclusion than football contest. Two days after the AFL and NFL title games, the *New York Daily News* in its New Year's Eve edition ran a banner headline proclaiming: "COLTS SUPER 16 OVER JETS."

The betting line had been set by Jimmy "the Greek" Snyder, who set in motion the notion of a Colts stampede. The point spread, described by the *Daily News* as "surprisingly big," was stunning since the Jets were believed to be fielding a better offense than either of the AFL's two prior representatives in the Super Bowl. Amazingly, the Jets were bigger underdogs than the College All-Stars had been against the Super Bowl champion Green Bay Packers the previous August.

Favored by more than two touchdowns, the Colts arrived in Fort Lauderdale on January 5. A carnival atmosphere soon enveloped their camp. Noll, who bossed a veteran defensive backfield and was in charge of stopping Namath's vaunted passing game, believed the Colts were being blinded by the media's hailing of them as the greatest team of all time.

Supremely confident, the Colts busied themselves signing autographs, holding press conferences, hitting the beaches, and awaiting the hour of their coronation. The team was surrounded by so many distractions that even a disciplinarian as strict as Shula found it difficult to get his team to focus in Florida. It was, he said, one of the most unpleasant weeks he had ever spent getting a team prepared to play a game.

Rosenbloom added to the distractions by hosting a victory party for his coaching staff days before the game. Weiss recalled it as an informal gathering around the large swimming pool at Rosenbloom's oceanfront home on Golden Beach, an exclusive enclave 45 minutes north of Miami. The party was a mere prelude to the celebration Rosenbloom had planned once his Colts crushed the Jets and were crowned world champions. Weiss, who was on the guest list, recalled Rosenbloom sparing no expense for what the NFL's P.R. director described as the "mother of all victory parties." Some 200 people were to be invited to a celebration that would be headlined by celebrity entertainers. Among those on the guest list were Spiro Agnew and members of the Kennedy clan.

Miami Beach at the time was Vacationland, USA, a playground where grand hotels such as the Fountainebleau and Eden Roc, the Sea Isle and Casablanca were frequented by leading personalities like Jackie Gleason and Frank Sinatra, J. Edgar Hoover and Meyer Lansky. A woman interviewed by Miami station WTVJ described the South Florida scene. "So clean and beautiful with the palms and everything," she said. "Just fabulous."

While the Colts seemed distracted by their circus surroundings, the Jets warmed to it. *Sports Illustrated* photographer Neil Leifer snapped a photo of Namath looking tanned and relaxed as he lounged poolside clad only in plaid Bermuda shorts. Informed that the betting line had risen to 17 points, Namath grinned. "That's crazy," he said. "We should only be favored by nine or 10."

The response was typical Namath. He spoke the truth as he saw it. A year earlier, most of the NFL and AFL players who had arrived in the Miami Orange Bowl for Super Bowl II between Green Bay and Oakland predicted the winner along league lines. One notable star dissented. "Green Bay is just better all-around," Namath said. "The Packers are one of football's great teams, probably the best ever." Broadway Joe proved an astute judge of football talent. Green Bay handled Oakland easily.

Namath had praised Lombardi's Packers, but he angered NFL traditionalists when he downgraded Baltimore and in particular Morrall, who like Namath was his league's MVP in 1968. Unlike Namath, Morrall was a journeyman quarterback enjoying a Cinderella-like season that saw him replace the injured Unitas and lead the Colts to the finest record in franchise history. Jets split end George Sauer Jr. thought Namath showed a "genius for leadership" when he punctured the Colts' air of arrogance by telling *New York Times* sportswriter Dave Anderson that there were "four or five" quarterbacks in the AFL better than Morrall.

"Including me," Namath said.

He added that only a few of the NFL's starting quarterbacks wouldn't be third-stringers on the Jets behind him and backup Vito "Babe" Parilli. He laughed at the belief that the older league was the better league. The AFL's top teams, he said, were just as good as the best teams in the NFL.

"If this sounds like I'm bragging," he said, "I am."

Even in the Age of Aquarius, when young voices spoke out in shocking self-expression, Namath's provocative chatter made for bold headlines. Writers from NFL cities snickered at Broadway Joe's shoot-from-the-lip style. "The man spoke arrogant junk," said Jerry Green of the *Detroit Free Press*.

Joe Willie was just getting started. He ventured into a Miami Bistro called Jimmy Fazio's and found himself in what became a highly publicized verbal battle with Colts placekicker Lou Michaels, who was also the younger brother of Jets defensive coordinator Walt Michaels. Some reporters played it up the next day as a near brawl. Ralbovsky compared it instead to the 1960 Nixon-Kennedy debates and placed Namath in the role of the smiling and confident JFK and Lou Michaels as the frustrated, beleaguered Richard Nixon.

Namath's biggest bombshell, however, didn't drop until the Thursday prior to the game. He attended a banquet at the Miami Touchdown Club in honor of his winning the AFL's MVP award. League president Milt Woodard, his white hair shining beneath the bright lights, introduced Namath, who was sitting at a table on the dais swigging scotch from a tumbler. Namath rose, thanked his family and friends for their support and added that unless anyone wanted him to sit down, he had a few more things to say.

A cry of "Siddown!" rose from the back of the room. Namath laughed. "Who's that?" he asked. "Lou Michaels?"

When the voice yelled back, "Hey Namath, we're gonna kick your ...", the playboy turned prophet.

"Listen," Namath snapped. "You don't know what you're talkin' about. We're going to win Sunday. I guarantee it."

Namath remembers his startling comeback not as something that was planned or premeditated. Just anger mixed with confidence.

"It was just something that I felt and said," Namath said. "It was my heart speaking, my feelings speaking. Those guys [the Colts] were overconfident over there."

Namath's response flashed like a lightning bolt and electrified fans and media alike. The *Miami Herald* ran a banner headline the next day: "NAMATH GUARANTEES JET VICTORY." Jets head coach Wilbur "Weeb" Ewbank, who had coached the Colts to consecutive NFL titles in 1958 and '59, supported his quarterback when confronted by reporters.

"That's the way he feels about it, and I'm for him," Ewbank said. "I wouldn't give a darn for him if he didn't think we could win."

Privately, he was outraged.

"I could've shot him," Ewbank said. "Some people were talking like the Colts were going to have a dynasty. But with Joe's quick release and our two great receivers, George Sauer and Don Maynard, we thought we could lick their defense. But we didn't want to say anything before the game."

Linebacker Larry Grantham, an original member of the franchise, understood Ewbank's anger. "I don't like Doberman dogs," he said, "but I'm not going to walk into the room and kick the son of a gun in the mouth. And that's what I felt Joe had done. I know Weeb was really upset."

Jets fullback Matt Snell was glad Namath hadn't gone any further with his guarantee, and hadn't said, "I guarantee we'll win... if they play the zone they've been playing all year."

The day the story broke, George Sauer Sr., the Jets' director of player personnel and father of the club's split end, stopped defensive end Gerry Philbin in the hotel lobby.

"Gerry, this is really going to stir the Colts up," Saver said.

Philbin said that at first he had thought the same thing. But then he remembered how in the first two Super Bowls, Kansas City and Oakland had kept saying how great Green Bay was. They didn't want to get the Packers mad. The problem was some of those players started believing it themselves.

"There's no way, George," Philbin said, "this team is going to beat itself."

Jets radio broadcaster Merle Harmon was climbing from a cab the Friday morning following Namath's brash prediction when he was approached by New York's return specialist Earl Christy. "Did you hear what Joe said?" Christy asked. "Did you hear?"

"Sure, Joe guaranteed the win," Harmon recalled. "But the whole team felt that way, and they had me believing it. The Jets were a good team. They were younger and faster than the Colts."

True to his style, Namath was unmoved by the commotion. If the Colts needed newspaper clippings to fire them up, he reasoned, they were in big trouble.

Namath's persona now overshadowed the game itself. Newspapers were filled with what Ralbovsky called a "montage of Namathania." Maury Allen thought Super Bowl III should be renamed the "Joe Namath Bowl." Broadway Joe's bachelor lifestyle, Kelly green Cadillac, and $5,000 mink coat became fodder for gossip columnists. His Manhattan apartment, famous for its white llama rug, black leather bar, and oval bed with satin sheets, was featured in the *New York Times*. Namath told reporters he liked his women blonde and his Johnnie Walker Red.

Namath had become the lightning rod for all things good and bad about the modern athlete. To many, he was as much a prototypical football player as Muhammad Ali was a prototypical heavyweight champion. The comparison was apt. Five years earlier, Ali, then a brash, outspoken 22-year-old still known as Cassius Clay, overcame 7-to-1 odds and shocked aging Sonny Liston to win the heavyweight title in one of sports' biggest stunners. It had happened in Miami, not far from where Namath would be looking to shock a Colts squad that had a Liston-like invincibility about it.

Signs and wonders pointing to another historic upset seemed to be everywhere. Ewbank was startled to see a church sign near the Orange Bowl that read "The Victor Will Be Whomsoever Jesus Nameth." A professional astrologer named Jonathan Booth drew up horoscopes for the Jets and Colts to determine the Super Bowl champion. He found that the Pisces Jets would have a great desire to win, while the Aquarius Colts would be plagued by overconfidence. Booth had never seen a football game, so he couldn't predict a final score. But, he added, "The Jets have 10 aspects going for them, the Colts only six. That could be it."

In Namath's home town of Beaver Falls, Pennsylvania, a 56-year-old woman left her job at Lane's Drug Store at 2:00 PM the day of the game and walked to nearby St. Mary's Church. Joe's mother, Rose Namath Szolnoki, had spent the morning opening Lane's Drug Store at 9:00 AM just as she did every Sunday. For five hours she listened to patrons telling her how badly her son would be beaten by the Colts that afternoon. Rather than go straight home after work as she usually did, she walked to church, lit a candle, and prayed to St. Mary and St. Jude. She was nervous but confident. Rose thought it a good omen that the game was being played on January 12, and that 12 was her son's uniform number. She would have been more confident had she remembered that the letters in his first and last name totaled 12, and that his room number that week at the Galt Ocean Mile Hotel—534—added up to 12. And Rose would have been particularly pleased to know that a bouquet of 12 red roses had been sent to her son's room.

Namath had made himself the center of attention on Super Sunday, but some of the Colts dismissed his brash guarantee as mere bluster. To them, he was a frightened young man who whistles when walking past a graveyard at night to quiet his fears.

"I thought he was scared, so I just laughed it off," said middle linebacker Dennis Gaubatz, who called the signals on the field for the Colts defense and would be matching wits with Namath at the line of scrimmage. "I figured, 'No way are they going to beat us.'"

"I didn't pay any attention to it," safety Jerry Logan said. "People say things, and if you pay attention to them, then you're not doing the things you need to do to prepare for the game."

Morrall told reporters Namath was just looking for publicity. "Some guys," Morrall said, "seem to thrive on that stuff." Cornerback and defensive captain Bobby Boyd thought Broadway Joe's boast had angered some of his Colts teammates. "It got under our skins," Boyd said. Bubba Smith, for one, sounded indignant. "Namath shouldn't talk like that," Smith said. "A professional doesn't say things like that." Privately, Bubba admired Namath's bravado. "If he wins, he's a fortune teller," Smith said. "If he loses, it's still a beautiful try."

Colts coach Shula welcomed the news. His players were conscious, he said, of everything that was being written. Namath had given them more incentive. "Joe has made it much more interesting," Shula said.

The Friday press conference at the Hilton Plaza was dominated by discussions of Namath's statement. Dozens of reporters were delighted to have a new angle to cover. One of those, Dave Anderson, thought the psychology of Super Bowl III had been dramatically altered. Even though he was an NFL man, Weiss privately loved Namath's bombast, loved every reckless syllable that spilled from Joe Willie's lips. Even if they had tried, Weiss thought, the NFL's best PR men couldn't have written a better script than to have a character like Namath confronting the all-conquering Colts. His guaranteeing a Jets victory had turned literally overnight what most observers felt was a serious mismatch into a must-see event. The Colts' colossal 18-point spread had been twisted into a promotional advantage: the AFL's green-and-white clad David pitted against the NFL's blue-and-white-uniformed Goliath.

NFL commissioner Pete Rozelle embellished the theme at what Weiss called Rozelle's "state of the NFL" press conference the Friday before the game. Namath's public boasting had also helped rekindle the strong feelings that still separated AFL and NFL loyalists, further fueling the hysteria surrounding Super Bowl III.

George Sauer Jr. wondered if the psychology of the Colts had been altered, as well. He heard scattered comments expressing indignation and attributed them to Baltimore players feeling scandalized that anyone would approach an event of such magnitude with such an attitude.

He believed the incident could affect their play, making them tense without intensity.

There was more to Super Bowl III, however, than Namath and his guarantee. Plots and subplots surrounded the game. Shula and Ewbank had a long history together; both were disciples of Cleveland Browns founder and coach Paul Brown. Ewbank had scouted Shula in college, had recommended that the Browns draft the kid from John Carroll University in Ohio. Shula began his pro playing career in 1951 as a defensive back with the Browns at the same time that Ewbank served as an assistant coach with the team. He later played under Ewbank in Baltimore. When Ewbank was fired as head coach by the Colts in 1963, he was replaced by Shula. For years, the Colts organization had served as a conduit of talent to the Jets. Offensive tackle Winston Hill and defensive backs Johnny Sample and Billy Baird had spent time in Baltimore's organization. Linebacker Larry Grantham had been drafted by the Colts, and punter Curley Johnson, special teams captain Mark Smolinski, and backup wide receiver Bake Turner also had ties with Baltimore.

Because Ewbank had coached both teams, the Jets and Colts had been built along similar lines. Namath and Unitas were the two most feared quarterbacks in football; Namath and Morrall were league MVPs in 1968. New York's Matt Snell and Baltimore's Tom Matte both hailed from Ohio State and were grinding runners who led their teams in rushing that season. Hill, a 275-pound road grader at left tackle, reminded some of former Colts left tackle Jim Parker, who had retired following the 1967 season. Philbin and Bubba Smith, both left ends, were the premier pass rushers for their teams. Both the Jets and Colts led their respective leagues in defense and were No. 2 in offense. New York averaged 30 points per game; Baltimore averaged 29. Baltimore's defense had allowed a league-low 10.3 points per contest, but the Colts were only plus-7 in takeaway-giveaway differential. The Jets, despite surrendering an average of 20 points per game, twice as much as Baltimore, also owned a turnover ratio that at plus-15 was more than twice as good as that of the Colts. The latter was a telling stat, if not an outright omen, of what was to come.

The Colts had captured consecutive NFL titles in 1958 and '59 by beating another New York team, the Giants. Rosenbloom envisioned football history repeating itself 10 years later, this time at the expense of the Jets. Lombardi's retirement and the decline of his aging champions in Green Bay had created a power vacuum in pro football. Who better to fill it than a Baltimore team that had been a championship contender since 1964 and had finally reached its full potential? The Colts fielded a blend of talented veterans and rising stars. Shula was the most promising young coach in the game, and he rode herd on a team that appeared unbeatable. Weiss thought the Baltimore offense was balanced and potent, its defense ferocious. And the Colts had Unitas, who despite being injured still struck fear in enemy defenders every time he strode on the field.

Yet as kickoff neared, one concern NFL adherents shared about the Colts centered on Morrall, their rags-to-riches quarterback. Don Smith, a longtime public relations director for the Giants, had watched Morrall perform for many years, and most intently during Morrall's three seasons in New York from 1965–67. During those years, his erratic passes had often led to undistinguished outings. When Morrall would have a bad day, Smith said, he really had a bad day. As he took his seat in the control booth next to Weiss in the Orange Bowl, Smith was anxious. Weiss saw it and thought Smith was more nervous than he had ever seen him. "Just a feeling is all," Smith told Weiss.

Some of the Colts shared that feeling. Orr and Hawkins both felt Morrall had played the 1968 season in something resembling a dreamlike state. Sidling up to Hawkins before the game, Orr said, "Señor, don't let Earl wake up today. Just let him sleep for three more hours." Hawkins nodded. He knew what Orr meant.

Both Shula and Ewbank arrived in Miami bearing conservative game plans. The Colts would emphasize the ground game early. After watching films of the Jets defense, Shula was confident his team could run and pass freely against a unit coached by Walt Michaels and Buddy Ryan. On defense, Arnsparger and Noll would stick with shifting zone defenses, mixing in an eight-man maximum blitz that had struck fear into NFL quarterbacks. The latter was a crucial element in the success of the Colts defense in 1968. Pro quarterbacks can find the holes in any zone scheme if given enough time to pass. Baltimore's blitz was designed to take away that time.

Ewbank's plan was geared to the most basic running plays, namely off-tackle slants and draws, and equally simple pass patterns of hooks, flares, and screens. For New York, this scheme marked a dramatic departure from its usual style. One observer noted that during the AFL season the Jets seemed to be using "10 receivers and three balls at once" and that Namath in two nightmarish games had thrown a combined 10 interceptions.

For the Super Bowl, Ewbank stressed poise and execution on each play. He had watched the first two AFL-NFL World Championship Games and had seen the Chiefs and Raiders lose their poise against the Packers after one key error turned the direction of the game. In what is now regarded as Super Bowl I, Green Bay free safety Willie Wood's interception of a Len Dawson pass on the first series of the second half set up Elijah Pitts' short touchdown run that blew open a close game and put the Packers in front 21-10 en route to a rout. The following year, Rodger Bird's fumble of a Donny Anderson punt late in the second quarter gave Green Bay field position for a Don Chandler field goal that turned momentum in the Packers' favor.

Ewbank knew Lombardi had fielded great teams, but he felt Kansas City and Oakland had been had by the Packers. He wasn't about to be had by the Colts. In his nine years as Baltimore's head coach, Ewbank had laid the groundwork for the '68 Colts, and he knew they were talented. But he didn't believe they were as awesome as the experts were proclaiming.

"Some people were calling the Colts the greatest team in the history of the game," Ewbank recalled. "They were not. They were a pretty good team, but they weren't *that* good."

Baltimore's rotating zone defense, so complex to NFL teams who were used to seeing man-to-man coverage, was easily deciphered by Ewbank and his offensive assistant, Clive Rush, both of whom had coached against the zone for many years in the AFL. Baltimore's defense was running many of the same schemes Ewbank had installed when he had coached in Baltimore. Their zone, which they used 90 percent of the time, was built to stop the long bomb but was very effective against short passes as well if not attacked properly. "We geared our passing game to cracking the zone," Ewbank said.

TV Guide previewed the Super Bowl in its "Close-Up" by highlighting the showdown between Broadway Joe and Baltimore's intimidating defense. Yet for all the hype paid to Namath's guarantee, NBC was half an hour into its pregame show before Gowdy even mentioned it:

> *"Namath has not been bashful this week. He's come down*
> *here to Miami and said the Jets are going to win. He doesn't*
> *predict it; he guarantees it."*

It was the Age of Aquarius; the age of audacity. Because of the high stakes surrounding it, because the future of the Super Bowl as the nation's premier sporting event hinged on its outcome, Gowdy believed he was about to call the single most important game in pro football history.

"We'll see how it all comes out," Gowdy told viewers as NBC closed its pregame show.

In the years that have followed, Super Bowl III has been remembered as one man's personal showcase. But it was much more than that—much more, in fact, than a game. Its outcome transcended sports and changed the future of pro football. The Super Bowl is what it is today—a mid-winter Mardi Gras—because of what happened in the Miami Orange Bowl on January 12, 1969.

It was an event that took its shape as much from the losing team as from the winning one, an event that served as society's mirror and still resonates today.

1

On Broadway

A wet Wednesday afternoon in New York and the skies over William A. Shea Stadium, home of the New York Jets of the American Football League, were filled with steel-gray clouds. If stadiums are living things that reflect their surrounding community, as writer David Boss once said, then Shea Stadium on this early autumn afternoon was very much New York: big and spacious, littered and in some parts grimy, but filled with interesting movements from its inhabitants.

Empty and near-empty beer and soda cans rattled noisily along the wet and shiny blue, orange, green, and yellow seats, and torn bits of newspaper were tossed by whipping winds through the upper deck. Discarded food from the previous day's New York Mets baseball game was spoiling, and the dank smell filled the moist air.

Located in Flushing Meadow Park, "Big Shea" as the stadium was known, was a 64,000-seat (for football) structure that opened in 1964, the year New York hosted the World's Fair. To observers like *New Yorker* magazine writer Roger Angell, Shea Stadium seemed to be an extension of the Fair itself, an exhibit with a cyclotron profile, gargantuan scoreboard, and mix of orange-and-blue-colored seats. Home to both the Jets and Mets, Shea was made compatible for football by sliding two suspended lower-level sections until they faced one another from across the field. On this day, the stadium floor was a glistening green as the Jets ran practice plays. The huge stadium lights, the brightest in pro sports, flared on the Jets' white-and-green helmets as players splashed through puddles of gray, stagnant water and cursed the mud that seeped into their low-cut cleats. Voices rose and reverberated throughout the vast near-empty stadium and were mixed at times with the rattle of the nearby IRT trains and passenger jets from LaGuardia Airport.

The bright spot amid the gloaming was a round-shouldered, red-vested quarterback who strode to his place behind center John Schmitt at the line of scrimmage. Joe Namath's trademark white-leather cleats were spotted brown and gray from the muddied water. As he crouched low behind center with his shoulders rolled, legs bent, and feet spread, he shouted a series of signals: "72Q, 72L, Ready, Hut, Hut."

Schmitt's right arm brought ball back quickly through his legs and into Namath's cupped hands. What followed over the next few seconds was a series of movements that by 1968 had become a signature style and one of the ornaments of the modern game:

Using a quick push-off step with his right foot, Namath took seven strides straight back into the protective pocket. The last four steps were an uneven gallop—left, right, left, right—with the left leg absorbing the strain. The ball was held chest-high and away from his body; he tapped it briefly with his left hand, like a marksman checking his gun sight. Turning his hips and coiling his shoulders, his right arm raised the ball straight up in one smooth motion. The ball was raised to a cocked position behind his right ear, and his right arm then whipped forward in an arcing motion. As the pass was released, Namath's arm slammed downward and across the front of his body, which was now balancing, flamingo-like, on his straightened left leg.

The entire sequence took just 2.8 seconds—the fastest in pro football history to that point—and ended with Namath's body in a 180-degree turn. The target was a streaking receiver some 40 yards downfield, but the ball was thrown with such power and accuracy that it spiraled through sharp crosswinds and damp, heavy skies. As the white laces blurred in revolution, the pass descended directly into the hands of the receiver, who grasped it in full, unbroken stride.

"God," an onlooker said softly. "Wasn't that beautiful?"

The quarterback, celebrated along the Great White Way as "Broadway" Joe, allowed a small smile to curl his black Fu Manchu mustache, then huddled up to call the next play. In 1968, Joe Namath was considered by football purists to be an artist, and the skies above AFL stadiums provided tapestries for his bold brush strokes. It was said at the time that while other quarterbacks could throw, Joe Willie Namath could pass. Namath, in typical fashion, said at the time that he took it for granted that he looked good passing and that he had good form. His motion was easy and natural; when it wasn't, when his motion felt awkward, he knew he was doing something wrong. It was the same principle that Jim "Catfish" Hunter, who threw a perfect game in the spring of '68, applied to pitching. The Oakland A's star and future Hall of Famer deliberately wore an oversized cap on the mound that he resettled after every pitch. If he found his cap was too much askew after each delivery, the Catfish knew he was overthrowing.

Namath played the quarterback position with elegance and flair. The sight of his deep spirals against a bright blue sky on AFL Sundays was aesthetically pleasing. Writer Bob Oates Jr. thought Namath's style highly refined. "There are no excesses and no disconnections," Oates wrote. "He has created a motion that is not only pleasing to watch but perfectly suited to the task he is faced with."

LeRoy Neiman was the Jets artist-in-residence in 1968. His beret and handlebar mustache became a familiar sight in the locker room after games, and he stalked the sidelines with pen and sketch pad in hand, capturing the season's key moments in splashy, expressionist paintings that were brilliant and raw. "Namath is a drawing," Neiman said. "He's contemporary, he's action. He's in a class by himself."

Jets fans agreed. One 19-year-old woman expressed her feelings about Namath in a letter to the *New York Times*:

"Forget the Blackout of '65. Joe Willie is here. We are united for 2½ hours in sports.... This is the center of the universe now, and nothing Ali or Frazier or Seaver or Tarkenton or Lindsay ever does from now on will even come close to the spiritual uplift Broadway Joe is giving to us 64,000 Jet fans."

Namath inspired a generation of young athletes. A budding young basketball star and fellow Pennsylvania steel town area native named Pete Maravich could relate to a gifted athlete like Namath; the Pistol thought Broadway Joe wanted sports to be unpredictable and fun. In time, Maravich would adopt a mop-top hairstyle and floppy socks as accoutrements to his dazzling skills. Namath helped Maravich believe that an athlete should bring his personality and excitement to his sport. Otherwise, athletic events would be little more than robots marching to the beat of the same drummer.

David "Sonny" Werblin, an owner of the Jets and an entertainment executive who recognized Namath's star power when he played for the University of Alabama, thought the quarterback was a product of his time. More than any other football player of his era, Namath reflected the riotous paradox that was 1968. It was a year of triumph and tragedy, a year *Life Magazine* described as a "paroxysm of rage and violence, and at the end, some not inconsiderable triumph."

Social consciousness permeated every fabric of American life in the 1960s, and pro football was not immune to the changing times. On August 2, the two-time defending Super Bowl champion Green Bay Packers opened the preseason schedule with a commanding 34–17 win over the College All-Stars in Chicago's Soldier Field. Later that month, the Second City took center stage as forces of the establishment again clashed with youth, this time at the Democratic National Convention on Michigan Avenue.

NBC news anchor Tom Brokaw covered the convention, which was taking place at the Hilton Hotel in Chicago. The winds of change that engulfed the Windy City that summer created an atmosphere charged with tumult and theater. Recalling the infamous Newark riots of 1967, Chicago police outfitted their jeeps with barbed-wire canopies and armed themselves with tear gas and clubs. Demonstrators and protestors prepared for battle by rolling bandages. Assigned to riot duty outside the Hilton, Brokaw was struck by the common age of the members of the police on one side and protestors on the other. America's future, he thought, was divided. Would it ever heal?

Historian Arthur Schlesinger Jr. wondered the same. To him, 1968 was "tragic and tumultuous." It was a year that witnessed rising opposition to the Vietnam War, increased demands for civil rights and a series of indelible images—the Tet Offensive and the Battle of Saigon; the assassinations of Martin Luther King Jr. and Bobby Kennedy; Apollo 6 and *2001: A Space Odyssey* both launched in April; the Beatles' White album; the Black Panthers; Nixon and Agnew; Rowan and Martin. The forces of tradition and upheaval clashed in 1968, and Namath was among those at the forefront of this societal collision. The 1960s saw America's popular culture embrace a new-style athlete, the athlete as anti-hero. The nation's youth was shedding convention as if it was their grandfather's camel-hair coat. A polite, self-effacing heavy-weight champion like Floyd Patterson gave way to Muhammad Ali, who taunted White America with his allegiance to the Black Muslims. In baseball, the corporate-like Yankees were down; the young, collegial Mets were on the rise.

The contrast was most striking in pro football. Balding, aging Y.A. Tittle figuratively hung up his high-top black cleats and retired from the Giants following the 1964 season at almost the exact time Namath arrived in New York as the thick-maned white-shoed senior from the University of Alabama. It was a symbolic passing of the torch, and Broadway embraced its flashy young star. Namath's flamboyant play and equally flamboyant lifestyle made him a hero to young people. Yet his talent and willingness to play with pain pleased traditionalists, as well. He was a hippie in a hardhat, and he found supporters among the political left and right. *New York Times* writer Marty Ralbovsky called him a "young Ike Eisenhower in English shag and shoulder pads." Namath laced on white cleats at a time when white shoes were considered by some to be effeminate. He grew long hair in an era when players wearing anything other than a brush cut were handed helmets two sizes too small, a not-so-subtle hint from management to get a hair-cut. When veteran sportswriters who covered the straight-laced NFL editorialized about Namath's flowing locks, sideburns, and mustache, he responded with a shrug.

"The greatest Man in the history of the world had long hair and a beard," he said.

The reply was typical Namath, who grew up in the no-nonsense world of western Pennsylvania. His hometown of Beaver Falls was a poor community located in the hills some 28 miles northwest of Pittsburgh. It was a shot-and-a-beer existence where immigrants from Europe's Ukranian countries sweated in America's mills, converted to Catholicism, and drank and danced in ethnic halls. Namath remembered it as the ultimate melting pot—Czechs, Croatians, Serbians, Syrians, Greeks, Hungarians, Poles, Italians, Germans, Irish, Blacks, Hispanics, Mexicans. He referred to his own ethnicity as "Bohunk."

Beaver Falls was a place where English was the second language of many kids' parents. It was also a place where hard work was a given. Many went to early graves with black lung disease. Those lucky enough to survive labored for a lifetime amid the grime and heat of Pennsylvania's hard-rock bowels and they developed a defiance that was passed on from one generation to the next.

Joseph William Namath was the youngest of five children and was born May 31, 1943, into a Hungarian family. His grandfather, A.J., was Hungarian-born. After arriving at Ellis Island, A.J. relocated to western Pennsylvania and found work in the steel and coal industries. Joe's parents, John and Rose, divorced when he was 12 years old. His father, however, made a lasting impression when he took young Joe to the Babcock and Wilcox Company steel mill where he worked for 40 years as a roller in the Number 2 hot mill. "Hell with the lid off" was one apt description of Pittsburgh's steel mills. The combination of fiery heat and noise inside the mill scared the boy. To him, it was hell with the lid on. "I never went back there after that one time," Namath said later. "Never."

Mill life nonetheless became a part of Namath. He developed the same defiance that his relatives and friends in Beaver Falls had, a defiance that allowed them to sneer at the stares leveled by America's disapproving aristocracy.

The divorce of Namath's parents when he was in the seventh grade left a poor family poorer. His mother worked as a maid in Patterson Heights, the upper crust section of Beaver Falls. At night, she stayed up late altering the old football and baseball uniforms Joe's brothers wore so they would fit him. Namath hustled to make money. He shined shoes for 50 cents a week, ran errands for bookies, and sold old newspapers and scrap metal to junkyard owners. In time he became street-smart, hanging around pool halls and hustling his way through adolescence. A black-and-white photo of the Beaver Falls baseball team shows Namath the only one wearing a pair of shades while his team-mates squint uncomfortably into the sun. Young Joe would get his cool on by cutting class, lighting up a cigarette, and heading to the Blue Room, a pool hall that sat on the main drag, Seventh Avenue. He would stride through the front door, pass through the luncheonette, and head to the back room where a dozen Gold Crown Brunswick pool tables offered a chance to hustle pocket change into a few dollars. He became one of the leading pool sharks in town. "Where I come from," Namath said once, "ain't nobody gonna hustle me, man."

The duality that became a celebrated part of Namath's personal-ity as an adult stemmed from his youth. He was an altar boy who smoked cigarettes, a skinny slouching kid with dark eyes who, accord-ing to classmate Gerald Astor, "ignored textbooks and studied girls." Sportswriter Dick Schaap stated once that being called an intellectual next to Namath was like being called a weightlifter next to Truman Capote. Namath wasn't interested in getting good grades in school. Unmotivated, he maintained a C average. To him, status in the world was gained on the field or in the street. He figured the only smarts that gained respect were street smarts, and the only guys who had all the answers were the wise guys.

Whatever Namath's shortcomings were when it came to books, he proved himself savvy on the streets and when it came to athletics. Jets receivers coach Ken Meyer would say later that Namath's football intelligence "must be in the genius range." His true loves early on, however, were basketball and baseball. His play on the court earned praise from an Ellwood City coach named Chuck Knox, who would go on to coach pro football. He was the best shooter on his team and also starred in baseball, hitting .450 as a senior to help Beaver Falls win a WPIAL Class AA title. Tommy Lasorda talked to him about pursing a career in the major leagues, and several teams, including the Chicago Cubs, Baltimore Orioles, and St. Louis Cardinals, bid for his services. The New York Yankees, Philadelphia Phillies, and Cincinnati Reds also expressed interest. Namath's baseball idol was Pittsburgh star outfielder Roberto Clemente, and the Pirates showed an interest in Namath, as well. But it was the Cubs who made the most serious offer—$50,000. Namath thought seriously of playing baseball; he also thought about a military career. He was talked out of both by his mother, who wanted him to get a college education.

As talented as he was in baseball, Namath seemed destined to play pro football. His boyhood sports hero was Johnny Unitas. When he tried out for the Beaver Falls High School football team, Namath asked for uniform No. 19, the number worn by the Baltimore Colts' star quarterback. Namath even wore his hair in a Johnny U-style crew cut. Unitas, he knew, had made the Baltimore Colts one of the great teams in NFL history by winning consecutive titles in 1958 and '59. Namath saw in Unitas not just a fellow product of western Pennsylvania, but a guy who had to fight for everything he had. Namath emulated Unitas' playing style, and young Joe's cool command on the field earned him the nickname "Joey U."

Beaver Falls head football coach Larry Bruno acknowledged the comparison between mentor and student when he said Namath called 99 percent of his plays, just like Unitas. "I watch him out there, pausing at the line of scrimmage, and I know he's calling an audible," Bruno told reporters after Namath engineered a 39–7 win over Sharon High. "He can pick a defense apart."

Namath led Beaver Falls to an unbeaten record his senior season of 1960, and the team earned its first western Pennsylvania championship in 35 years.

"He was Number One on our team," Bruno remembered. "First one in, last one out. He was a real, honest-to-goodness player. He listened to everything I told him and tried to make us win."

He also listened to his older brothers, whom he credited in a 1972 *Time* magazine piece with teaching him his elegant throwing motion. "They taught me a single motion—simply throwing from your ear," he said. "I don't have any wasted motion."

His brothers got the credit for his throwing motion; opposing defenders were responsible for his quick drop back and release, developed, he said, strictly out of fear. "When you see those sons-abitches coming at you," he told *Time*, "you get rid of it."

Scholarship offers poured in from 52 colleges and universities, including Notre Dame, Ohio State, and Penn State. He preferred the University of Maryland because he thought it was down South. "I was stupid," he said later. "I didn't know from outside Pittsburgh."

Namath's score of 745 on the college board exams was five points less than Maryland's academic standard. Maryland officials contacted legendary University of Alabama football coach Paul "Bear" Bryant, who had formerly coached at Maryland. Namath was picked up at his house by Crimson Tide assistant coach Howard Schnellenberger and driven to Tuscaloosa to meet Bryant. The Bear was tough, a strict disciplinarian, but he was also fair. He paced the field with a leathery, lined face and a plaid fedora pulled low on his brow. He impressed his players with his commitment to winning. "Everything I am," Namath said later, "I owe to that man." Bryant returned the compliment, calling his recruiting of Namath the "best coaching decision I ever made."

Namath blossomed under Bryant's stern guidance. The man whom the Bear later called the "greatest athlete I have ever coached" was only a sophomore when he led the Crimson Tide to a 17-0 upset of Bud Wilkinson and Oklahoma in the 1963 Orange Bowl. Not widely known outside the South at the time, Namath was sipping a soda in the locker room after the game when a reporter asked him for the spelling of his last name. Before the young quarterback could answer, Bryant's booming voice cut through the din of the dressing room. "N-A-M-A-T-H!" he shouted. "And I don't think you'll have to ask next year."

The 6'2", 185-pound Namath developed into one of the top college quarterbacks in the nation. He was also one of the most controversial. He crashed his car into a tree when he lost control on a rain-slicked road and was suspended from the 1964 Sugar Bowl game against Mississippi after he was spotted drinking alcohol in town. Namath's mother and some friends rallied to his side. They begged Bryant to reconsider, and the Bear did.

In his 1964 senior season, Namath's future as a pro player was again in doubt. In an October game against North Carolina State, he rolled to his right, cut left, and felt his right knee buckle beneath him.

Crumpling to the ground in pain, he was forced to leave the game. Ice was applied to the swollen knee, and the Tide's team surgeon alleviated some of the pain by draining excess fluid from the leg. Namath returned to play half a game against Tennessee, but his right knee collapsed beneath him again the following week against Florida. Traces of blood were found amid the excess fluid drained from his knee. Steve Sloan took over at quarterback for the Tide, but when 'Bama fell behind Texas 14–0 in the Orange Bowl, Namath limped to where Bryant stood on the sideline. "I'll play," he said.

Namath's appearance in the game stunned friend Ray Abruzzese. "He was limping real bad on the leg, and he was in real pain," Abruzzese said. "I don't know how he went out there."

The torn ligaments in his leg caused excruciating pain every time he delivered a pass. With his right knee encased in a brace, Namath brought the Tide back with touchdown passes to Wayne Trimble and Ray Perkins. The desperate Longhorns tried several defensive strategies—including six- and seven-man coverages—but the gimpy Namath still picked them apart. With a minute remaining in the game and Alabama trailing 21–17, Namath began a drive that carried the Crimson Tide to the Texas 1-yard line. The miracle comeback ended when Namath, who rushed for 15 touchdowns in his career at Alabama, called his own number on a quarterback sneak and was stopped short of the goal line by All-America linebacker Tommy Nobis. The defeat didn't detract from Namath's gritty performance. He had thrown for 255 yards on one good leg and confounded the multiple defensive looks thrown at him by Texas coach Darrell Royal.

"We tried to rush him, but it didn't work, he'd hit us with those quick ones," Royal said. "We tried dropping back, he still hit it. He's fantastic about anticipating the route his receiver runs. The second the receiver makes his cut—boom! Namath lets go."

To Royal, what made Namath special wasn't just how he avoided the rush and delivered the ball quickly, but also his instincts for the passing game. "He won't seem to be watching a man, but he'll whirl and throw to a spot and the man will be there," Royal said.

The *New York Times* article on the game the next day said the 72,647 fans that jammed the Orange Bowl were "privileged to witness an exhibition that has hardly been surpassed in artistry, unruffled poise, and deadly targetry."

Among those in the Orange Bowl that New Year's Day night was Werblin and Jets coach Weeb Ewbank. "This Joe Namath can be great," said Werblin, who had been part of a syndicate that purchased the bankrupt New York Titans franchise in 1963 and renamed the team the Jets.

"He's exciting to watch when he steps back in those white shoes and tosses those long passes," Werblin told reporters. "He could bring people into the park to watch the Jets and the entire American Football League. He'd have people watching the American Football League on television. He can be as important [to the AFL] as Red Grange was to the NFL when it got started."

When someone asked what he saw in Namath, Werblin didn't hesitate.

"A star," he said. "Someone people will knock down gates to see. He's always been a winner. He can make winners of the Jets."

Jets linebacker Larry Grantham is one of just 19 players who played in the AFL for its entire 10-year existence. Grantham survived the lean years in New York when the franchise was still called the Titans and the organization seemed to be forever teetering on the brink of bankruptcy. He could see the impact Werblin was having in making the Jets respectable. Grantham thought Werblin was doing a great job of selling AFL football to the nation's largest and most influential media market—New York. The AFL might have survived with or without Namath, Grantham said, but Namath's signing led many young people in New York to become fans of the Jets and not of their aging NFL rivals, the Giants. Namath, Grantham said, "really helped younger people to identify with us."

Merle Harmon, who had arrived in New York to broadcast Jets games on WABC Radio in 1964, knew Werblin's signing of Namath meant instant prestige for the Jets and the AFL.

"Sonny wanted to make headlines all over the country," Harmon said. "He wanted to put football on the same level as baseball. Sonny wanted a star system. He was a star-maker, and he was promotion-minded."

Harmon recalled that after the Yankees won the 1964 American League pennant, Werblin had a large sign posted near Yankee Stadium offering the Yankees congratulations from the Jets. Yankee Stadium was, of course, also home to the New York Giants football team, and Werblin made sure to add a little something extra to his congratulatory sign—a not-so-subtle dig at the Giants:

"Congratulations to the Yankees from the New York Jets. Come see the Jets play."

Ewbank was as impressed with Namath as Werblin was. Namath, he said, had a presence about him. The Jets coach had noticed fans in the Orange Bowl moving to the edge of their seats when Namath entered the game. Ewbank said he had never seen anything more exciting than Namath. An incredible statement, considering the fact Ewbank had coached Johnny Unitas in the 1958 overtime classic in Yankee Stadium. "I see in him," Ewbank said of Namath, "the same things I saw in Unitas."

Ewbank noted that even though Namath couldn't play at his best from a physical standpoint against Texas, he had still managed to provide his teammates with a tremendous emotional lift. "That's leadership," Ewbank said.

Namath left Alabama owning several school records, including most passes completed (237), most yards passing (3,054), and most touchdown passes (28). The Tide's record during his three years as a starter was 29-4. They had also gone to three bowl games. Namath's slingshot arm had dazzled some of college football's best defenses and frustrated coaches and players alike. When a University of Mississippi coach asked his defensive back why he couldn't stop Namath's passes, the flustered player remarked, "He gets back and throws so quick, you don't have time to cover a receiver."

Namath's stay in the South earned him a reputation as college football's top quarterback. He also developed a new accent—a down-home Southern drawl that one writer said would suggest his forefathers had fought under the banners of Breckenridge and Beauregard. He also adopted a good ol' boy nickname, "Joe Willie." The latter helped teammates forget he was from up North. Eastern writers called him "Joe

Willie White Shoes." Namath responded by referring to media on the other side of the Mason-Dixon Line as the "Northern" press.

Jets scout and later director of player development George Sauer Sr. had followed Namath's progress on the field, and he delivered a glowing report. He gave Namath a No. 1 rating in tangible qualities such as size, agility, quickness, reaction time, coordination, and intelligence, as well as intangibles such as aggressiveness, pride, and potential. Namath was given a No. 2 rating in strength, speed, durability, and character. He received the highest evaluation—1-plus—on the pro rating guide. Sauer wrote that Namath was an "outstanding passer with big hands and exceptionally fast delivery. Has good agility and sets up very well. Throws the short pass very well and also throws the bomb with great accuracy. Is smart and follows the game plan perfectly. Is a fine leader and the team has great confidence in him. Will be everyone's number-one draft choice."

Sauer underlined the last line. At a time of heightened tension between the leagues, the importance of signing Namath was understood by both the AFL and NFL.

To get Namath, the Jets had to first move up in the AFL draft and then outbid the NFL. The Houston Oilers had finished last in the Eastern Conference in 1964 and thus were ahead of the Jets in the draft. The Oilers were also in the market for a young quarterback. The AFL at the time remained a parochial league; club owners looked to attract fans by signing college players their fans were familiar with. Houston was interested in Tulsa quarterback Jerry Rhome, who had played against the University of Houston. Oilers fans knew Rhome; he led the nation in passing and would finish second to Notre Dame's John Huarte in the Heisman Trophy vote. They knew less about Namath, except that he ran Bear Bryant's offense at Alabama and had suffered a serious knee injury his senior season.

The Jets had acquired the rights to Rhome the previous year in the AFL's redshirt draft. Werblin, who craved a star quarterback and didn't see Rhome as the kind who could command attention in New York, was more than happy to make a deal with the Oilers. Houston, which owned two high picks in the draft, was just as eager to in effect swap Namath for Rhome. On November 28, 1964, the Oilers chose Baylor end Lawrence Elkins with their top pick after the Jets took Namath with the first overall choice. In the NFL draft, the St. Louis Cardinals also selected Namath.

Bryant asked both the Jets and Cardinals to wait until the end of Alabama's regular season to speak with Namath, and both sides agreed. The Tuesday after the season was over, Werblin was in a Birmingham hotel talking terms with Namath and his lawyer, attorney Mike Bite. The Cardinals surprised Namath by sending two representatives to his dormitory.

"What would it take to sign you?" they asked.

"Uh, yeah, $200,000," he answered.

Shocked, one of the Cardinal reps fell backward on Namath's bunk bed. "Oh, $200,000!"

Namath wasn't finished.

"And a new car," he added.

Seemingly put off at first by his requests, the Cardinals agreed. They asked Namath to sign with them that day. He refused. "No, I have to get a lawyer. I'm not signing anything 'til after the Orange Bowl, and I need to talk to the New York Jets before I commit to anyone."

Behind the scenes, there was maneuvering going on within the NFL to have the Cardinals sign Namath and then trade him to the Giants. Such a move would serve to make up for the Giants losing Ohio State fullback Matt Snell to the Jets the year before and would all but guarantee that the Giants, and not the Jets, would remain the football kings of New York. Namath knew the Giants were prepared to step in and make a deal with the Cardinals.

Namath and Bite eventually met with Cardinals vice president Bill Bidwill. Each time an important point was raised, Bidwill excused himself from the table, left the room, and called his brother, Stormy, who was team president. In what stands as a vivid display of the seriousness of the signing war between the AFL and NFL, Stormy was also acting as an intermediary between the Cardinals and Giants.

The bidding war escalated. Namath said later that the Cardinals eventually went as high as $400,000. They also asked if he'd be willing to play for the Giants. Namath didn't like the way the Cardinals did business, and he didn't like the fact that their offer included a stipulation that he would host a radio show.

"Man, I'm just a football player," Namath told St. Louis team officials. "And what I make will be for football only."

Prior to the Orange Bowl, Namath had dinner with Werblin. "Mr. Werblin," he said, "I knew three weeks ago that the Giants were dealing for me. I just wanted to tell you not to worry about anything you hear. I'm going to play for the Jets."

The Jets had lost more than $1.4 million in 1963-64, but Werblin believed the team was one star player away from filling Shea Stadium to its capacity every game day. He sold Namath on the idea of being that star, on the benefits of playing in New York, and of playing in the AFL, where he would be free to express himself and wouldn't have to conform to standards. Namath liked wearing white leather cleats—they made his feet feel quicker than black shoes. He liked that Werblin accepted him for who he was, that the AFL played a wide-open brand of ball, and that Ewbank had once coached his idol, Johnny Unitas.

What Namath also liked is that the Jets had a connection to western Pennsylvania. Offensive line coach Chuck Knox had previously been a coach at Ellwood City and had befriended Namath in ninth grade. Knox helped negotiate the deal between Namath and the Jets, and Namath said later that the Pittsburgh connection gave him a level of comfort. To him, Knox represented not only the Jets, but something more. He represented home; he represented western Pennsylvania.

The Jets announced the signing the next morning in a press conference at the Miami Harbor Inn Hotel. "We don't care to divulge the figures," Werblin remarked, "but I believe it is the largest amount ever given to an athlete for professional services."

In time, the stunning details of the then-record $427,000 deal would shock the sports world. Namath would receive a base salary of $25,000 for four years; a signing bonus of $200,000; $30,000 to cover Bite's attorney fees; scouting positions for Namath's brothers, Bob and Frank, and brother-in-law Tommy Sims at $10,000 apiece for three years; and a Lincoln Continental, valued at $7,000. Namath showed up for the press conference outfitted in a pink sports jacket, white shirt, dark tie, and dark slacks.

He grinned when someone asked about the fancy pink car that was said to be part of the deal. "It's green," Namath said. "Jet green."

The hefty contract brought swift reactions from the sports and entertainment worlds. Cleveland quarterback Frank Ryan, who had just guided the Browns to a startling 27–0 upset of the Colts in the NFL championship, scoffed at the big money the Jets were paying an unproven rookie.

"If that kid is worth $400,000," Ryan said, "then I'm worth a million." Comedian Bob Hope used the Namath signing as material for his stand-up routine. "Joe Namath's the only quarterback in history," he said, "who will play in a business suit."

In Baltimore, Johnny Unitas' wife, Dorothy, read the headline heralding Namath's signing: Ewbank Says $400,000 Quarterback Another Unitas.

She smiled. "Yeah," she thought. "Only richer."

Los Angeles Rams defensive end David "Deacon" Jones, who in 1964 was in the fourth year of his Hall of Fame career, thought Namath's contract was "crazy." So, too, did Kansas City Chiefs veteran quarterback Len Dawson. An NFL castoff, Dawson had led the then-Dallas Texans to an AFL title in 1962, beating two-time defending champion Houston in the longest game in pro football history to that point.

"Four hundred thousand dollars to play football, well, that's ridiculous," Dawson said. "Football players said it was ridiculous. Everybody said it was ridiculous for somebody to pay that kind of money. But what it did accomplish is to get everybody to look at the American Football League. Finally, they said, 'I'm going to watch this.'"

Green Bay Packers assistant coach Dave Hanner frowned on the deal. Any bonus baby who makes that kind of money before he plays a single down as a pro, Hanner said, won't be willing to pay the price necessary to succeed at the game's highest level.

Namath disregarded such talk. You don't play four years under Bear Bryant, he said, without paying a price. Bryant, too, dismissed questions about Namath's ability to make it in the pro game. Namath was not only the greatest athlete he had ever coached, the Bear said, he was the greatest he had ever seen. "He's quick as a cat, perfectly coordinated, and has a trigger mind," Bryant said. "He should be a great pro."

Almost immediately after his signing, Namath underwent surgery on his right knee. Werblin had *Sports Illustrated* do a four-page feature on the operation and Namath's recovery for one of its February 1965 issues. For the cover of its July 19 issue, *Sports Illustrated* ran a picture of a smiling Namath posed, in his Jets uniform, at the intersection of Broadway and Seventh Avenue. That it was the same spot where actor James Dean had been pictured in a photo titled "Boulevard of Broken Dreams" was not lost on Namath.

In 1963, The Drifters recorded a hit song titled "On Broadway" that told the story of a young man trying to make his way amid the neon lights:

> *They say that I won't last too long*
> *On Broadway*
> *I'll catch a Greyhound bus for home, they all say...*
> *But no they're wrong, I know they are*
> *And I won't quit till I'm a star*
> *On Broadway*

When a writer from the *New York Times* asked Namath, "Hey kid, suppose you don't make it?" the western Pennsylvania product showed some steel city resolve.

"You can forget all about my injury, the pressure on me, everything," he said. "Throw them all out, because I am going to make it."

The Jets' signing of Namath altered the balance of power between the AFL and NFL. The *New York Times* Pulitzer Prize winner Arthur Daley wrote of Werblin: "With one gesture, he saved the Jets, saved the AFL and set the wheels spinning inexorably along the road to merger." A Giants fan was said to have told his Jets counterpart on a subway ride, "You were minor league until you got Namath." AFL insiders agreed. NBC's television contract with the league and Namath's signing forced the NFL to take their rival seriously.

After spending four years in Tuscaloosa, Namath quickly acclimated himself to New York City. He rented an apartment in Manhattan's fashionable Upper East Side for $500 a month and turned it into a personal Xanadu at a cost of $25,000. His chic surroundings included an oval bed with satin sheets and Siberian snow leopard throw pillows;

a wall-to-wall white llama rug 6" thick; a fully-stocked black leather bar; and an elaborate stereo system. He bragged that he had the same decorator as Frank Sinatra. The *New York Times* was impressed enough to feature Namath's apartment on its fashion pages.

Drawn to New York's nightlife like a mariner to a siren's song, Namath escorted various blondes to celebrity nightspots like the Pussycat, Dudes 'n Dolls, Mr. Laffs, P.J. Clarke's, and Small's Paradise. *Time* labeled him the "lion of the single bars." He was New York's biggest hell-raiser since Babe Ruth, who used to cruise Broadway in a coonskin coat. Namath was the last rebel; he once spilled his drink on Sinatra. Cash flowed freely. He estimated at the time that he spent $25,000 a year "on nothin', man." With his long hair and sunglasses, he seemed more rock star than football star. Writer Dan Jenkins proclaimed Namath "pro football's very own Beatle."

Namath drew the attention of a new generation of fans. People who cared little for football cared about Namath. Men loved his swagger; women loved his sex appeal. Celebrities were caught up in Namathania. Actress Connie Stevens, a platinum blonde who knew something about sex appeal, smiled coyly when asked about her interest in Broadway Joe. "Why would I want to date a guy," she smiled, "with two bum knees and a quick release?"

The attention Namath received in his early years with the Jets didn't always sit well with the team's veteran players. There was an undercurrent of resentment among some players concerning Namath's money and publicity. Don Maynard was a veteran who didn't share those feelings. To him, Namath's contract could only help to raise salary levels not only on the Jets, but around the league.

"I thought, 'If Joe's making all that money, I can make more, too,'" Maynard said.

"I know the linemen and the special teams guys who were making $10,000 or $11,000 a year didn't resent Namath's contract," Merle Harmon said. "They knew it changed the whole financial structure in pro football. When Joe signed for $400,000, everybody's contract went up."

Jets offensive tackle Winston Hill had traveled a tough road to pro football. He had been cut by the Colts in 1963 and then by the Jets. He was kept on New York's taxi squad before becoming a starter and eventually one of the best linemen in AFL history. He was in his third year with the Jets when Namath was signed.

"I've always thought that you had three kinds of players—the bad, the good, and the great," Hill said. "And then you had players who used greatness as a springboard to becoming something special."

Hill was impressed by Namath's work ethic and by the fact that Broadway Joe didn't act like a star around his teammates. Because of his bad knees, Namath was excused from running laps and sprints after practice with the rest of the team.

"He could have gone to the training room and no one would have said anything about it," Hill said. "Instead, he would be over on the sidelines doing hundreds of sit-ups. He didn't have to do that, but he did. To work with Joe and be around him was a great experience. It was special; people like Joe make you want to be better at what you do."

Hill recalled there being "some dissension" on the team concerning Namath's contract during that first training camp. "We had a team meeting and Namath got up to speak—he was the last one—and he said, 'Some of you are concerned about how much I'm making. I'm getting from the Jets as much as I can, same as you. We're all doing the same thing, we're all playing a game we love. So don't be angry with me.'"

Namath's speech, Hill said, had the desired effect. "It diffused a lot of concerns," he said.

Initially, there was also some concern about Namath's ability to develop some touch on his passes. Everyone acknowledged the strength of his throwing arm. "He could throw a ball through a wall," Jets center John Schmitt said. The finesse, the feel and touch on short passes, however, was lacking. Jets punter Curley Johnson watched Namath work out and thought the kid "didn't throw the ball that damn well." Maynard and George Sauer, New York's starting wide receivers, had their doubts, as well. Maynard thought Namath fired the short pass when he didn't have to. "He'd knock us over on short patterns," he said. Sauer felt Namath needed to improve not just his touch but also his timing on short- and medium-range passes. Namath didn't know how to throw on the break, Sauer said. The ball was always early or late.

Namath's statistics his first two years in the AFL gave credence to the concerns of his teamates. He threw for a combined 37 touchdowns

in 1965 and '66 but was intercepted 42 times. Still, he won AFL
Rookie of the Year honors in '65, and two years later, he put all the
elements of his game together. He completed 15 consecutive passes
in one game and became the first pro quarterback to pass for more
than 4,000 yards in a season when he totaled 4,007 in 1967. His 258
completions were bettered by just two other quarterbacks in pro history. Namath was just 24 years old, but he was already accomplishing
things few others had ever done.

"Joe has come along even faster than we expected," Ewbank said
at the time. "It takes three or four years to make a pro quarterback.
There's too much to learn. You can't do it in less time."

Namath was unusually quick at reading AFL defenses, one of the
benefits of a deep drop that saw him set up eight-to-10 yards behind
the line of scrimmage. Most quarterbacks at the time were dropping six
and seven yards deep.

"Weeb had him set up in a seven-step drop, and that meant it took
the defense an extra two or three seconds to get to him," Harmon said.
"His arm was so quick and powerful it was tough for blitzers to get to
him. By the time they got near him, the ball was gone."

Namath's quick progress was even more impressive considering the
fragile state of his knees. By 1968, Broadway Joe's knees may have been
the most famous in the history of the American Medical Association.
Since joining the Jets in 1965, he had twice undergone surgery to repair
cartilage and ligaments in his knees. The operations were successful,
but the pain persisted. It was a dull throb mostly, but at times during
games the pain would flare up and vibrate through his legs.

His knees were girded every Sunday in steel and rubber, "like radial
tires," *Time* magazine said. In postgame locker rooms, Namath would
slowly strip the adhesive tape that held the steel and rubber braces to
his knees, revealing joints that were red and swollen. Sports columnist
Elinor Kaine thought Namath had "Achilles' knees" and that the
original shape of them was almost unrecognizable after games. "He has
played in pain more often than not," she wrote. Namath would limp
to the trainer's room, where Jeff Snedeker was waiting to insert long
needles into the quarterback's knees to drain excess fluid. The man
some saw only as pro football's playboy would limp back to his locker,

where he would lower himself onto his stool and apply ice bags to his scalpel-scarred knees.

Ewbank told Namath that by the time Joe turned 40, he'd have an arthritic knee like someone who was 75. "That's the price he is paying to play football," Ewbank said.

Namath didn't miss a game due to injury during his first five years in pro football, but then the brutalities of the sports caught up with him. He was sidelined for 28 of a possible 56 games from 1970-73. When he did play, he would sometimes have his knees drained at halftime so he could continue playing. Years of constant injury and insufficient recovery time damaged the cartilage in his knees and left him in a debilitated state later in his retirement years. In April 1992, he had total knee replacement done on both legs.

In 1967, *Pro Football Illustrated* called Namath a "portrait of pain and pride" and featured him and Unitas on the cover of its AFL-NFL preview issue. Comparisons of the two men dominated the 1967 off-season. *Sport* magazine declared that Namath's rapid development as a pro quarterback would have been unrivaled had Unitas not done the same in the 1950s.

"In the past 15 years, only Johnny Unitas established himself faster as a quarterback," wrote the editors of *Sport*. "But not even Unitas became a superstar at the box office so quickly."

"Traveling with Joe was like traveling with a rock group," Harmon said. "It was quite an experience. He was a major attraction, not only in Shea Stadium but also on the road. We'd go into hotels on the road, and the lobby would be jammed with fans. It was unbelievable how he would draw people. He was like The Beatles. They were famous, but they could *play*. And Joe was like that. He was famous, and he could *play*. Joe never lost sight of what his job was, and that was to pick the Jets up by their bootstraps and make them winners."

While many looked at Namath and saw little more than Broadway Joe, Harmon knew there was more to the Jets quarterback than his earthy good looks and playboy image. In the mid-1960s, the Buffalo Bills featured one of the great defenses of the era. Led by Tom Sestak, Mike Stratton, Butch Byrd and Co., the Bills of 1963–66 became the only team in AFL history, and the only pro team of the decade, to reach the postseason four straight seasons. In 1964–65, they joined the 1960–61 Houston Oilers as the only AFL teams to win consecutive league titles.

Harmon recalls Namath routinely struggling against the Bills' rugged defense, especially in games played in Buffalo's infamous War Memorial Stadium, a depression-era structure known as the Rockpile.

"In one game up in Buffalo, Sestak buried Joe in the mud," Harmon said. "Joe had mud and blood over his face. After the game, reporters asked Sestak if he had something against Namath. Sestak said, 'No. If you don't play your best against Namath, he won't respect you.'

"Reporters then went to the Jets' locker room and asked Namath if Sestak had taken any cheap shots. Joe told them, 'He didn't take any cheap shots. He's my friend, and I respect him.'"

The answer was typical Namath: honest and direct. In the language of the times, he was cool and hip, but he could also be sharply self-critical. After throwing five interceptions in a loss, Namath greeted reporters at his locker with the words, "I stink." When a reporter tried to console him in defeat following a different Jets loss, Namath became angry. "No fault of mine?" he shouted. "I'm the quarterback. You kiddin' me? We didn't get enough points on the board. That's my job, man. I'm the quarterback."

"That's how Joe was," Harmon said. "He was a competitor. Everybody thought of him as Broadway Joe, but he told me once, 'If I did all the things people said I did, I would've been dead five years ago.' Joe never got credit for knowing the game. He could pick a defense apart. He would check off [audibilize at the line of scrimmage] all the time. Drove Weeb crazy."

Few knew that Namath kept a movie projector in his luxurious bachelor's pad, and that he studied game films for hours. Namath watched so much game film that he said he dreamed in 8 mm.

"He paid the price," Maynard said. "He worked as hard and studied as much film as anybody." Maynard would watch Namath show up early for practice and stay late. The veteran wide receiver thought the kid quarterback was doing all the right things, the things that would help speed his acceptance by teammates. Namath, Maynard thought, not only came to play—he came to win.

Namath had enjoyed a record-breaking season in 1967, and Harmon began noticing an interesting phenomenon that would take place in AFL games at Shea Stadium. The fans were totally into Namath. When Namath trotted off the field in his customary slope-shouldered, head-bowed manner, fans would leave their seats and head to the concession stands. If the Jets defense forced a turnover, fans would turn around in the aisles and wait to see if Broadway Joe could get them a score. Jets fans, Harmon realized, were only interested in watching that one man. Jets beat writers noticed something else. The whole Shea Stadium throng would stand at the first sight of Namath going into his backpedal. *New York Times* writer Gerald Eskenazi thought it showed the amount of anticipation fans had for what was about to happen when Namath had the ball.

At the start of the 1968 season, Namath was named offensive captain by the same teammates that had doubted him just years earlier. Having convinced them of his abilities as a passer, he was now being asked to make the transition from being a great quarterback to being a great leader.

Namath was initially suprised to be named captain. To him, it was one of the most flattering things a player could achieve. Curley Johnson told him that his teammates wanted him to have more responsibility. At first Namath thought Johnson was kidding. Then he realized that getting voted captain by your teammates shows that they like your work ethic. Next to being on a championship team, Namath thought it was the highest honor he could earn.

Broadway Joe was taking center stage for the 1968 season. But at the same time a new star was rising on Broadway, an old one was receding in Baltimore.

The career of Colts great Johnny Unitas was suddenly in serious jeopardy.

2

The Old Master

On an early autumn afternoon in Baltimore's Memorial Stadium, Colts quarterback Johnny Unitas took the snap from center, began the quick, shuffling drop into the pocket that served as one of the signature styles of the National Football League in the 1960s, and threw a short peg of a pass intended for a receiver no more than a dozen yards away.

"*Uunnnhh!*"

Unitas' involuntary groan was the result of what happens when pain and advancing age mix in a man's system, when torn muscles send shock waves against nerves so raw they might have been scraped by sandpaper. Ripped from deep inside the usually stoic Unitas, the loud grunt startled everyone at the practice session. Horseshoe-adorned helmets snapped in the direction of their legendary leader.

In Unitas' long career, his strong psyche had been exposed to extreme pain before. In a 1958 game against the Western Conference rival Los Angeles Rams, Unitas wore a 9-lb. corset made of molded aluminum and sponge rubber during games to protect two cracked ribs and a collapsed lung. He was diagnosed with pneumothorax, and rumors flew that he had been given last rites of the church in the hospital. Yet he suited up for the game against the Rams in what amounted to an aluminum suit of armor.

"With that vest around him," former Colts coach Weeb Ewbank said, "John really looked like one of the knights of old, riding to rescue the fair damsel.... John was our knight in shining armor." On the first play from scrimmage, Unitas dropped back and fired a long touchdown pass to halfback Lenny Moore.

Unitas only wore the protective vest for a short time, but the target he bore never left him. In an era when quarterbacks weren't protected by the rules, Johnny U was a marked man. "If they fall behind," Rams sack specialist David "Deacon" Jones said of the Colts, "then Unitas has to throw deeper and that's when we get him. That extra split second John needs to get rid of the ball is just what we need." NFL Films president Steve Sabol, a cameraman in the 1960s, would keep his lens on Unitas after the pass was thrown. He was astounded by what he saw. After virtually every delivery, Unitas took a hit—in the throat, in the mouth, in the stomach, across the knees.

The punishment he took would, in time, leave the fingers on his famous right hand without strength. He would be rendered unable to lift a hammer, button buttons, or use zippers. In retirement, he was forced to use his other hand, his left, to do such everyday things as brush his teeth, hold a cup of coffee, or answer a telephone.

His condition was the direct result of life in pro football's wrecking yard. In a 1960s game against the Chicago Bears that was infamous for its brutality, Unitas was so beaten up his teammates couldn't even bear to look in his direction. Blood poured from his face after he was belted during a blitz. Baltimore's team trainer tried to take him out of the game. Unitas spat blood on the ground. "If you take me out," he said, "I'll kill you." Disdaining medical treatment, Johnny U scooped a handful of mud from the ground and stuffed it up his nose to stop the flow of blood. He fired a touchdown bomb on the next play.

Johnny Bridgers, who coached the Colts offensive and defensive lines in 1957-58, thought that while Unitas had a strong and accurate arm and could throw any type of pass—the hitch, the slant, quick outs, square-ins, fly or go passes, deep posts, sideline and corner routes—his most outstanding attributes were what Bridgers called the three C's:

concentration, confidence, and courage. Unitas had the ability to take punishing hits and continue to perform well despite pain and injuries that would have sidelined most NFL quarterbacks. "He showed tremendous concentration and courage," Bridgers said.

Ernie Accorsi, who worked in the Colts' PR department during the Unitas era, believed the purest definition of leadership was watching John Unitas get off the team bus. To many, Unitas was not only *a* Baltimore Colt, he was *the* Baltimore Colt. And he was not only *a* quarterback, he was *the* quarterback. He could feather short passes like Joe Montana would decades later, spiral deep bombs like Dan Marino, and scramble when necessary like John Elway. He didn't master the 2-minute drill like Roger Staubach or Tom Brady later would—he *invented* it. Yet what made Johnny U remarkable wasn't his arm or his skill, Accorsi thought. It was what was inside his stomach—pure guts.

"He would take the hits, get knocked down, get up, and dust himself off," Colts left guard Glenn Ressler said. "Even when there was tremendous pressure on him, he was always in command. That was John."

"John led by example," Colts linebacker Mike Curtis said, and playing through pain helped Unitas earn the nickname Mr. Quarterback. Even his surname inspired leadership—Johnny Unite-Us. Colts fans bedecked Memorial Stadium with banners proclaiming "Unitas We Stand." He would throw for 290 touchdown passes and more than 40,000 yards in an era when NFL rules didn't favor the passing game, when his receivers could be mugged while running pass routes, when defensive linemen like the Deacon could head-slap their way past his blockers and exact revenge on the man known as the Golden Arm. Unitas, however, never seemed fazed. Legendary Baltimore sportswriter John Steadman thought Johnny U was beyond intimidation, immune to pressure. "Totally immune," Steadman added.

Unitas had arrived on the national scene at the same time as another young swashbuckler, golf champion Arnold Palmer. Their careers, their styles, paralleled one another to a certain degree. Both captured their first major title in 1958—Arnie at the Masters in April, and Johnny U in Yankee Stadium that December. But this was 1968, not 1958, and Unitas was no longer the crewcut, 25-year-old kid fresh from the rock-strewn fields of semi-pro ball. He still wore the high-top fade and high-top cleats, but he was 35 now, and his angular face with its taut skin and high Slavic cheekbones was weathered and bearing the marks of life in the NFL. His nose bore a scar across its bridge, a byproduct of being pro football's most marked man. A surgeon had cut into his knee in 1965, and he had played through a painful shoulder injury in 1966 and a sore right elbow in '67.

Dick Szymanski, a 13-year NFL veteran who played center and linebacker for the Colts, believed Unitas to be the toughest player he had ever known. Teammate Preston Pearson thought Johnny U's toughness and talent made him the undisputed leader of the offense. "He'd get hit in the mouth, get bloodied, get knocked down, and get beat up. Then he'd get up, call the play, and throw a touchdown. He was the master."

Linebacker Dennis Gaubatz had played against Unitas as a member of the Detroit Lions before he was dealt to Baltimore in 1965. The trade had pleased Gaubatz for several reasons, not the least of which was that he now played on the same side as Johnny U rather than against him.

"He was something else," Gaubatz said. "We could be down by 20 points late in a game, and we would win. It was all Unitas. He took some hits, had a few injuries, but he always came back."

But even Johnny U was discouraged by this most recent injury, one that occurred suddenly and seemingly without explanation in the Colts' final preseason game, a September 7 outing against Dallas in the Cotton Bowl. Unitas played the first quarter, found tight end John Mackey for an 84-yard score, and then took the second quarter off to allow newly signed backup Earl Morrall to gain needed playing time. Unitas returned to start the third quarter, and on his first attempt of the second half, he snapped off a pass to Mackey. In the midst of his follow-through, Unitas actually heard something rip in his right arm. He later described it as a "tearing sound." Shock waves of pain shot up his arm. He lost feeling in his fingers. Morrall looked at Unitas, saw his eyes narrow and his lips tighten, and knew something was wrong. Unitas played on, but his passes floated instead of zipped, and his passing form—which Morrall thought was classic—was now suddenly altered. Absent was the exaggerated wrist movement as the ball left his right hand, an inside-out flip in which his wrist rotated counter-clockwise until his palm was facing out and his fingers were pointing to the right.

Anxiety was growing on the Baltimore sideline. Teammates heard defensive leader Bobby Boyd tell a team doctor, "Get him outta there! He's gonna ruin his arm!"

Unitas played through the third quarter and into the fourth. The score was tied at 10 when Unitas, facing a third-and-25, tried to throw deep. The ball traveled a slow, humpbacked course and fell far short. All eyes on the Colts sideline turned and looked at Unitas. His left hand was gripping his right elbow. Morrall finished the game, and in the days that followed Unitas' arm swelled and turned black and blue beneath the elbow. His pain was such that he had trouble bending his elbow or raising his arm above his head; it was difficult to even straighten it out. The Colts tried numerous treatments—ice packs, heat lamps, massages, whirlpool baths—but it not until the following Thursday that Unitas even attempted to again throw a football. He tried two or three tosses to head coach Don Shula, then had to stop.

Unitas' final pass that day fell several yards short of its intended target and took a nosedive into the infield dirt. As the ball bounced along the scruffy, divot-laden turf of Memorial Stadium, pro football's most revered quarterback lowered his bright white helmet with the royal blue horseshoe in disappointment and kicked at the baseball infield with the toe of his black hightop cleats.

"Oh hell," he muttered. "Damn!"

Watching from the sidelines was writer Larry King. A biographer of Louis Armstrong and Bill Buckley, King was in Baltimore to do a story on the trials of the Colts' future Hall of Famer. As Unitas walked off the field with shoulders sagging, King noticed that the quarterback's right arm, once tanned and muscular, seemed shrunken in diameter and slightly discolored. The sight of Unitas, in this moment of agonized failure, stirred inside King painful memories of a night at Madison Square Garden 17 years prior, a night that had seen a balding Joe Louis knocked out of the ring by a young bull from Brockton, Massachusetts, named Rocky Marciano. It was, King would write, a "sense of things all wrong and out of place."

King's sentiment reflected the high regard observers had for Unitas. His was a heroic story, the saga of an athlete overcoming all odds to achieve startling success. If Broadway Joe Namath was the fifth Beatle, then Johnny Unitas was a throwback to the era of Elvis. If Namath was Broadway, a complex live-and-let-live figure moving easily among a colorful backdrop of love beads, long hair, and loud music, Unitas blended comfortably into Baltimore's shot-and-a-beer surroundings. With his sandy brown U.S. Marine-style brushcut hair and rugged face, Unitas was the favored son of Baltimore's bar patrons. The swing-shift crowd that lifted beer glasses to toast Maryland governor and vice president-elect Spiro T. Agnew also toasted Johnny U.

Paul Wiggin, a defensive end for the Cleveland Browns in the 1960s, thought Unitas bridged the gap between the 1950s and '60s and that Johnny U belonged to his era in the way that Broadway Joe belonged to his. While Namath favored flowing hair and a Fu Manchu mustache, Unitas was as clean cut as a Kiwanian. Namath was, in the language of the Sixties, a swinger; Unitas was as square as the dice that hung from the rearview of a '57 Chevy. Namath knocked back Johnnie Walker Red scotch; Unitas sipped an occasional beer. Broadway Joe tooled around town in a Lincoln Continental; Johnny U drove a Pontiac. Namath lived and moved amid New York's hustle and bustle; Unitas resided in a quiet Maryland suburb with his wife and children.

On the surface, there seemed to be few similarities between pro football's two leading men. If their personalities and personal styles differed, then so, too, did their business interests. Unitas owned a Maryland restaurant called The Golden Arm. Namath was part owner of a New York singles bar, Bachelors III.

Beneath their surface exteriors, however, Johnny U and Joe Willie shared common ground. Both had been born into large immigrant families from Eastern Europe and were raised in western Pennsylvania towns just 25 miles apart. Unitas was one of four children born to a Lithuanian coal miner; Namath was one of five children born to a Hungarian mill worker. Both men suffered the absence of a father. Unitas was four years old when his father died of pneumonia; Namath was 12 when his father left the family following a divorce. Both had been raised by industrious mothers. Unitas' mother took control of her late husband's coal delivery service and even drove the truck herself. She would later work as a cleaning woman in downtown Pittsburgh offices and take a second job in a restaurant and a third in a bakery. Namath's mother, too, would work as a domestic to help feed her family.

Johnny U's last name—pronounced early in his career by some as "Uni-tahs"—was a phonetic transliteration of a common Lithuanian surname, Jonaitis. He grew up in a Pittsburgh suburb that was less than an hour's drive north from Namath's hometown of Beaver Falls. Both starred at quarterback in their respective high schools, and both eventually matriculated at southern universities after failing entrance exams at the original schools of their choice. Unitas went to Louisville but would have preferred the University of Pittsburgh; Namath went to Alabama after failing to make the grade at the University of Maryland.

With his father gone, Unitas helped his mother run the family business. At age 8, he was hauling coal through the streets. He inherited his toughness from his mother. "We did what we had to in order to get along," he said once. "We didn't panic."

He played quarterback at tiny St. Justin High School and beat out former Pittsburgh Steelers chairman and then North Catholic quarterback Dan Rooney for All-Catholic first team honors. Unitas went on to the University of Louisville, where his college coach, Frank Camp, remembered the teenage quarterback as a "little kid, skinny, with that same crewcut." The skinny kid compensated for his unimpressive physical stature with a personality of pure steel. Playing against the University of Houston, Unitas faced a fourth-and-2 at his own 40-yard line late in the game. The score was tied at 21, and Louisville's fullback asked Unitas to give him the ball on the next play. As a younger player, Unitas could have shirked responsibility for controlling the huddle and just handed the ball off. Instead, he leveled a cold glare at his teammate. "When I want you to take it," he said, "I'll tell you." Rather than hand off, Unitas delivered a 40-yard touchdown on the next play.

The daring play, the deep strike, would become a Unitas trademark. "I don't know what he uses for blood," Hall of Fame coach Sid Gillman once remarked, "but whatever it is, I'll guarantee you it isn't warm." NFL defenses swore Unitas spit ice water, but the truth is he wasn't always perceived to be an emotional giant.

After graduating from Louisville, Unitas was chosen by his hometown Pittsburgh Steelers in the ninth round of the 1955 NFL draft, the 102nd overall pick. Dan Rooney had remembered him from his high school days and pushed for the Steelers to draft him. "We don't want him playing against us," Rooney told Steeler scouts.

Pittsburgh coach Walt Kiesling took one look at the gawky, gaunt Unitas, saw his 170 pounds stretched over his 6'1" frame, and thought the Rooneys were nuts. The word around Steelers camp that summer was that Unitas was so excitable he couldn't even call plays. Veterans called the wiry kid "Clem Kadiddlehopper," a mocking reference to the country bumpkin played by comedian Red Skelton on his TV show. Kiesling mistook Unitas' excitably for lack of smarts. "The kid's just too dumb to be a pro quarterback," he said. "He'll never amount to anything."

Art Rooney Jr., however, said later that Kiesling never gave Unitas a chance. Every time it was Unitas' turn to pass, the coach would look at the clock and blow his whistle. When Kiesling cut him, Johnny U fumed. He had never been given a chance, he said. The Steelers went on to suffer a long series of losing seasons. The Colts went on to win four NFL championships. Some call what happened to the Steelers the Curse of Unitas, the NFL's equivalent to the Curse of the Bambino that afflicted the Boston Red Sox for decades after they dealt Babe Ruth to the New York Yankees. There just might be something to it. Johnny U's final NFL start came in 1973 at Pittsburgh. The Steel Curtain sacked him six times in the first half, and he was taken out of the game. He retired in 1973, and with Unitas gone from the NFL, the Steelers would, one year later, win the first of four Super Bowl titles they would claim in the next six years.

Unitas was married by the time he was first cut by Pittsburgh. He had wed Dorothy Jean Hoelle. The young couple had a child and was expecting a second. After being released by the Steelers, Unitas returned to Pittsburgh. To save the $10 the Steelers had advanced him for travel money, he hitchhiked his way home. He took a $100 a week job operating a pile driver on a road construction crew. One of his duties was to be monkey man for the crew, and he would shimmy up rigs as high as 125 feet in the air to grease the chutes. It was a hard, dirty job, and it exhausted 12 hours of his day, every day. Years later, he shrugged at the memory of the long hours and the tough work. It left him time at night, he said, to play football.

He joined the Bloomfield Rams, a semi-pro team in the Steel Bowl Conference. Their field at the Arsenal School in Lawrenceville was strewn with rocks, broken glass, gravel, and lead musket balls that still remained from the explosion of the Allegheny Arsenal during the Civil War. In the summer, the grassless dirt bowl had to be oiled to keep the dust storms down. Because he joined the team after the season started, Unitas had to rummage through a pile of used uniforms and old equipment in order to suit up and play. He dressed in a nearby shack and after games would carry his mud-caked uniform home to be cleaned. There were no team trainers to massage his tired and aching muscles, no whirlpools to soak in to alleviate soreness and pain. Still, Unitas said later that what mattered most were not the bush-league conditions associated with semi-pro ball, but the fact that there was a football team that wanted him.

The Unitas legend has long held that he played with Bloomfield for $6 per game. In fact, the man who would later become pro football's greatest quarterback only earned $3 per game with the Rams. And the $6 figure? That, Unitas once grimly recalled, represented championship game money, not regular game pay.

Opponents welcomed the gangly kid into the Pittsburgh Greater League in typical fashion; forced to scramble, Unitas was heading toward the sideline and relative safety when he was driven by defenders into a concrete wall that stretched the length of the playground's sideline. Standing over him, an opponent sneered. "Welcome to the Steel Bowl Conference." Teammates could be just as tough. When Unitas told Fred Zangaro in the huddle to cut over the middle for a short pass, Zangaro spat into the grimy turf. "Kiss my ass," Zangaro said.

Unitas later told *Sports Illustrated* NFL writer Paul Zimmerman that while it may have been called semi-pro football, it was actually a sandlot game. Just a bunch of guys, Unitas said, knocking the hell out of each other on an oil-soaked field beneath the Bloomfield Bridge. Disabled millworkers and ex-mill workers helped fill the rosters. Tackle Clay Dalrymple remembered his offensive line as "five guys, seven arms."

Unitas spent the fall of 1955 playing semi-pro ball and made enough of an impression that word reached the NFL that the skinny kid playing quarterback for Bloomfield might be worth a second look. Unitas received a phone call the following January from Colts general manager Don Kellett. Considered the most famous phone call in NFL history, Kellett invited Unitas to camp for a tryout. Unitas had also been contacted by Cleveland Browns coach Paul Brown, who was a year away from drafting another young talent, Syracuse running back Jim Brown. Had he not opted for the Colts, Unitas might have been teamed in the same Cleveland backfield with Jim Brown. Instead, Unitas signed with Baltimore, prompting Kellett to forever proclaim his 80-cent phone call the "best buy in the history of football."

There are more revisions to the Unitas legend. It has long been believed that Kellett contacted Unitas after a Colts fan wrote the GM and told him to "look at a great quarterback playing for the Bloomfield Rams." The Colts did indeed receiver a letter—Ewbank wondered if it came from Unitas himself—but Kellett had, in fact, been scanning the NFL waiver wire list in 1956 seeking a backup quarterback for starter George Shaw. Second-stringer Gary Kerkorian was planning to retire soon, and Kellett came across Unitas' name on the waiver list. He contacted Steelers assistant coach Herman Ball. "The kid can throw the football," Ball told him. Kellett then had Ewbank contact his friend and Unitas' former college coach at Louisville, Frank Camp. Camp assured the Colts that Unitas was worth a tryout, and Kellett placed his famous phone call.

Signed as a backup, Unitas won the starter's role in the fourth game of the 1956 regular season when Shaw went down with an injury. It became the NFL's version of New York Yankees first baseman Wally Pipp taking a day off and giving his lineup spot to Lou Gehrig, the man who would become known as the Iron Horse after playing in a then-record 2,130 consecutive games. Like Gehrig, Unitas became a fixture in the starting lineup, relegating Shaw, like Pipp, to a backup role. When healthy, Johnny U would remain the Colts starting quarterback for the next 17 seasons. To teammates and Colts fans, he was the Main Man.

Ewbank was impressed with Unitas' ability and attitude. "He could throw short or long," Ewbank recalled. "He had guts. He wasn't afraid of being tackled." Ewbank said Unitas looked the way a quarterback should look; his passing form—with his left arm extended and his right arm drawn back like an archer—was a model for others to copy. One measure of the man was that while other pro quarterbacks were compared to Unitas, he was never compared to anyone. There were other great quarterbacks in the NFL at the time—future Hall of Famers Bart Starr, Y.A. Tittle, Sonny Jurgensen, and Fran Tarkenton—but Unitas stood out.

"There were few men, if any," Ewbank said, "who could surpass him as a football player and a leader."

Even his appearance was unique. He was listed at 6'1" but his stooped, rounded shoulders made him appear shorter. Bridgers didn't think Unitas measured up to his listed height or weight of 190 pounds. Unitas' long arms hung loosely at his sides. His feet toed in, and he walked with a bow-legged gait. He wore his white football pants so high that his belt was buckled just beneath the large number 19 on his blue-and-white Colts' jersey. His black hightop cleats, usually reserved for the linemen of the era, gave his long, thin legs a weighted appearance. Former Dallas Cowboys executive Gil Brandt, however, believed people looked at Unitas and recognized a hero. Maybe the cleats weren't stylish for a quarterback, but it was fitting that he wore linemen's shoes since he played the game with the mindset of a pulling guard. He stood tall in the pocket, looking statuesque in his high-waisted white pants, and despite the furious, frenzied rush of defenders clawing their way toward him like hungry lions toward an antelope, Unitas would defiantly hold the ball for an extra split second, seemingly daring the defense to come get him.

Famed New York sportswriter Jimmy Cannon marveled at Unitas' calm amid the storm. "His serenity," he wrote, "suggests contempt for the people trying to get their hands on him."

One of those people was 6'5", 280-pound defensive tackle Merlin Olsen, a member of the Los Angeles Rams' famous Fearsome Foursome. Olsen said that while the Rams celebrated defense, which included fellow Hall of Famer Deacon Jones, could intimidate other

NFL quarterbacks, it was impossible to intimidate Unitas. Olsen had high regard for Unitas' passing arm and football smarts. But what made Johnny U stand out from the rest, he said, was one thing. "His courage," Olsen said. The great Rams lineman often heard that Unitas would hold the ball a second longer than he had to, just so he could take the hit and laugh in the defender's face.

Brutal, physical defenses ruled the day in Green Bay and Chicago, Detroit and Minnesota, Los Angeles and New York, but Unitas seemed immune to the pain they inflicted. Vikings defensive end Jim Marshall thought that while other quarterbacks might have good and bad days on the field, Unitas always lived up to being Unitas. "He was always on top of his game," Marshall said. George Allen served as defensive lieutenant under George Halas when the Bears rode one of the decade's great defenses to the 1963 NFL championship. Allen later built the Rams' Fearsome Foursome that won division titles in 1967 and '69. To Allen, Unitas was the most difficult man he ever tried to draw up a defense for, more difficult even than Jim Brown. Allen thought Unitas became even more dangerous after he was hurt than he had been before.

"We tried to slow him down by beating on him until you'd think he couldn't get up," Allen said. "But he'd get up and knock *you* out."

Unitas could be as tough on his teammates as he could be on opponents. If an offensive lineman wasn't doing his job, Johnny U would call him out. "Damnit, what are you trying to do, get me killed? C'mon, do your job."

"If you got beat physically, John never said a word," said Ressler. "But if you made a mental mistake, that was another thing. He didn't tolerate mental mistakes."

He didn't tolerate any backtalk in the huddle, either. A story favored by some of the Colts from the 1950s involved Unitas and the Colts great halfback, Lenny Moore. In a 1958 game against the 49ers, Unitas called Moore's number for half a dozen consecutive running plays. Moore, a slashing runner, was gaining good yardage, but he finally told Unitas, "Hey, man, cool it. I'm getting tired."

Unitas fixed Moore with a flinty stare. "Listen, asshole, nobody tells me to cool it. I'll run your ass 'til you die."

The shaken Moore had the fear of God put into him. "Forget I said anything, John," he stammered. "Give me the ball, please. Give me the ball on every play."

Unitas, who considered Moore to be a natural talent that comes along once in a lifetime, remembered there was no stopping his half-back that afternoon. Moore, he said, even ran one in backwards from 20 yards out.

In a time when the AFL-NFL rivalry was white-hot, the Colts quarterback was often cited as the difference between the warring leagues. "We don't have Unitas," Lou Saban, coach of the AFL champion Buffalo Bills, said in 1964. "But 13 other NFL teams don't have him, either." Washington Redskins coach Bill McPeak thought the distinction between Unitas and other quarterbacks was that Johnny U had more of a physical impact on every game he played in. "He's not looking to eat the ball or throw a harmless incompletion if the pocket is invaded," McPeak said. "He's more willing to take off and find a secondary open spot to throw to."

Unitas helped bring color to an era when NFL games were still being broadcast in black and white. He took what defenses dished out, stared them down with an icy glare, and froze them with convincing pump-fakes. Like Bill Haley and the Comets, Unitas could rock around the clock. Packers All-Pro cornerback Herb Adderley recalled Unitas taking a physical beating for almost four full quarters and still throwing the winning touchdown in the waning moments. "Maybe you're tiring, but he isn't," Adderley said. "He's standing in there to knock you out, and he usually does."

Unitas personified Hemingway's ideal of grace under pressure. When he broke in with Baltimore in the fifties, the idea of "cool" was defined by Elvis the Pelvis and James Dean. Like a 1950s drag racer, Unitas would take the wheel of his souped-up offense and, with the convertible top down and Top 40 hits turned up, burn rubber through the NFL's best defenses. In late-game situations he was like greased lightning, driving his team to numerous game-winning scores.

Johnny U's competitive fire burned brightest on December 28, 1958, when the Colts and Giants met in the NFL Championship Game. A cold dusk had descended on New York City. Inside majestic

Yankee Stadium, however, players on both sides thought the dark clouds avoided the cathedral-like structure; it seemed instead to glow with wealth and prestige.

Playing in his first title game, Unitas directed the Colts to an early 14–3 lead. Throughout the first half, Johnny U had played the quarterback position as if he was inventing it; here was Beethoven conducting his Fifth Symphony. But the Giants famed defense, coached by Tom Landry and including such famous surnames as Huff, Robustelli, Grier, and Tunnell, rose up in the second half and snatched the momentum from the young maestro. They stopped the Colts on a crucial goal-line stand in the third quarter and held them scoreless while New York's offense surged to a 17–14 lead.

With 1:56 remaining in regulation, Baltimore got the ball back for one final drive. Unitas and Co. were backed up to their 15-yard line. Fronting them was the NFL's best defense and a huge crowd that shook historic Yankee Stadium with tribal chants: "Dee-fense... Dee-fense..."

The howling mob and a nationwide television audience knew Unitas would have to engineer a masterpiece of a march to tie or win the game. He would, in fact, produce two such drives. Relying on his entire repertoire, Johnny U began a play sequence that became the standard for two-minute marches. On NBC Radio, Joe Boland called one of the most dramatic drives in NFL history:

> *"Baltimore is 85 yards away from a touchdown... Unitas back, sets, looks, throws out to the right... good to his flanker man Moore at the 25... A minute-fifteen to go. Unitas sets, throws, it's good to Berry in the middle of the Giant secondary, shakes one man shakes another and is caught up at the 50-yard line by Sam Huff..."*

Fifty years later, a review of NBC's original telecast shows the young Unitas, dazzling in his white Colts' uniform, dropping back in the pocket and then rolling out and waving his receivers past the first-down yard markers as he coolly scrambles away from the Giants rush. As Baltimore drove downfield and toward the tying score, Boland described the drama:

> *"Unitas fakes, throws to Berry, who is tackled at the 35-yard
> line of New York... Forty seconds left... Unitas back to throw,
> does throw, it's good to Berry. He's down at the 13-yard
> line..."*

These were Colts on a fast track and Johnny U was a jockey who didn't spare the whip. The second-year quarterback was operating in a white-hot creative state, and a national television audience, one that included President Eisenhower, had tuned its dials to NBC to witness the future of pro football unfold in front of them. Even the players on the field, even the Giants themselves, were struck by what they were witnessing.

"You're just a spectator, but you're watching and you know that the Colts have Unitas, Berry, [Alan] Ameche, and Moore, and that we had one of the top defenses in the league, and we had to shut them down," said Don Maynard, a Giants return specialist who was also a backup flanker and defensive back. "And a whole nation was watching this."

Even though he was on the opposing team, Maynard, an offense-minded player, appreciated the unique chemistry between Unitas and Berry, who were combining to frustrate the game's greatest defense.

"I was a backup defensive back, too, so I'm watching and thinking that our defense has to overlap, cheat a couple of steps to stop Unitas and Berry," he said. "Huff was thinking that he would drop off a little to his right [from his middle linebacker position], but Unitas is thinking, too."

The chess match concluded with Colts kicker Steve Myhra tying the game at 17 in the final seconds with a 20-yard field goal—no easy thing for Myhra, who made only 4-of-10 field goal attempts during the regular season. The tie forced the first sudden-death overtime in NFL championship history. When Baltimore got the ball back following a New York punt, Boland's broadcast partner Bill McColgan painted vivid word pictures for his listening audience:

> *"It's 4:35 here in the east, and the lights in Yankee Stadium
> are invaluable now because dusk is falling. It's a wonderful
> picture... First-and-10 for the Baltimore Colts... Unitas gives*

to [L.G.] Dupre off-tackle. Dupre still on his feet, comes across the 30 to the 32-yard line...

"Some fans have moved to the sidelines now... Unitas calls the signals, going back to throw, he throws the flare pass to Ameche... Unitas back to throw, starts to run with the ball, now he throws... It's good to Berry, he's at the 45... The fake to Dupre, handoff to Ameche, he's at the 30, the 25, down at the 20-yard line...

"Many of the fans are surrounding the gridiron... Unitas throws the quick one to Berry, makes a fine grab at the 10-yard line... A tremendous football game... Unitas throws a flare pass out to the right... It's good to [Jim] Mutscheller at the 1-yard line!... Unitas has been sensational this afternoon..."

Steadman watched the action unfold on the field below and thought Unitas was calling plays with the delicate touch of a surgeon wielding a scalpel. He probed away at the Giants, cutting here, taking away there, and setting up the next spot he would strike. To Steadman, the magnificent Giants defense was like a patient under local anesthetic; they knew what was happening but were powerless to stop it.

Down on the sidelines, bundled against the cold in his overcoat and fedora, Ewbank was struck by his quarterback's skill and poise. "We're in the driver's seat now," he thought. Still, the Colts coach nearly fainted when he saw Unitas deliver the diagonal pass to Mutscheller in the flat. An interception by the Giants could have resulted in a score for New York. Later, Unitas calmly—almost coldly—told reporters he would have thrown the ball away if his receiver had been covered.

"When you know what you're doing," he stated, "you don't get intercepted. Mutscheller was there. All I had to do was hit him."

The Colts were in field goal range, but Unitas was still throwing not because strategy dictated it, but because that was Johnny U's style of quarterbacking—daring, ingenious, clutch. "You have to gamble or die in this league," he told *Sports Illustrated*'s Tex Maule. "I don't know if you can call something controlled gambling, but that's how I look at my play-calling."

Under the circumstances, one writer noted, Unitas couldn't have moused it any more than Van Gogh could have done postcard landscapes. The Colts were on history's doorstep, and a national audience was on the edge of its collective seat. Johnny U bowed his helmet into the huddle and called "19 Power," an off-tackle slant. Chuck Thompson provided the historic call on NBC-TV:

> *"Here come the Colts to the line of scrimmage... Unitas over the center... the ball is snapped, given to Ameche, he is over for a touchdown! The Colts are the world champions!"*

It's called the greatest pro football game ever played, and maybe it wasn't, but no game was ever more important to creating interest in NFL than the '58 classic. "This is the game that did it for NFL football," wrote the editors of *The First Fifty Years: The Story of the National Football League*. "As John Unitas crafted the sudden-death drive to its bravura touchdown, pro football was exploded into the mind of America."

Beau Riffenburgh, author of the *Official NFL Encyclopedia*, called the overtime march the "best single drive in NFL history." Writing for the *New York Times Magazine*, Stephen J. Dubner called the drive the "13 plays to glory, as they are known in the football canon." One could make an argument for the greatest drive being Bart Starr's late-game heroics that defeated Dallas and the elements in the 1967 epic, the "Ice Bowl;" Joe Montana's march against the Cowboys for the '81 NFC title that was capped by "The Catch;" or John Elway's classic series against Cleveland in the '86 AFC Championship Game, remembered in NFL lore as "The Drive." But it was Unitas who had set the precedent.

He inspired a generation of future greats. "If you were a quarterback," said Paul Krause, a future Hall of Fame safety for the Minnesota Vikings in the 1960s and 1970s, "you wanted to be Johnny U." Starr spent hours studying game films of Unitas; Namath wore his uniform Number 19 in high school in honor of him. Dan Fouts thought Unitas was head and shoulders above everyone else in his era. "There was no doubt when he was playing who the best quarterback was," Fouts said.

Even Hall of Famers who preceded him deferred to Johnny U. Chicago Bears legend Sid Luckman said the elements of the Unitas style—how he dropped back to pass, how he held the ball, how he threw—were textbook perfect. Luckman also liked Unitas' courage. "He just said, 'I'm going back, come get me.' He was better than me. Better than (Sammy) Baugh. Better than anyone."

Johnny U's creative genius created the concept of what a modern quarterback should be. The position became defined as he played it. His style of pump-faking the ball was often imitated but never duplicated. Lee Grosscup, a quarterback for the Giants and New York Titans in the 1960s, thought the Unitas influence was wide-spread. "Nearly every young quarterback who sees Unitas wants to copy him," said Grosscup, who attempted to imitate Unitas in 1961 after watching him on film. Grosscup tried to emulate the way Johnny U shuffled back after taking the center's snap, then planted his right foot, pump-faked, and threw. But while Unitas did it in a flowing seamless rhythm, however, Grosscup felt his imitation was awkward. Giants coach Allie Sherman watched Grosscup trying to copy Unitas in training camp in '61. "You can't be Unitas," he said. "You've got to be Grosscup."

When it came to the NFL, Unitas bridged the gap between the fabulous Fifties and psychadelic Sixties. On December 9, 1956, he threw a touchdown against the Rams in a 31-7 loss. The strike served not only as the lone score for Baltimore, but as the beginning of a historic streak that would see Unitas throw at least one touchdown in the Colts next 47 games. His consecutive-games record is pro football's answer to Joe DiMaggio's Major League Baseball record 56-game hitting streak. Unitas' streak ended on December 11, 1960, almost four full years to the day after it started and against the same team, the Rams. Again the Colts lost, this time by a score of 10–3.

Unitas' rise to greatness paralleled the NFL's rise to its status as the nation's top spectator sport. He set 22 NFL records, reached the gold standard of passing for 300 or more yards in a game 26 times, and played in 10 Pro Bowl games. He and Berry perfected the sideline pattern and are one of several pass-catch combinations—along with Namath/Maynard and Joe Montana/Jerry Rice—to be enshrined in the Pro Football Hall of Fame.

Working tirelessly together, Unitas and Berry turned their passing plays into precise patterns. It was estimated during their era that an NFL quarterback needed an average of 2.5 seconds to deliver the ball.

Realizing that, Unitas timed his shuffling retreat on the sideline out pass to Berry to require no more than 1.2 seconds. That gave him 1.3 seconds to look for Berry. Figuring the ball would be in the air for one second, Unitas and Berry timed their out patterns to be completed in just 3.5 seconds. The Colts scientific passing game left defenses struggling to cope.

In Ewbank's system, Unitas had different depths on his drop back passes. The three-step drop was used for patterns that took 1.5 to 2.3 seconds—hitch passes, quick outs, and slants. Patterns timed between 2.3 and 4 seconds required a five-step drop. Unitas' initial drop was deeper than the depth from which he threw. As soon as he planted his back foot on the final step of his drop, he would slide his back foot forward and then step with his front foot in the direction of his intended receiver. For their quarterback to be effective, Colts linemen had to prevent defenders from breaching the area behind the line of scrimmage that Bridgers referred to as "no-man's land"—three yards from behind the line of scrimmage to a depth of 10 yards and a width from the outside foot of the left tackle to the outside foot of the right tackle.

If Unitas was pressured by the defense, he would wait until the last second to release the ball. One reason was his field vision; he could spot alternate receivers in a split second. Regardless of how close the pass rusher was, Unitas would still step forward to deliver the ball. He knew he would take a terrific hit, but by ignoring the defender and stepping forward, he also knew his pass would be on target. "You can depend on John Unitas to stay in the pocket and he still won't hurry his throw," Olsen said. "He waits until the last second, and just when you think you've got him, he lets go right on the button."

Despite his celebrity, Unitas always remembered hard times past. He never let fame get in the way of his hunger to achieve. Norm Van Brocklin, a tough quarterback who passed the Philadelphia Eagles to the 1960 NFL title game and dealt Packers boss Vince Lombardi his lone championship game defeat, admired Unitas' work ethic. "He's a guy who knows what it's like to eat potato soup seven days a week as a kid," Van Brocklin said.

Cannon admired Unitas because he didn't try to dramatize his profession. He never celebrated a Colts score, and when the game was over,

Johnny U would dress in a shirt and tie and pack his public persona in the same canvas bag that held his football gear. "There is no actor in him," Cannon said. "No comedian, no poet. He is all quarterback."

Unitas credited his quiet and unassuming manner to his upbringing. "My mother had real challenges raising us without a husband and father," he said once. "Playing football couldn't compare." His lack of emotion impressed teammates and coaches. Bridgers would watch Unitas in interviews and thought Johnny U never exaggerated his role as a quarterback, never sought to emphasize how difficult it really was to determine the right play to call. Instead, he answered reporters' questions as succinctly as possible. His favorite expression to explain how he beat camouflaged coverages was, "Hit the single coverage." Translation: Throw to the receiver who had only one man covering him.

Thompson, who covered the Colts on radio and TV throughout Unitas' career, received some insight into the man following the season-ending 1967 loss to the Rams in the Coliseum. The defeat devastated the team since it eliminated Baltimore from the playoffs. The silence in the locker room afterward was eerie. Thompson had learned to avoid contact with distraught players after the game and was leaning against a wall with his head down. All of a sudden he felt a finger under his nose, a gesture designed to lift up his head. Thompson looked up and found himself staring into the eyes of Johnny U. Unitas didn't say a word, but his gesture spoke volumes: No matter how badly the loss hurts, you can't take it with you. "That brief encounter," Thompson said, "told me a lot about the man."

Rookies gained quick respect for Unitas as well. After safety Rick Volk was drafted out of the University of Michigan and joined the Colts in 1967, he lined up against Unitas in training camp. "I realized how lucky I was to be on the Colts and not have to play against him on Sundays," Volk said. "But what was unique about John was that he wasn't above anyone on the team. He was a regular guy, and that's how he carried himself."

If the job of a pro quarterback is to win, as *Houston Post* sportswriter Mickey Herskowitz once wrote, then Unitas did his job despite playing in arguably the most competitive era in pro football history. The game wasn't as complex then, and situational substitution was limited, but there were only 12 teams in the NFL when Unitas broke into the league in 1956, and with fewer teams and fewer roster spots, talent was at a premium. Unitas not only competed against some of the game's greatest defenders and many of the all-time top defenses, but he also shared the same Western Conference with the NFL's team of the decade, the Lombardi Packers. Lombardi called Unitas the best football player he had ever seen.

"I can't relax when Unitas is out there," Lombardi said once. When Shula replaced Ewbank as head coach of the Colts in 1963, the former defensive coordinator for the Detroit Lions told reporters he was glad to be working with Unitas rather than against him. "Who else," Shula asked, "was ever able to start out with a Unitas? We were scared to death of him in Detroit."

Still, Unitas and Shula clashed on occasion. While Shula felt that he and Unitas had a good, honest relationship, the two men were never as close during their years together in Baltimore as their contemporaries—Lombardi and Bart Starr in Green Bay; Allen and Roman Gabriel in Los Angeles; Bud Grant and Joe Kapp in Minnesota. Becoming close to Unitas, Shula said, was something only a few people had succeeded in doing.

Shula had coached against Unitas and respected him as a player. To him, Johnny U had overcome tremendous obstacles to become the first of the great modern quarterbacks, and he set a standard for all who would follow. After arriving in Baltimore as head coach, Shula came to know him as a man. Unitas, he thought, was a loner in every sense of the word. When things didn't please Unitas, he showed it. He once said, "You don't become a real quarterback until you can tell the coach to go to hell."

Teammates remembered plays being sent in by Ewbank and later by Shula and Johnny U ignoring them. When Ewbank told him not to throw against Detroit cornerback Dick "Night Train" Lane, Unitas frowned. Hell, he thought, I'm not going to give the guy a day off. Johnny U would test the Night Train. Maybe Lane would pick one off, but Unitas knew there were some things he could do against the great cornerback. By his own admission, Unitas was a stubborn guy who wanted to manage the game on his own. He rarely asked for help from coaches. All he wanted to know were the blitz tendencies of the opposing defense. Otherwise, he said, just leave him alone.

Colts players recall Ewbank, who was a nervous wreck on game days, meeting with Unitas on the sidelines during a timeout.

Unitas: "Whad'ya got?

Ewbank: "Whadda *you* got?"

"Ah, c'mon, Weeb..."

"Well, John..."

Ewbank would hesitate on which play to call, and Unitas would finally say, "I'll get the first down," and head back on the field.

Years later, in a game against rival Green Bay, Shula thought the Packers defense was going to blitz and signaled in a play to Unitas. Johnny U made a call to beat the blitz, but the Packers instead dropped into coverage and Unitas' third-down pass was batted away from the intended receiver. The Colts would have to punt, and as he walked toward the sideline, Unitas glared at Shula and kicked the dirt.

"Listen, it wasn't my fault," Shula said. "They crossed us up, and I blew it by sending in the wrong sign."

"Unless you're sure of what you're doing," Unitas snapped, "don't interrupt my play-calling."

Under Unitas, the Colts had won NFL championships in 1958 and '59, and he was named the league's Most Valuable Player in 1959, 1964, and 1967. The latter followed a campaign in which he led Baltimore to an 11-1-2 record and set career marks with 255 completions and a 58.5 percent completion rate. The man who was as identifiable with the 1950s as Ike, *The Honeymooners*, and hula hoops was aging with the grace of a fine wine. Yet the status of his health changed suddenly in the summer of 1968, when he injured his throwing arm against the Cowboys.

Johnny U's football future was in doubt. So, too, were the Colts dreams of an NFL championship.

3

Jet-Setters of the AFL

1968.

It was a year when hopes rose and dreams died, when national leaders were felled by bullets that symbolized man's failures, and national heroes William Anders, Frank Borman, and James Lowell were raised by rocket boosters symbolic of man's success.

It was a year of black militants and white flower children. It was the counterculture on the rise in San Francisco's Haight-Ashbury and New York's East Village, and it was rioting in cities and revolts on college campuses.

There was no sense of revolt, however, at Hofstra University in Hempstead, New York, the sight of the Jets' training camp. For years, the Jets had trained in Peekskill, but the cramped quarters, humid conditions, and bad food had been distractions for the team. Flanker Don Maynard recalled players sitting around their rooms in Peekskill and griping nightly about the lousy food and small rooms. Head coach Weeb Ewbank's insistence on a new training site with improved conditions marked the first step in creating team harmony. Hofstra offered air-conditioned dormitories, good food, and a first-rate practice field. Maynard remembers everything about Hofstra being first-class and players sitting around at night focused on football rather than on their surroundings.

"It was the greatest move Weeb made at the beginning of the season," said Maynard, who thought the change helped forge team togetherness and helped every player focus on the primary team goal of winning the AFL's Eastern Division championship after having come so close the season before. For much of the 1967 campaign, New York appeared to be on track to its first division title and a berth in the AFL Championship Game. The Jets had been buoyed by the fact that they were the only team in the league during the regular season to defeat the Western Division leaders, the Oakland Raiders, who eventually finished with a 13-1 record that was the best in AFL history.

Fronted by quarterback Joe Namath, who was filling the air with footballs, the high-flying Jets led the league in passing offense and total offense. By season's end, Namath had fire-bombed enemy defenses for 4,007 passing yards, the first pro quarterback to ever throw for more than 4,000 yards in a season. Split end George Sauer led the league with 75 catches, and Don Maynard was second with 71. It was the only time in AFL history that two receivers from the same team finished the season ranked first and second in receiving.

The Jets were 7-2-1 when injuries caught up with them. Fullback Matt Snell injured his knee in the season opener and missed the next eight weeks. Halfback Emerson Boozer carried the ground game and rushed for 10 touchdowns through the first half of the season. Yet just as Snell was preparing to return to the lineup, Boozer suffered an injury that caused him to miss the rest of the season.

With the Jets rushing attack crippled, opposing defenses geared up to stop Namath. New York dropped three of its last four games and finished 8-5-1, one win behind the division champion Houston Oilers. The Jets journey back from that bitter disappointment began on a hot July morning in Hempstead. From the first day of camp, New York was a team on a mission.

"It was something you could sense," Ewbank remembered, and it was Namath who helped set a tone. Older and more mature, Namath realized it would take more than a rifle arm and rapier release to win a championship. He still wore his hair in a hippie-style cut and he still had long sideburns and a Fu Manchu mustache, but his maturity could be found in his exhibiting more patience on the playing field. He was learning to speed-read coverages and to parry and attack the multiple movements of AFL defenses.

Teammates noticed Namath's new-found maturity, and it struck a responsive chord with them. Maynard saw Namath as a natural leader, and the club knew it couldn't win without him. "We sort of told Joe that it was up to him to take us all the way," Maynard said.

His teammates voted Namath offensive team captain prior to the season opener and, following his lead, vowed in a show of solidarity not to shave until they had won the Eastern Division. They grew sideburns and mustaches, long hair, and afros. In time, their unshorn looks helped endear the Jets to a new generation of football fans. Like the rock group the Young Rascals, the young Jets would find themselves groovin' on Sunday afternoons. Veteran linebacker Larry Grantham, who had been with the franchise since its inception as the New York Titans in 1960, told reporters at the start of the season, "This is the best team I've ever played with."

Pro football experts liked the Jets as well, but for different reasons. In his preview of the 1968 AFL season, writer Berry Stainback picked New York to win the East and listed several reasons for his selection. Namath, he wrote, was the best quarterback in the division; the return of Snell and Boozer gave the Jets the best running game in the East; the receiving trio of Maynard, George Sauer, and Pete Lammons was excellent; and the defense was improving. Stainback had one more reason for picking the Jets. "Probably the biggest thing the Jets have going for them," he wrote, "is that there is no dominant team in the East."

New York Daily News sportswriter Larry Fox previewed the Jets chances for a division title two days prior to the September 15 regular-season opener:

"The Jets are a team that could win a championship... even the Super Bowl... or finish deep among the also-rans. A lot depends on Boozer. More depends on Namath. When he's hot—with receivers like Don Maynard and George Sauer—he can beat anybody, even the Packers. He also is capable of throwing six interceptions a game."

The worth of the experts' opinions would be tested early when the Jets traveled to Kansas City for their 4:00 PM (EST) opener. AFL founder Lamar Hunt's organization had been one of the AFL's best since winning the 1962 league title as the Dallas Texans in a dramatic, double-overtime victory over two-time defending champion Houston. The game eclipsed the 1958 Colts-Giants overtime classic in the NFL title as the longest in pro football history. Hunt relocated his team to Kansas City the following year to avoid continuing to compete for ticket sales and publicity with the NFL's Dallas Cowboys.

Just as they had ended the Oilers two-year run as AFL champions in 1962, the re-named Chiefs stopped the Buffalo Bills from winning three straight league titles with a 31–7 win in the 1966 championship game. Fittingly, it was Hunt's team that represented the league in the first AFL-NFL World Championship Game in January 1967, and though Kansas City lost to Green Bay, the Chiefs remained one of the AFL's top contenders. Oddsmakers rated the Chiefs as 6 ½-point favorites and were no doubt aware that the Jets had lost three in a row to the Chiefs, including a 42–18 romp in Kansas City in 1967 in which the Jets took a physical beating.

Fox stated in his preview in the *Daily News* that Ewbank and his team were "in awe" of Kansas City's tremendous natural talent. "To beat a team such as this—and on the road too—would turn championship dreams into realistic hopes," Fox wrote.

On a dazzling, sun-drenched afternoon, a record Kansas City sports crowd of 48,871 crammed every corner of Municipal Stadium. The interest in this season opener featuring two of the AFL's most dynamic teams was such that a corner terrace of the stadium was filled with 2,833 fans who paid $5 each to stand and watch.

New York sprinted to a 17–3 halftime lead after Namath found Maynard for scoring passes of 57 and 30 yards. His first score had come courtesy of a strategy that served to emphasize Broadway Joe's development as a strategic passer. He fired two straight sideline passes in Sauer's direction to tighten the Chiefs' secondary and get man-on-man coverage with Maynard. When Kansas City obliged, Namath dropped deep in the pocket and watched Maynard get a step on cornerback Goldie Sellers. Broadway Joe unfurled a perfect, sky-scraping bomb that Maynard caught in full stride for a 57-yard score. Jets fans listening to the game on WABC Radio in New York thrilled to Merle Harmon's call:

> *"Namath back to throw, dropping way back, looking and throwing long for Maynard, he's out there at the 20, 15, 10, 5... Touchdown! He got behind Goldie Sellers by a step. Joe Namath went for the bomb on second down and inches, a bit of a surprise element possibly... Sam Walton doing great pass-blocking for Namath as he dropped back deep, and the Jets go for the bomb and make it."*

Jets defensive coaches Walt Michaels and Buddy Ryan came up with a plan to counter Chiefs coach Hank Stram's imaginative offense. Kansas City's flashy running game, which had rolled up 204 yards in its season-opening 26–21 win over defending Eastern Division champion Houston the weekend before, was kept out of the end zone by the Jets and limited to 118 yards. When the Chiefs went to the air, defensive tackle John Elliott dropped quarterback Len Dawson twice. New York sacked Dawson four times and limited him to 98 yards passing on the day.

The Jets led 10–3 in the second quarter when the Namath-to-Maynard combination struck again late in the second quarter.

> *Harmon: "Now it is second down and 10 on the Kansas City 30 with 1:55 left to play in the first half... Namath calls it for New York, drops back to pass, looking, throwing far for Maynard at the 5 and... He's got it! He's in! Touchdown!"*

Stymied on the ground and in the air, the Chiefs rode the right leg of kicker Jan Stenerud and his four field goals to pull within a point of the Jets at 20–19 late in the fourth quarter. Six minutes remained in the game when the Jets offense took over in the shadow of its own goal post. Calling audibles on virtually every play, Namath completed four clutch third-down passes to maintain a marathon 14-play, 62-yard march that exhausted the clock and preserved New York's one-point win. The drive was highlighted by this crucial third-down play:

> Harmon: "*Crowd trying to spur that defense on now with third down and 11 on the New York 4... Sauer wide to the left, Maynard wide to the right... Namath back in the end zone to throw, throws slant-in to Maynard at the 15! Don spinning and going to the 20, brought down at the 20-yard line and the Jets got out of the hole.*"

The late-game march stunned Stram. "The last drive by Namath was fabulous," Stram said. "There was no way I thought they could go from the [5]-yard line and maintain possession until the end of the game."

Later, he would add, "Joe Willie gave us a breathtaking demonstration of control football for the final seven minutes of the game.... The kid was amazing."

Dawson, who had been nursing a sore arm since training camp had begun in July, agreed with Stram. Namath, he said, did a fantastic job in the last seven or eight minutes of the game. He controlled the ball, came up with the big third-down play, and kept the drive going until he ran out the clock.

Namath's play calling and precision passing, Maynard's then-career-high 203 yards on eight catches, Boozer's return to form and game-high 75 yards rushing, Jim Turner's clutch field goals, and the stingy play of the defense were all positive signs for a club considered to be a contender. Namath still regards that victory as the turning point of the Jets season, even though it was only the first of 14 regular season games. To Jets cornerback Johnny Sample, the victory marked a big step that the team needed to build its confidence.

Boozer told WABC Radio analyst Sam DeLuca after the game that the key to victory was the play of the Jets defense. "We have something this year that we didn't have and that's defensive togetherness," Boozer said. "I think the defensive unit played real fine. They held Kansas City to no rushing touchdowns, and that means a lot to stop that Kansas City offense."

New York's defense fueled the Jets rise to the top of the Eastern Division. Coached by Michaels and Ryan, the Jets yielded an AFL-low 3.2 yards per carry, surrendered the fewest first downs, and forced 43 turnovers, second most in the league. New York finished the season ranked first in the AFL against the run, second against the pass, and first overall.

Harmon stated during a broadcast that the Jets defense was a key reason why New York was able to progress from being a good team to a great team. Namath credited the defense with helping his development as a passer. In past years, he had tried to force passes in order to generate points. But the way New York's defense was playing in 1968, he could afford to throw the ball away, take the field goal, and let the opposing offense make mistakes.

No one appreciated New York's success on defense more than Larry Grantham. Lacking size and speed, Grantham was one of the unlikeliest pro football players in the 1960s. Yet along with Maynard and fullback Billy Mathis, he was one of just three of the original Titans who had survived the early years of the AFL and was still with the team in 1968. The trio also owned membership in an exclusive club known as "The Originals"–19 players who had started with the AFL in its inaugural 1960 season and were still on the league's active rosters in 1969, the AFL's final year of existence before its merger with the NFL.

Grantham was a success story typical of the AFL. Talented enough to play both offensive and defensive end at the nationally ranked University of Mississippi, the 6', 195-pound son of the South was concerned his lack of size would prevent him from going pro. After Ole Miss beat Louisiana State University 21-0 in the Sugar Bowl, Grantham was selected in the 15th round of 1959 NFL Draft by the Baltimore Colts. The Colts were reigning NFL champions, and Grantham was told by the team that of the 30 rookies they were bringing to training camp, they would only keep two or three. Since he had also been drafted as a first-round choice of the Titans, Grantham felt he would have a better chance of making it in the AFL.

"I knew I'd have a chance to play in the new league," Grantham said. He signed with New York for a $1,000 bonus and though his weight had increased to 194 pounds, he was still one of the smaller players among the 125 who showed up in the Titans first camp. Grantham was initially tried out at offensive end, but his experience at that position was limited. He had been used mainly as a decoy for the

Ole Miss squads and had caught less than 10 passes in his three years with the team. Grantham struggled so much in the Titans training camp that he began checking return flights to Mississippi. But Titans line coach John Dell Isola changed the course of Grantham's career and his life when he took him aside one day during practice.

"I saw you in the Ole Miss films," Isola said. "You played good defensive football there. How about trying defense with us?"

Converted to right outside linebacker, Grantham developed quickly. He earned All-AFL honors in 1962 and 1964. Four years after being drafted by Ewbank in Baltimore, Grantham wound up playing for Ewbank in New York when the latter was hired as coach in 1963. By the end of the '68 season, the two would take the field together against those same Colts.

Nicknamed Chugger, Grantham earned the respect of his teammates by playing through pain and injury. He was tough and durable. He took off his ankle cast and played against Houston with a broken bone in his leg; played against Buffalo despite a broken wrist; played against the Oilers on another occasion with a broken rib; and practiced despite a split finger. He missed just seven games in his 13-year career, and three of those were due to an Army recall during the 1961 Berlin crisis.

Grantham was an inspirational leader, and his fiery spirit and intelligence made him the leader of the Jets defense on the field and their player representative off of it. He was a holler guy, and he was smart; he called the team's defensive signals. Grantham would look at the yards, the down, and the distance, and then determine how far the opposing offense had to go for a first down. Then he would remember from film study what the quarterback had called in a similar situation. He would then set the defense to counter what he believed the offense was going to try.

Grantham was rarely caught out of position, rarely fooled by an end reverse, rarely beaten on a screen pass. He reacted well to the ball and enjoyed every aspect of the game, the physical as well as the cerebral. He was football's version of Eddie Stanky—he played bigger than his size. He would be remiss, Grantham said, if he didn't acknowledge that he liked the contact inherent in the game. In playing linebacker, he found that just about on every play the ball was coming at him. Blockers would be trying to get at him to clear a path for the runner, and it was a case of somebody hitting him while he was hitting them. "I enjoy the hitting," he said.

He still counts his AFL experiences as among the more meaningful in his life.

"The AFL meant a lot more to me than to a lot of guys because it provided me with a way of life and an income that I might not otherwise have enjoyed," he said.

Grantham was there for the Titans lean years in 1960, '61, and '62, when players literally raced one another to the nearest bank to cash their checks before team owner Harry Wismer's account ran dry. He was there for a particularly cold night game when it looked to the players like no more than 50 people had showed up to watch a Titans game at their home stadium, the rust-caked Polo Grounds. Grantham, the team's spiritual leader, stood up that night in the locker room to address his teammates. "No introductions tonight, fellas," he said. "Instead, we're going to introduce the fans to the players."

Wismer used to announce an attendance of 20,000 fans, but the players knew better. "I'll bet there was a hot dog vendor for every customer," Grantham said. "I told the guys, 'Let's go up in the stands and shake their hands.' But I had a lot of fun at the Polo Grounds; there was so much history there. I remember I used to stand in center field and remember this is where Willie Mays made his famous catch [against Cleveland's Vic Wertz in the 1954 World Series]. I felt at home there."

Still, the AFL was such an unknown entity at the time that when Grantham would arrive home in Crystal Springs at season's end, neighbors would ask him where he had been for the past several months.

In an era of great outside linebackers, Grantham did not fit the classic mold as shaped by Kansas City's Bobby Bell or Houston's George Webster. He compensated by studying the game and learning the correct angles to take to play the run and the pass. "When I joined the pros," he said, "I realized that because of my smaller size I had to be a little smarter, a little sharper."

Grantham studied game films at home, watched how the great line-backers played the game, and learned how they handled various situations. He also studied offenses and learned their inclinations. Along with fellow linebackers Al Atkinson and Ralph Baker, Grantham became adept at reading plays and reacting to them. Because of the strong rush of the front four—Philbin, Elliott, Verlon Biggs, and Paul Rochester—Jets linebackers were free to drop into short coverage zones on passing downs. Grantham, Atkinson, and Baker were so active in pass coverage that it was said at the time that the Jets secondary appeared to be using seven defensive backs at a time. Carl McAdams proved invaluable as a backup who was versatile enough to play on the defensive line or linebacker. When Atkinson was sidelined early in the season with a bone bruise in his leg, McAdams split time spelling Biggs and Rochester on the front line and backup middle linebacker Mike Stromberg.

The Jets experience allowed Michaels and Ryan to employ a "key" defense in which players looked for small tips an offensive player might use to indicate the type of play and its direction. As the weakside line-backer, Grantham would key the stance and positioning of the offensive tackle, guard, and running back on his side of the field. He would then make the defensive call based on this few seconds of observation. The potential danger in playing a key defense is that offenses design false keys to influence the flow of the defense in one direction and then run a counter play against the grain.

Making calls in the defensive secondary was Johnny Sample. A member of Baltimore's NFL title teams in 1958 and '59, Sample was the most experienced player on New York's defense. He used his knowledge to diagnose offensive formations and signaled the appropriate pass coverage with hand signs: a clenched fist held high indicated a blitz; two fingers called for a weakside zone rotation; three fingers indicated regular zone coverage; four fingers called for a weakside "double" where the end, linebacker, or cornerback covered the short zone on the flanker; and five fingers called for a strongside double.

New York fronted its rotating coverages with a standard 4-3 alignment of four linemen and three linebackers. Michaels occasionally called for a "mixer"—a change of pace that might be a three-man line or five-man line, depending on the situation. The Buffalo Bills had used a three-man defensive front against the San Diego Chargers in the 1965 AFL Championship Game. The Bills confused the Chargers by using agile defensive end Tom Day as a fourth linebacker who could either drop into pass coverage or rush quarterback John Hadl. The novel alignment instituted by head coach Lou Saban and defensive coordinator Joe Collier helped Buffalo shut out Chargers coach Sid Gillman's high-octane offense, 23–0. Two years later, the 3-4 alignment was adopted by the Oakland Raiders en route to their AFL championship.

The mixer used by Michaels and Ryan in New York in 1968 was an overshifted front that placed a defensive tackle, either Elliott or Rochester, over the opposing team's center. The odd front was an AFL staple, popularized by Kansas City and Oakland. Michaels kept his front four fresh by substituting McAdams, a speed rusher, at the end or tackle positions. Blending strategy with skill, Michaels and Ryan molded the Jets into one of pro football's best defenses. After holding the powerful Chiefs in check in the opener, the Jets rode cornerback Randy Beverly's 68-yard interception return for a score and Turner's team-record four field goals to a 47–31 win over Boston in Birmingham, Alabama.

The Jets headed to Buffalo's War Memorial Stadium in Week 3 as 19-point favorites. Instead, it was the Bills who rocked the Rockpile. Harassed by defensive end Ron McDole, who gave rookie right tackle Sam Walton fits all afternoon, Namath threw five interceptions, three of which were returned for scores. The 37–35 defeat did not sit well with New York's defense, which surrendered just one touchdown in the loss.

Maynard heard Philbin tell Namath the week after the game, "Hey Joe, remember, we're wearing *green* uniforms this week."

One week later, Beverly and the Jets defense took center stage in New York's Saturday night home opener at Shea Stadium on October 5. An AFL-record crowd of 63,786 showed up for what was expected to be a shootout with Western Division contender San Diego, whose offense featured John Hadl, Lance Alworth, Gary Garrison, and Dickie Post.

Beverly turned in the game's first big play.

> *Harmon: "Hadl back to pass, third-and-19, Hadl throwing*
> *for Garrison... Intercepted by Beverly at the 35! Down to*
> *the 25, down to the 20, down to the 15... He slips, rolls out*
> *of bounds..."*

Three field goals by Turner gave New York a 9–7 lead at halftime, and Snell's 3-yard scoring run made it 16–7 in the third. San Diego surged back and took the lead in the fourth, forcing the Jets offense to produce a late drive. A leaping grab by Maynard and a clutch catch by Mark Smolinski on a slant-in helped New York march to the Chargers 1-yard line, where they faced fourth down with just 1:47 remaining.

> *Harmon: "The Jets come out of the huddle... Namath calls*
> *it, the crowd standing, fourth-and-1 at the goal line... Here's*
> *a handoff, a dive... Touchdown! Boozer made it! Emerson*
> *Boozer over the top for a touchdown... A handoff to Emerson*
> *Boozer, up over the top he went and it's a happy band of*
> *Jets..."*

New York led 23–20, but because no lead was safe against San Diego, it was left to the Jets defense to seal the deal. Michaels called for a prevent defense. With time running out and San Diego driving, Sample stepped up and picked off a Hadl pass to rookie Ken Dyer at the goal line.

> *Harmon: "Hadl back to pass, getting the protection, now*
> *being rushed, now throwing long for Dyer... It is intercepted*
> *by Sample! Sample at the 5, up to the 10, up to the 20, run-*
> *ning easily, killing the clock..."*

In the locker room after the game, Sample cradled the game ball, which had been awarded to him moments before by Namath. It was a special moment between the two men, both of whom had somewhat surprisingly been named captains of their respective units prior to the start of the season.

Interviewed by DeLuca, Sample told WABC listeners that beating San Diego was big, since the Jets had "given the game away to Buffalo" the week before.

The victory proved but a brief reprieve for Namath. The Jets were 20-point favorites to beat Denver at Shea Stadium the following week. The Broncos had won just one of their first four games. But in what amounted to a replay of his disastrous day in Buffalo just two weeks prior, Namath—pressured by defensive end Rich "Tombstone" Jackson and tackle Dave Costa—was intercepted five times in a 21–13 loss. The upset stunned the 62,052 fans in attendance, and their displeasure with Namath was so loud that their boos reverberated throughout Shea Stadium.

New York's locker room after the game was morgue-like; for the second time in three weeks, the offense, and in particular Namath, had given away a game the Jets should have won. The Jets locker room was divided into four parts so that players at like positions had dressing stalls close to one another. On their side of the room, members of the defense were shocked and angered. Safety Jim Hudson, Namath's roommate for road games, sat on a stool in front of his locker; his head bowed, he dragged on a cigarette. Sample, standing at the adjacent locker, kept shaking his head in disbelief. Horrible day, he thought. Philbin, his eyes flashing with anger, bit his lip.

Through the first half of the season, it was the Jets low-profile defense that was playing solid football; its high-gloss offense was erratic. Facing Eastern Division rival Houston beneath the artificial sky of the new Astrodome, New York's defense held the defending division champions scoreless for the first three quarters.

Michaels and Ryan had prepared a game plan designed to take advantage of the inexperience of second-string quarterback Bob Davis, who was subbing for injured starter Pete Beathard. Believing that the Oilers would rely more on running back Hoyle Granger, who had fueled the AFL's leading rushing offense in 1967, Jets linebackers were instructed to play close to the line of scrimmage in what amounted to a seven-man front.

Granger ended up missing the game with a sore back, an injury that wasn't disclosed until game time. Michaels and Ryan figured that a heavy pass rush would rattle Davis and help the Jets secondary. They figured right. An interception by Beverly set up New York's first scoring drive, and Davis was roughed up and finally knocked out of the game following a hit by Biggs. Don Trull rallied the Oilers in the fourth, and with New York clinging to a 20-14 lead with less than a minute to play, Philbin put the game on ice with a big special teams play.

> Harmon: "Zeke Moore and Larry Carwell are deep for Houston... Here comes Curley Johnson [to punt], downfield comes the football... High, end-over-end, it's going to be taken by Moore on the 5, to the 10, to the 15, to the 20... He fumbles as he is hit and the Jets recover on the 27! Gerry Philbin hit Zeke Moore and really whacked him and shook that ball loose... I have never seen a harder whack than Philbin gave Moore, right in the breadbasket on a shoulder tackle and the ball went flying right on up the field..."

Philbin played in a decade dominated by high-profile defensive ends—Deacon Jones, Willie Davis, Bubba Smith, Carl Eller, Jim Marshall, Jerry Mays, Ben Davidson, and Rich "Tombstone" Jackson. And while he didn't receive the accolades afforded others, it's Philbin who is generally recognized as the greatest end in AFL history. He overcame physical problems—"His shoulders popped out of place more times than a runaway toaster," Murray Olderman wrote—but he waged a vendetta against quarterbacks for more than nine seasons. A steady diet of malteds, soybeans, and weightlifting helped Philbin survive the AFL wars. He was nicknamed "Puppy Dog" by Ewbank because of his propensity for chasing the ball. "He's got the knack of penetration, getting to the passer," Ewbank said at the time. "He never quits, he always rushes. He's got heart and pride, a will to win. He's always chasing the ball." In 1968, Philbin succesfully chased down AFL quarterbacks 19 times.

The Jets returned to Shea to face Boston, and the defense had another big outing. Tying a team record with five interceptions and holding the Patriots to 44 rushing yards, the Jets scored their second-highest total in team history in a 48-14 romp that raised their record to 5-2 at the season's midpoint.

New York's defense, once maligned, was coming of age. Its maturity was evident not only in its play but also in its appearance. By Week 7, Biggs, Elliott, and Hudson were all sporting discreet goatees. Though the AFL had a league rule prohibiting beards, Ewbank told the *New York Daily News*, "I like the spirit of the thing."

Hudson said it was Biggs who started the trend when he said he wasn't going to shave until after the Jets had won the Eastern Division title. Biggs' statement and action was significant, since he was considered by teammates to be the most introverted member of the team.

Biggs and Elliott had something in common other than their goatees. Both were explosive off the ball in their pursuit of the play. "There's only one way to play," Elliott said, "and that's to charge full speed ahead when the ball's snapped. You don't guess. You just go." Elliott believed that if he penetrated the offensive backfield quickly enough, he could mess up a running play. If it was a pass, he could sack the quarterback or hurry his throw.

The Jets esprit de corps was not only winning games, it was winning over fans, as well. Seven-year-old John F. Kennedy Jr. watched the victory over the Patriots from New York's team bench. The Kennedy's party, which included his friend Douglas Woo, his uncle Stephen Smith, and three Secret Service agents, had arrived at Shea without tickets. The club, however, found room for the group. Kennedy talked with Namath on the sidelines and said he had previously been a fan of the Packers but was now switching his allegiance to the Jets.

New York's defense provided the Kennedy party with quite a show. Philbin forced three fumbles that were recovered by New York and turned into touchdowns. Powerful fullback Jim Nance was held to 14 yards rushing, and the Patriots as a team were limited to just 44 yards on the ground. The Jets sacked Boston quarterbacks seven times for minus-50 yards and allowed just eight first downs.

"The Jet defense," Fox wrote in his game story, "was superb."

Grantham saw New York's success as a blend of skill and strategy.

"In the early years, we didn't have a lot of talent," he said. "Even in 1968, we didn't realize at the beginning of the season how good we were. The Kansas City game was a turning point for us."

Sample agreed that the win over Kansas City had a carry-over effect for New York. On paper, the Chiefs had the best team in either the AFL or NFL and were picked to win the Western Conference. Beating them was the big step the Jets needed. "It built up our confidence," Sample said.

Leading the East midway through the regular season, the confident Jets were halfway home to a division title.

4

The Colts Go from "Rags" to Riches

Three hundred miles south of the Hempstead headquarters where the New York Jets had taken their first step toward a date with destiny, the Baltimore Colts began their long journey to the summit of pro football in their training camp at Western Maryland College in Westminster, Maryland.

Despite the hundreds of miles of separation, the Colts could feel kinship with the Jets in at least one respect. Like New York, Baltimore had endured a bitterly disappointing conclusion to what had been a most promising 1967 campaign. Aging like a fine wine, 34-year-old quarterback John Unitas enjoyed a vintage season in '67 by completing an NFL-best 57 percent of his passes and earned his third league MVP award.

Playing like he had in his breakthrough 1958 season, Unitas directed the Colts to victories over Green Bay and Dallas, two teams that went on to meet for the NFL championship in the epic Ice Bowl game in Lambeau Field. A 30–10 victory over New Orleans on the season's penultimate weekend gave Baltimore an 11–0–2 record heading into their season finale against their Coastal Division rivals, the Los Angeles Rams. In the era prior to expanded playoffs, only the NFL's four division champions advanced to the postseason. With a division title and playoff rematch with the Packers within their grasp, the Colts played their worst game of the season and were routed by the Rams, 34–10, in the Los Angeles Coliseum. It was a devastating loss. Despite owning the second-best regular season record in the NFL, the Colts missed the playoffs for the second straight season.

"We went out to Los Angeles and they beat us, so they got to the playoffs and we didn't," cornerback Bobby Boyd remembered. "It was discouraging, but we had to live with it."

Baltimore's defeat in the big game marked the continuation of a troubling trend for a team that had not won a playoff game since repeating as NFL champions in 1959. In 1964, the Colts posted the league's best record at 12–2 and led the NFL in most points scored (428), fewest points allowed (225), and takeaway/giveaway differential (plus 22). Fueled by seven future Hall of Famers, including head coach Don Shula, Baltimore was a heavy favorite to beat the Cleveland Browns in the NFL title game. Instead, the Colts high-powered offense was shut out and its stingy defense shredded in a shocking 27–0 upset.

Baltimore's Western Conference playoff loss to Green Bay the following season can be partly excused. The Colts had lost Unitas and backup quarterback Gary Cuozzo to injuries during the regular season and were forced to convert halfback Tom Matte to quarterback. Baltimore made another run at the postseason in 1966, but losses to Green Bay in the Colts two most important games of the season gave the Packers the Western Conference title and a trip to the NFL Championship Game and the first Super Bowl.

By the start of their training camp in 1968, the Colts disappointment in falling short of an NFL title for four straight seasons was palpable. When they arrived in Westminster, they showed the same steely resolve as another 1967 near-miss, the New York Jets. "We aren't going to miss this time," Bobby Boyd vowed to reporters.

"We wanted it bad in '68," Boyd said, looking back.

At a team luncheon prior to the start of the regular season, several of the Colts stood and spoke of their determination not to let the title slip away from them again. When it came time for offensive tackle Sam

Ball to speak, the native Kentuckian drawled out his words slowly for emphasis:

"In my part of the country, we've got an expression that covers this situation: 'Let the big dog eat.'"

His audience roared its approval, but Ball didn't crack a smile. He was grim and serious. The whole team was. Watching the scene, Earl Morrall thought the big dog was mighty hungry.

For the second time in a decade, the Colts and their fans were about to experience a Cinderella-like season from an unlikely and unexpected source. In 1958, a young Unitas had emerged from his sandlot surroundings to lead Baltimore to its first NFL title. Ten years later, Morrall, a 34-year-old veteran playing quarterback for his fifth NFL team, would play the rags-to-riches role in Baltimore. It was a fitting role for Morrall, whose nickname was Rags.

A 6'2", 209-pound product of Muskegon, Michigan, Morrall was drafted in 1956 by the San Francisco 49ers after leading Michigan State to a Rose Bowl victory over UCLA. An outstanding athlete at Muskegon High School, Morrall earned a dual football-baseball scholarship to Michigan State. His decision to opt for football came after he committed five errors playing third base against Wisconsin. The 49ers made Morrall a first-round pick, and he spent his rookie year seeing limited playing time as a backup to Y.A. Tittle.

In 1957, Morrall was traded to the Pittsburgh Steelers. Despite playing in all 12 regular season games and throwing for 1,900 yards and 11 touchdowns, he was dealt to Detroit the next year where he played through the 1964 season.

Morrall received a career break in 1965 when he was traded to the New York Giants. Ironically, the man he was replacing at quarterback in New York was his former 49ers teammate, Tittle, who had decided to retire following the 1964 season. Stepping into the starter's role, Morrall passed for 2,446 yards and 22 touchdowns to lead the Giants back to respectability with a 7–7 record. Morrall's performance was impressive; New York had finished 2–10–2 the season prior to his arrival.

Giants coach Allie Sherman thought Morrall was the perfect quarterback for a young team. "He had poise, control, and confidence," Sherman said.

Just as Morrall seemed on the verge of establishing himself as a starting quarterback, he suffered a broken wrist halfway through the 1966 season. The injury reduced him to a backup role, and the Giants traded for Fran Tarkenton in 1967. The scrambling son of a minister, Tarkenton took over as the starter, and Morrall attempted just 24 passes during the regular season.

On August 22, 1968, Morrall was resting in his room in the Giants training camp in Fairfield, Connecticut, when there was a knock on his door. In walked assistant coach Ken Kavanaugh, the "Turk" whose job it was to inform players they had been cut or traded.

"Coach wants to see you," Kavanaugh said.

When Morrall met with Sherman, he was told he had been dealt to Baltimore. "Why Baltimore?" Morrall asked. "Don Shula will explain it to you when you get there," Sherman said. "It has something to do with Unitas."

Morrall had been a backup for four teams, and now he was being traded to a team whose quarterback was arguably the greatest in NFL history. Depressed, Morrall thought about quitting the game and discussed retirement with his wife Jane. "It seemed this was a good time," he said.

Had he not driven himself through a rigorous off-season conditioning regimen, Morrall might have retired rather than report to Baltimore. Physically, he felt he was ready for his best season ever. All he needed, he thought, was a chance.

His chance came September 7 when Unitas injured his passing arm in the final preseason game. Dame Fortune was frowning on Johnny U but favoring Morrall. Shula called Morrall into his office and told him Unitas' arm injury was causing the quarterback tremendous pain and that he would likely miss the regular season opener against San Francisco. Unitas confirmed the seriousness of his injury when he met with reporters on September 10. The surroundings for Unitas' announcement was ironic; it took place in his Baltimore restaurant, The Golden Arm.

"I can't raise it or straighten it out, and it hurts when I try to do something with it, like lifting," Unitas said. "It's real sore, puffed up, black and blue.... It hurts more than it ever has. I couldn't even throw a pop pass. What next? I really don't know. All I know is that I don't expect to be doing any throwing for awhile."

One practice session with Unitas was enough to convince Morrall of the extent of Unitas' injury. "The first time I worked out with the Colts I knew Johnny wasn't right," Morrall said. "He spent most of the time just lobbing the ball back and forth on the sidelines. His arm seemed to be hurting him all the time."

The three weeks between his arrival in Baltimore and the Colts opener against the 49ers in Memorial Stadium saw Morrall work harder than he had at any time in his 12-year career. He had less than a month to grasp a system of play-calling that was completely new to him.

Some Colts had their doubts about Morrall. Special teams player Alex Hawkins said that early in the season not much was expected of the newest addition to the team. Because of what he had gone through in 1965 when he had to adjust to playing quarterback, Matte could relate perhaps better than anyone to the adjustments Morrall had to make.

The main problem Morrall had, Matte thought, was the Colts numbering system. It was directly opposite the one Morrall had used as a member of the Giants and the Lions. New York and Detroit used hole numbering systems that listed even numbers to the left and odd numbers to the right. The Colts system was in reverse order. The backfield numbering system was also reversed. When Morrall would call a play in the huddle, he would be thinking one play while his teammates were thinking something else. Morrall compared it to thinking of your right arm as your left and your left arm as your right, and then being told to raise your right arm. You would do it, Morrall explained, but you would have to stop and think for a second. And in the NFL, that second can be disastrous.

Prior to the season, Matte told Colts radio and TV announcer Chuck Thompson that it was going to be "a little difficult" for Morrall to adjust. "He's going to have to think out there on the field all the time," Matte said, "and we're going to have to help him."

All-Pro tight end John Mackey knew that Morrall had to familiarize himself with Baltimore's system and that it would take time. Play-calling was only one part of Morrall's adjustment to a new team. The Colts offensive system was more complicated than any he had ever encountered. Baltimore used more plays and more formations, and since certain plays were only to be used against specific defenses, Morrall had to be careful to read the opposing defense and read it correctly, and then call the right play to counter it. In the past, the teams he had played for had allowed him to use his own judgment when it came to calling plays. In Baltimore, however, the play-calling was spelled out for him.

If the strongside linebacker and middle linebacker both blitzed, the Colts scheme called for the quarterback to look for Mackey, who would be in single coverage against a smaller defender, the strongside safety. If the play was designed as a pass to split end Jimmy Orr and Morrall walked to the line of scrimmage and saw that the weakside safety was preparing to cover Orr, then Morrall was supposed to look to his other receiver, flanker Willie Richardson, who was on the opposite side of the formation.

So Morrall not only had to learn new plays, new formations, and new terminology, he also had to concentrate harder on reading defenses and calling the correct play. Compared to the Colts complicated system, he thought the Giants offense was child's play.

Baltimore's coaches paid the same attention to detail. End coach Dick Bielski studied how his receivers ran their patterns to make certain they weren't using the same moves each time. If a pattern called for a receiver to make a break to the outside and he was consistently veering in before he made his break, Bielski would make the receiver vary his route. Colts receivers were also taught to run very specific patterns. Most NFL teams at the time had a primary receiver, secondary receiver, and a third receiver on each pass play, and the quarterback was coached to look for his receivers in that order.

Baltimore, however, used a system in which each of the routes run by receivers was staggered so that each man came open in sequence. On his previous teams, if Morrall's primary receiver was covered, he would then look for his secondary receiver. Often, however, that receiver would have already made the break on his route and would then be covered just as Morrall was looking for him. Because of the Colts sequenced system, Morrall seldom found himself in that situation.

Morrall thought Baltimore's offensive game plans offered another example of the team's thoroughness. The basic plan was mimeographed on sheets of paper and handed out to the players. A dozen or so plays that the coaches felt confident about in made up the "ready list." There were evaluations of each member of the opposing defense and a look at the frequencies, listed in percentages, of the opponent's team tendencies. How often do they stunt or use a zone? How often do they blitz on first-and-10 or second-and-long?

Some NFL teams based their game plans on scouting reports and their own reviews of three or four game films. Colts coaches, however, studied film from the previous six, sometimes seven, games. Their in-depth study made for a far more comprehensive plan than Morrall was accustomed to, and he spent a great deal of time huddling with offensive coach Don McCafferty in order to properly digest what he called the "new mass of information" before each game.

Morrall's debut in Baltimore blue-and-white began ominously. On his third play from scrimmage, Morrall's pass was tipped by 49ers defensive tackle Roland Lakes and plucked from the air by end Stan Hindman, who returned it 25 yards for a score. Morrall was so jittery he said he felt "like a rookie starting out all over again." He was still unsettled on the Colts next series but tried to bluff his teammates in the huddle. "Let's get this one back," he said. "Let's not get excited."

Colts center Bill Curry thought Morrall was almost humorous in his attempt to command the huddle. Whereas Unitas had such absolute command of the huddle that no one spoke but him, Curry said Morrall would lower his helmet in the huddle and with a puckish grin and a very slow and deliberate manner of speech say, "Okay, let's calm down. Everything is under control." At that point, one of the Colts would speak up. "Yeah, Earl, call a play, would ya?"

Struggling to learn the Colts' system, Morrall at times launched into some tortured play-calling:

"Out left, flank right, split... No, out right, flank left? Uh..."

On such occasions, Matte would make the correct call. "Out left, flank right, 36 on one!"

"Right!" Morrall would say. "That's it!"

One of the Colts key plays was "34-slant." In Baltimore's scheme, it was a handoff to the halfback, who would then hit off right tackle. But the Giants also had a play called "34-slant" and in their system it was a handoff to the fullback who would hit off left tackle. When Shula sent the play in, Morrall lapsed into Giants terminology. He turned the wrong way at the snap and saw Matte running in the opposite direction, away from the handoff. Both men quickly recovered, however, and improvised. Morrall tossed a soft lateral to Matte, who ran for a first down. On a play designated as "Ride-35," Morrall was supposed to hand off to Matte. Again, lapsing into the Giants play-calling system, Morrall turned and shoved the ball into the stomach of his surprised fullback, Jerry Hill. "It was like I had slipped him a hot poker," Morrall said. Hill took it and kept running, but as Matte wheeled by he yelled at Morrall, "I get the ball!"

Morrall was shaky in his start against the 49ers. Some of his old doubts nagged at him. The Giants had given up on him; the Lions had preferred someone else. And he hadn't won the Colts starting job, he had only gained it by default because Unitas was hurt. Maybe Sherman was right. Morrall could feel tension building up inside him. This was his first start in almost two years. Could he handle the Colts system?

Less than two minutes of the 1968 season had passed and already the Colts were trailing by a touchdown because Morrall's pass was intercepted and returned for a score. Is it going to be one of those days? Morrall wondered. Even worse, is it going to be one of those years?

Unitas stepped in and worked with Morrall on the sidelines, laying out formations and suggesting audibles. He can read defenses, Morrall thought, like most people can read a calendar. He didn't know another quarterback who could come close to Unitas in that skill.

On the Colts next offensive series, Morrall found Orr for 25 yards and then lofted a high 18-yard pass that Ray Perkins made a spectacular diving grab of at the 1-yard line. Matte plowed to paydirt, and Lou Michaels tied the game with an extra point. As he came off the field, Morrall drank in the revived atmosphere. The crowd that had sat in stony silence following his turnover minutes before was now cheering wildly. Morrall thought of his teammates, thought of how no one had panicked in the huddle or shown any anxiety, and instead had met an early challenge, a crisis, with a 72-yard touchdown drive of their own. He had even more respect now for his new team, and he felt confident that they had more respect for him. It was an important turning point, he thought, in the game and in the young season.

Baltimore took the lead for good in the second quarter. Morrall culminated a 58-yard drive with his first touchdown pass as a Colt. Bill O'Donnell called the play on the Colts' radio station:

> "Third down, a yard to go for the first down, the ball at the San Francisco 8-yard line... Here's Morrall faking to [Terry] Cole, flips over the middle... Mitchell's got it at the 5-yard line, all alone... Touchdown Colts!"

In the third quarter, Morrall threw his third touchdown pass of the game, a 16-yarder to Orr, and Michaels added two field goals to complete a 27–10 final. The win was personally satisfying for Morrall for two reasons: it marked the first time he had played a complete regular season game in two years, and it gave him a victory over his former teammates. Voted the game ball in the locker room, Morrall left Memorial Stadium feeling 12' tall. He knew his teammates hadn't voted him the game ball because of his performance. He felt he had made a million mistakes. They did it because they wanted him to feel accepted.

Morrall followed by guiding the Colts to a 28–20 victory over Atlanta by overcoming three interceptions with three touchdown passes, including a flea-flicker pass to Jimmy Orr for a crucial score. Morrall then engineered a 41–7 win over another former employer, the Steelers, in sun-bathed Pitt Stadium. He played his best game of the young season in Week 4. Throwing for 302 yards and four scores, Morrall dissected a physical Chicago Bears defense, 28–7.

> O'Donnell: "Here are the Colts, breaking from their huddle... Morrall sending Orr out to the right, Richardson just as wide left. So, from the Bear 38-yard line, Morrall, play-action fake here to Hill, Earl rolling out to his right, he's back to the 45... Morrall throwing deep down the right side, headed for

> *Jimmy Orr... Caught at the goal line! Touchdown Colts! It's*
> *now Baltimore 20, Chicago 7..."*

One week later, Morrall beat his former 49ers teammates again, this time by 42–14. Preston Pearson gave Baltimore an electrifying start in Kezar Stadium.

> O'Donnell: *"Pearson waiting for the kickoff and has it at the*
> *4-yard line... He's up the middle to the 10, Pearson to the*
> *20-yard line...Four blockers in front of Pearson now as he gets*
> *to the 30... Cutting back to his left at the 35, has blockers*
> *ahead of him, here's a block by Cornelius Johnson... Pearson*
> *at the 50... [Timmy] Brown throws a block for Pearson at the*
> *49ers' 40-yard line... Pearson to the 30, he's being chased by*
> *Johnny Fuller... Pearson to the 20, Pearson to the 10, Fuller*
> *dives for him at the 5-yard line, he doesn't get him... It's a*
> *touchdown for Preston Pearson, a 96-yard touchdown return!*
> *And here's Pearson in the end zone, he's mobbed and hugged*
> *by Bill Curry and Roy Hilton and Alex Hawkins."*

With 11 minutes left in the game and the Colts leading 28–17, Unitas made his first appearance of the regular season. His passes lacked their normal power and speed, but he compensated with his play calling. He crossed up the 49ers defense with his play-action fakes and delivered two touchdowns.

But it was Morrall who found himself in the midst of an MVP-caliber season, and Baltimore poet Ogden Nash took time off from tending his dogwood trees and mint bushes to sing the praises of the Colts' new quarterback in his *Life Magazine* article:

> *"Once a grim second-stringer, a sad Giant castoff,*
> *Earl today is the spark of a thundering blast-off.*
> *Though the fables of Aesop still wear a green laurel,*
> *They end where the Colts now begin, with a Morrall.*
> *For it's Morrall to Mackey, yes, Morrall to Mackey,*
> *A refrain that is driving the corner men wacky.*
> *They lock up against Richardson, Perkins and Orr,*
> *Then it's Morrall to Mackey, right through the front door.*

Perhaps it is hindsight, perhaps it's a sophistry,
But the Colts owe a lot to Giant front-offistry."

Like the Motown group, Martha and the Vandellas, the Colts had their fans dancing in the streets from Baltimore to D.C.

"The people in Baltimore knew the Colts' players, we were part of their family," left guard Glenn Ressler said. "And we were very close as a team. The Colts were a family. The players were truly friendly with one another, and that's an important part of a winning team, associating with each other off the field. It was truly a unique situation."

Baltimore was in a feel-good mood, and even the strict Shula relaxed on occasion with a joking remark. "The good thing about Earl Morrall," he said of his well-traveled veteran, "is that we always have a homecoming for him."

Turning serious, Shula said Morrall had "an enormous amount" of adjusting to do. "But he did it because of his great poise and intelligence," Shula said. "Morrall was fantastic."

To his credit, Morrall downplayed the revenge factor when facing former teams. When he was pressed on the issue by reporters, he would run a hand through his dark crewcut and smile. "I just wanted to prove I can still play in this league," he said. "After so many ups and downs, it's nice to win."

Surrounded for the first time in his career by a strong supporting cast, Morrall made the most of the talent at his disposal. The left side of the Colts offensive line featured Ressler at guard and All-Pro Bob Vogel at tackle. Curry had started at center for Vince Lombardi's 1966 Super Bowl champion Packers, and right guard Dan Sullivan and right tackle Sam Ball paved the way for Matte, Hill, and Terry Cole to combine for 1,400 yards rushing and 13 touchdowns.

"We knew Earl would need a strong running game to help him with his passing," Shula said. "So we put more emphasis on it."

Hill said the entire offense realized that Morrall needed their help. "It had to be a cooperative effort without Unitas," he said.

Baltimore's top running play in 1968 was "Draw Play, Center Lead." The effectiveness of this play hinged on Curry's ability to make a difficult cutoff block on the middle linebacker. At the snap of the ball,

Curry would loop behind Sullivan and into the designated hole. Matte delayed while the pass rush developed, then took Morrall's handoff. Timing Curry's seal block on the linebacker, Matte would slip into the running lane between Sullivan and Ball. The play was based on timing and finesse—two factors which suited Matte, who was a shifty but not speedy runner.

Handing off to his backs and throwing to a receiving corps that included Mackey, Orr, and Willie Richardson and combined for 111 catches and 19 touchdowns helped smooth Morrall's transition.

"This is a guy we feel has the greatest ability to do the job, and we hope he can do it for us," Matte said at the time. "He has all the experience of a great quarterback. He just didn't have a great team behind him and now he does."

Pearson respected the way Morrall dealt with the difficult spot he was placed in as Johnny U's replacement.

"To come in and do what he did, replace 'The Man,' that was something," Pearson said.

"Earl was a unique person," Ressler said. "I don't like to call him a journeyman quarterback because he was a great quarterback. He had just been with teams that were limited. He was a nuts-and-bolts quarterback. He didn't always throw a pretty pass, but he got the job done."

Members of the ferocious Colts defense were gaining confidence in their surprising quarterback, as well. "I thought Earl was fantastic," Boyd said. "I had all the confidence in the world in him. He was a very good player, very smart."

Unitas told Chuck Thompson late in the season that he was impressed with the way Morrall had handled himself since arriving in Baltimore.

"I don't think you can say enough about Earl Morrall," Unitas said. "He came from another team to an organization that was completely foreign to him, and he's picking things up like it was nothing and getting our system under control. He's been doing a fine job all year."

Baltimore had won its first five games of the season, but some Colts veterans still harbored hopes that Unitas would soon return as the starter. "Each week, our rallying cry was, 'John will be well next week,'" Hawkins said.

Unitas did return in Week 6 when Baltimore hosted Cleveland amid brilliant fall weather. The unbeaten Colts were favored to beat a Browns team that brought a mediocre 3-2 record to Memorial Stadium. An audience of 60,238 was on hand for the expected rout, but Cleveland quarterback Bill Nelsen silenced the big crowd for much of the afternoon. Nelsen hit the seams in the Colts zone and halfback Leroy Kelly gouged out consistent gains on the ground to give the Browns a 14-7 halftime lead. With his team trailing at the break, Shula told Morrall he was going to make a change at quarterback. "John will start the second half," he said.

Unitas' aching arm produced just one completion in 12 attempts, and three of his passes were intercepted in an eventual 30-20 Browns win. The stunning loss was Baltimore's first of the season and dropped the Colts to second place in the Coastal Division behind the defending champion Rams. Up next for Baltimore was a home date with L.A., which was 6-0 and had beaten the Browns 24-6 four weeks earlier.

Fresh in the collective memory of the Colts was the 34-10 defeat they had endured in the Los Angeles Coliseum in the final game of the 1967 regular season. For Baltimore and its rabid fans, the rematch with the Rams offered nothing less than an opportunity for redemption.

It was, as Thompson liked to say in his Colts radio broadcasts, "Time to go to war, Miss Agnes!"

5

Go to War, Miss Agnes

TIME WILL NOT DIM THE GLORY OF THEIR DEEDS.

The stainless-steel lettering that appeared on the brick façade of Baltimore's Memorial Stadium gleamed in the autumn sunlight on the afternoon of Sunday, October 27. Football fever filled the streets of the city's east side as the 2:00 PM kickoff for the Western Conference showdown with the Los Angeles Rams neared.

Fans crunched through showers of gold, red, and brown leaves that fell along 33rd Street in front of the stadium. Ellerslie Avenue, Ednor Road, and East 36th Street were crammed with cars that made one take pride in Detroit engineering. There were Ford Thunderbirds with sloped hoods and a Diamond Lustre finish that advertisements of the day would boast "lasts and lasts, without waxing." There were four-door Bel Airs, two-door Impalas, along with Corvairs and Fairlanes. Ads proclaimed the latter was designed "expressly for the young of all ages who desire the dash of a sports car and the open-air freedom of a two-door hardtop."

What each car owner had in common this day was a desire for a parking place. Memorial Stadium's parking lots, however, could not accommodate a capacity crowd, and cars could be seen jockeying for position on side streets like Frisby and Homestead. Some fans chose to park near Johns Hopkins University and hop the No. 3 bus line to the stadium.

As fans pushed through the turnstiles and walked up the concrete ramps into the stadium, they got their first glimpse of the field below. Some looked up and thought it a good omen that the bright skies were Colt blue [pronounced "Coat" blue in the accent of Baltimoreans]. Smoke from cigars and cigarettes swirled in the sunshine and mixed with the scent of grilled food to create an unmistakable aroma.

The setting stirred memories of the lines from Ray Bradbury's poem on pro football, "All Flesh is One: What Matter Scores":

> In this mild romp we teach our lambs and colts
> Ascensions, swift declines, revolts, wild victories,
> Sad retreats, all encompassed in the round
> Of one autumnal October afternoon.

City fathers built Memorial Stadium as testimony to America's fighting men. Colts fans saw it as a shrine to their Sunday warriors. A multipurpose park, Memorial Stadium played host to the Colts and baseball's Orioles. The stadium floor was infamous for its scruffy crab-grass and sizable divots. Pittsburgh Pirates outfielder Roberto Clemente would complain bitterly about the pock-marked condition of right field during the 1971 World Series. The football field ran north-south; its end zones were located in center field and behind home plate, respectively. A row of bright green Lombardy poplar trees lined an embankment beyond the fence of the north end zone.

Memorial Stadium's most visible and famous feature was the shadow-streaked cinder corner of the end zone called "Orrsville." It was named for Jimmy Orr, a wide receiver who played for Baltimore from 1961–70 and seemed to catch the majority of his touchdown passes in that area of the field. At the close of Colts practice every Thursday, Orr would work with his quarterbacks on timing patterns that ended in Orrsville. Colts quarterbacks would stand at the opponent's 40-yard line and throw deep passes that Orr would gather in on the cinder track.

"I was comfortable there," Orr said. "The guy on the road playing there maybe once a year was not."

Colts home games were special events for the city's fans. Baltimore was the only NFL team that started its home games at 2:00 PM rather than 1:00 PM. Everything about a Sunday afternoon game at Memorial Stadium reflected the team and its surrounding city. The stadium was shaped like a horseshoe and its concession stands were operated by kindly women who referred to each customer as "Hon." The atmosphere on game days was electric. A white horse named Dixie and her female rider bolted up and down the sideline, and the stadium itself seemed to shake from the combination of rallying cries and raucous chants. Visiting media marveled at the scene. Steve Bisheff of the *Los Angeles Herald-Examiner* called Memorial Stadium an "outdoor zoo."

"The outdoor insane asylum," Colts halfback Tom Matte said with a laugh as he recalled Memorial Stadium. "Baltimore was a blue-collar town, and at that particular time, we were blue-collar workers. We weren't above the fans, and we weren't below them, either. We were a part of the community, and we were very active in the community. We put a lot back into it."

Colts cornerback and defensive captain Bobby Boyd thought Baltimore's fan base made Memorial Stadium special. "To me, it was the greatest place in the world to play," Boyd said. "We had well over 100 games in a row that were sellouts. It was a unique time in a unique place. I know opponents didn't like to come there. They knew it was going to be a hornet's nest."

The fans were raucous, linebacker Mike Curtis said, because the Colts were so damn good. "They all went ballistic, that's just the way it was," Curtis said. "They supported a winner. I'd go over to east Baltimore and have a beer with them. I enjoyed it because I grew up in an area like that."

"Once the fans get behind you, they're behind you," safety Jerry Logan said. "I would stack those people up against anybody as far as a fan base goes. I always loved to play there because I knew the fans would be there and they would be loud."

The zoo was at it most riotous when the Rams arrived for a mid-season collision of Coastal Division powers. Fans crowded into the Colts' Corral cheering sections located throughout the stadium. "They had the Corrals all over," middle linebacker Dennis Gaubatz said. A sign was held up that read "Slam the Rams." Down on the field, five Baltimore cheerleaders carried small placards, each bearing a letter of a word they would spell out to the accompaniment of loud chants: C-O-L-T-S.

Colts home games carried the feel of a college campus, and every Sunday was Homecoming. Just as most college stadiums are built into the campus, Memorial Stadium sat amid surrounding neighborhoods of stucco-and-stone Tudor-style row homes. Adding to this collegiate-like atmosphere was the Baltimore Colts Marching Band. Dressed in blue and white uniforms, they represented the most famous marching band in pro football. When they paraded to midfield at Memorial Stadium, they brought the capacity crowd to its feet. Their theme song, penned in 1947 by Joe Lombardi and Benjamin Klasmer, was known to every Colts fan:

> *"Let's go you Baltimore Colts*
> *And put that ball across the line*
> *So, drive on you Baltimore Colts*
> *Go in and strike like lightning."*

Founded in 1947, the year the Colts joined the All-America Football Conference, the Colts Band has survived despite losing its team on two occasions—from 1951-52 and from 1984-95. The Band was renowned enough to be invited to play in other teams' halftime shows as well as at the Pro Football Hall of Fame Game each July in Canton, Ohio, and in parades and concerts.

While the Colts Marching Band entertained fans with music on autumn Sundays, radio announcer Chuck Thompson entertained listeners with a voice distinctive for its richness and resonance. Born in Palmer, Massachusetts, Thompson grew up in Reading, Pennsylvania. He began his career as a vocalist but realized early on that his future would not be as a singer. He took up broadcasting and began what became a Hall of Fame career when he was hired while still in high school to do sports reports at WRAW, a 250-watt station in Reading. Thompson graduated to reporting on college sports and began broadcasting games from nearby Albright College. He was hired by WBIG in Philadelphia and was covering local sports when he entered the army during World War II. He served with the 30th Infantry's Recon Troop in the Battle of the Bulge, and it was during his service time that he realized that his career lay in sports broadcasting. "That was one of the good things about the army," Thompson said. "It gave you time to think."

Thompson returned to Philadelphia after the war. He broadcast Phillies and Athletics baseball games, as well as college football and high school basketball. His association with Baltimore sports began in 1949 when he was hired to cover the Colts. When the St. Louis Browns baseball franchise relocated to Baltimore in 1954 and became the Orioles, Thompson became one of the few sports broadcasters at the time to cover both the NFL and major league baseball on a full-time basis. That same year, Thompson did his first weekly national NFL telecast when he broadcast Saturday night games on the Dumont Network. In the mid-1950s he teamed with Ernie Harwell on Colts radio broadcasts.

Fate smiled on Thompson again four years later. Standing in the office of NFL commissioner Bert Bell on Friday, December 26, 1958, Thompson called "heads" when the commissioner flipped a coin into the air. The coin toss was to determine whether Thompson or NBC-TV broadcast partner Chris Schenkel would call the first half of the Baltimore Colts–New York Giants championship game the following Sunday. Most announcers preferred to broadcast the second half, since the final two quarters usually proved climactic. Thompson and Schenkel were each hoping to receive that choice assignment, and when the commissioner's coin landed on "tails" it went Schenkel's way. Thompson's seeming loss turned into a huge gain when the game ended in a tie after four quarters. Thompson took over and called the first sudden-death overtime in NFL Championship Game history, and it was Thompson who broadcast Colts fullback Alan Ameche's game-winning one-yard plunge for a touchdown.

Along with Bob Wolff, Bailey Goss, and Joe Croghan, Thompson was one of National Bohemian beer's "Four Horsemen" serving as the radio and TV voices of the Colts. By 1968 he was teamed with Bill O'Donnell. Thompson also hosted a weekly TV show, *Corralling the Colts*. He punctuated his home-spun broadcasting style with phrases that became his trademark. He would put the exclamation point on key plays by exclaiming in his rich, baritone voice: "Go to war, Miss Agnes!" and "Mmmm, ain't the beer cold!" In 1965, Baltimore lost a divisional playoff game to Green Bay in part because a disputed field goal by the Packers Don Chandler was ruled good by referee Norm Schachter. For months afterward, Thompson would conclude his radio show with a bitter remark. "And good night to you, Norm Schachter, wherever you are."

Thompson, the Colts Marching Band, and a large Memorial Stadium crowd were all on hand for Baltimore's midseason meeting with the Rams in 1968. The game featured a battle between the NFL's two most dominant defenses, but it was the Colts unit that stood out this day. Baltimore's defense sacked Rams quarterback Roman Gabriel five times and held Los Angeles to a net of just 148 yards in a 27–10 win. Thompson later said that the Colts defense played with a "controlled fury that was at times frightening to watch."

Keying Baltimore's defensive effort was Mike Curtis. Known around the league as Mad Dog and The Animal, the All-Star outside linebacker set an early tone when he stopped a sweep by fighting past pulling guard Joe Scibelli, then spinning away from fullback Tommy Mason's attempt at a block, and pulling down halfback Dick Bass for a loss. Later, Cutis came on a blitz, went airborne over a Rams lineman, and wrapped his padded forearms around Gabriel's black-and-white helmet. Like a rodeo cowboy wrestling a steer to the ground, Curtis twisted the 6'4", 220-pound Gabriel to the turf and caused a fumble.

Teammate Alex Hawkins said Mike Curtis played as if he was "full of fury," and the Mad Dog's ferocious tackle on Gabriel was preserved in all its fury by the camera lens of Malcolm Emmons and the words of sports writer Larry Merchant, who was covering the game for the *New York Post*:

> *"For a moment you weren't sure if it was the ball or Gabriel's head rolling around. Mike Curtis, a linebacker for the Baltimore Colts, was a history major at Duke. After yesterday's performance against the Los Angeles Rams, it was obvious who his favorite people in history are—Genghis*

> *Khan, William the Conqueror, Sitting Bull, Bonnie and*
> *Clyde, and Vince Lombardi."*

The Associated Press described Curtis' performance against the Rams as "tough, quick, volatile" and named him its NFL Defensive Player of the Week. A native of Washington, D.C., the 6'2", 235-pound Curtis grew up in Rockville, Maryland, in the shadow of the Colts franchise and epitomized the story of a local boy who makes good. A standout athlete at Richard Montgomery High School, he went on to play fullback and linebacker at Duke University. Pro scouts rated Curtis the second best linebacker in the 1965 draft. Number one was Dick Butkus of Illinois.

After Baltimore was routed by Cleveland, 27–0, in the 1964 NFL title game, the Colts decided to draft defensive help. Curtis was a first-round choice by the Colts and a third-round pick of the AFL's Kansas City Chiefs. His decision to play in Baltimore was not a difficult one.

"I didn't know I'd be drafted number one," Curtis said. "I wanted to play close to home, and the Colts were a fine team with a winning tradition. I might have gotten a better deal with the AFL, I don't know. The AFL was a new league, obviously. The prestige of the NFL was the reason I went there. I was really happy with the Colts and pleased with the deal they offered me."

Curtis had led Duke in tackles during his senior season despite playing with a separated shoulder. NFL scouts raved about his ability. Pat Peppler of the Packers was impressed with Curtis' quickness and intensity. "He hits," Peppler said. Peahead Walker of the Giants wrote in his scouting report that Curtis would make an outstanding pro linebacker. Curtis, he wrote, was a "fierce tackler with fine pursuit."

Mike Curtis was so good that Baltimore head coach Don Shula initially had trouble deciding just where to play him when the rookie arrived in camp. Shula knew Curtis was a good linebacker, but he was also aware Curtis had set a team rushing record while at Duke. Curtis was tried out in Colts camp as a backup fullback, but his struggles were obvious. When he ran the wrong pass route in practice, quarterback John Unitas drilled the rookie in the back of the helmet with the football. Game films from the Colts 1965 campaign show Curtis running awkwardly with the ball, and he had trouble cutting back across the grain as pro backs must when the original lane is closed down by the defense.

"I was a flop as a runner," he said. "I wasn't making any progress."

Curtis' difficulties on the field led him to become withdrawn off it, and he rarely said more than a few words at a time to teammates during his entire rookie season. As his confidence sagged, old feelings of inferiority began to surface. He had always battled his insecurities with a drive to be the best, but the realization that he wasn't a good pro fullback haunted him. He fought off his self-doubt with a dedicated training regimen that dropped his weight from 230 pounds to 220 entering the 1966 season. He figured the lighter weight would help his quickness, but when an assistant coach told him that Shula wanted to see him, Curtis' first thought was that he would be playing fullback for another team.

Told that he was going to be switched to linebacker, Curtis finally relaxed. He would still wear the uniform number of a fullback—32—but could now put his Mad Dog mentality to use on defense. He would pull his Colts helmet low on his forehead and squint until his eyes appeared to be no more than slits. He became one of the quickest linebackers in the game—he ran the 40-yard dash in 4.6 seconds—and pysched himself to a fever pitch by repeating mantras: "Be quicker. Move quicker. React quicker."

Mike Curtis opened the 1966 season as a third-string linebacker behind starter Steve Stonebreaker and backup Jackie Burkett. But injuries to both allowed Curtis to earn his first NFL start at his new position in the season's fifth week in a game against Detroit. The Lions tested him immediately by sending a sweep in his direction. Curtis fought off two blockers and stopped the ball carrier for a loss. Later, he batted down a pass. Baltimore won, 45–14, and Curtis was given the game ball.

His confidence restored, Curtis responded when teammates teased him about the string of injuries it took to get him into the starting lineup. "It doesn't matter whether I get hurt or not," he told them. "I'm going to play. I'm not about to give up my job to anybody."

Primed for a big season in 1967, Curtis injured his knee against San Francisco in the third game of the season and had to undergo knee surgery. Any questions concerning his play in 1968 were answered in a preseason game against the AFL's Miami Dolphins. Curtis responded to a Dolphins sweep by knocking the blocker back into the ball carrier so hard that both Miami players had to be helped from the field.

By the mid-point of the 1968 season, Curtis had established himself as one of the game's best outside linebackers. Colts defensive coach Chuck Noll said Curtis was the quickest linebacker in the NFL and had instincts that could not be taught. There was no limit, Noll said, to how good Curtis could be.

A fan sent Mike Curtis a statue of John Wayne, and the Colts linebacker at times seemed as if he was delivering his own brand of frontier justice to ball carriers.

"I guess I'm branded, I'm like the old Western gunslinger," Curtis said at the time. "Everybody wants a crack at me because I'm supposed to be mean and tough. Off the field, I'm a gentleman. But when I'm on the field, I'm an animal. I don't know what makes me so aggressive."

Curtis' dual persona was expressed in a studio brochure he made for his modeling career. The front of the brochure showed the curly-haired Curtis in thoughtful repose, resting his chin against his thumb and forefinger beneath the words, "This man is a GENTLEMAN!" Beneath the photo ran the words "He is also..." and when the page turned, the legend read, "an ANIMAL!"

Colts linebackers coach Hank Bullough thought Curtis' duality stemmed from an inner drive to succeed. "Some people watch him and misconstrue his actions as animalistic," Bullough said. "I call it competitiveness. He longs to play the perfect game."

Shula called Curtis "one of the main differences between the Colts championship team of 1968 and the one we had in 1967. He worked his way into the starting lineup and did a great job."

Curtis returned the compliment. "Shula was a great coach whether you liked him or not, and I liked him," he said.

Shula liked what Curtis brought to the game. Even at his playing weight of 232 pounds, Curtis was as fast as many of the running backs in the NFL at the time. Baltimore was able to double-cover wide receivers because Curtis had the speed to stay with a tight end throughout his route.

Curtis was also intelligent and had a mean streak. On the field, he saw himself as a rugged individualistic, a conqueror—"a Viking or a Cossack," he said—and his on-field fury was always on full display. After Bubba Smith made three consecutive tackles to force a punt, Curtis hurled his helmet to the ground in frustration. "I was glad Bubba made the tackles," he told reporters. "But I get emotional by the time a game starts. I want the Colts and myself to be the best in the world. I despise being second in anything."

The mean streak that Shula admired sometimes worked against Curtis. "Mike Curtis was one of those guys who practiced like it was the Super Bowl," Preston Pearson said. "I remember Shula had to kick him off the field one time."

The incident occurred during the 1968 season. In a practice session, Curtis leveled rookie fullback Terry Cole without warning. Shula considered the offense so blatant he banished Curtis to the sideline for an hour. Curtis also had on-field confrontations with his roommate on the road, center Bill Curry. On one occasion, the two engaged in a slugging match. "Sometimes," Curry said, "he just loses control." Curtis said their disputes never lingered long, however. "Bill and I always make up." Still, teammates were wary of the Mad Dog. Jimmy Orr, whose stall was next to Curtis' in the locker room, made it a point to dress quickly and leave. "I usually get out of here in a hurry," Orr said, "so he doesn't hit me."

Baltimore's victory over Los Angeles began a streak of defensive excellence that was near perfect. The Colts blanked the Giants, 26-0, in Yankee Stadium the following week, Baltimore's first shutout since 1964. In Detroit, they sacked Lions quarterback Bill Munson four times in a 27-10 win highlighted by Preston Pearson's 102-yard kickoff return for a touchdown. The Colts followed with their second shutout in three weeks when they intercepted five passes and battered St. Louis, 27-0.

Against Minnesota in Week 11, the Colts sacked Vikings quarterbacks five times and made a great goal-line stand that stopped back Bill

Brown twice from the 1-yard line in a 21–9 win. Baltimore's defense tied an NFL record one week later by recording its third shutout of the season with a 44-0 victory over Atlanta. On the regular season's penultimate weekend, the Colts headed to Green Bay and earned a 16–3 win over the three-time defending NFL champions on a bright but cold December 7. Because of the historic nature of the day, Lambeau Field was filled with more than 50,000 Packer Backers waving tiny American flags in the chill, windy weather.

The Packers were hampered by the retirement of head coach Vince Lombardi after Super Bowl II and the loss of quarterback Bart Starr to injury, and Baltimore's defense made life difficult for Starr's backup, Zeke Bratkowski. Bill O'Donnell called the key defensive plays on the Colts' radio station:

> *"Third down, Brat back to pass, he's firing, knocked down incomplete and the defensive play has been made by Bobby Boyd...*
>
> *"Fourth down [and] seven from the 7... Zeke back to pass, he's being rushed, it's incomplete! The pass rush was made by Bubba Smith. He made him force a pass and he threw it low, and the Colts defense has held here in Green Bay and has bailed the Colts out again..."*

The victory over the Packers clinched the Coastal Division championship and climaxed a seven-game stretch in which the Colts defense shut out three opponents and surrendered just 32 points and two touchdowns. It was a run of excellence made possible by a unit that blended experience with youth, skill with strategy.

Baltimore's front four didn't have a catchy nickname like L.A.'s Fearsome Foursome or Minnesota's Purple People Eaters. But it did have a pair of 12-year vets in right end Ordell Braase and left tackle Billy Ray Smith. All-Pro Fred Miller started at right tackle, and Charles "Bubba" Smith, who had been moved from his defensive tackle position prior to the start of the season, was an anchor at left end.

"You can have all those fancy nicknames," Smith, a homespun Arkansan, said at the time. "What we play is called defense and nothing else."

The linebacker corps of Curtis, Gaubatz, and right outside line-backer Don Shinnick comprised a unit that ranked with Green Bay's trio of Ray Nitschke, Dave Robinson, and Lee Roy Caffey as the NFL's best. Gaubatz was the ringleader, calling the defensive signals sent in by coordinator Bill Arnsparger. He had come over from Detroit, where he started at outside linebacker and occasionally moved to the middle, and he immediately felt at home in Baltimore.

"Detroit was very cliquish," Gaubatz said. "In Baltimore, they took you under their wing. It was a thoroughly different atmosphere. When I got to Baltimore, Shula looked at my time in the 40-yard dash and wasn't impressed. I said, 'Put your fastest guys out there and I'll race 'em for 20 yards.' He did. One guy beat me by like two inches. I beat the other guys. I wasn't fast, but I was quick.

"When Unitas got hurt, we knew we had to suck it up on defense and not let the other team score. I called the signals sent in by Arnsparger, but if I didn't like the call, I'd check out of it."

Gaubatz said if he did change the play and it didn't work, he'd have to answer for it—not to Arnsparger, but to Shula. "He was a good coach, fair but tough. He'd say, 'Gaubatz, what was that last call?' I'd say, 'Hell, I don't know.' He'd jump all over my tail."

Gaubatz liked to hit opponents high and hard; clotheslining a ball carrier was not the infraction in the 1960s it is in the modern era. "Today, I'd be thrown out of the game in two plays," Gaubatz said.

Shinnick was the best ball-hawk among NFL linebackers in his era. He tied for the league lead with seven interceptions in 1959 when the Colts repeated as league champions, and he would eventually hold the career record for picks by a linebacker with 37. But it was an acquired skill. His first two years in the league he had quite a few deflections but just two interceptions. He quickly realized that holding on to the ball was the most important thing.

In 1964, Shinnick held on to a pass thrown by Starr on a play that proved pivotal to Baltimore beating rival Green Bay and winning the Western Conference title. The Colts were clinging to a 21–20 lead late in the fourth quarter, but the Packers were driving for the go-ahead score. Starr had success all afternoon with a square-out pattern to end Max McGee. The Colts decided to drop Shinnick into short coverage in front of McGee. It was a gamble. With Shinnick vacating his area in the flat, the Packers were free to run one of their patented routes and have a back circle out of the backfield. Starr called the play Baltimore feared, and halfback Tom Moore was all alone in the flat. Starr, however, threw instead to McGee, who was bracketed short and long, and Shinnick intercepted. The Colts ran out the clock to win the game.

Shinnick's method of success was to try to camouflage his coverage. "I tried to make myself scarce when the opposing quarterback was setting up," he said. "If he couldn't find me, I had an important advantage." Whenever possible, Shinnick would move up and down the line behind his defensive linemen in the hope that he would get lost in the crowd.

Bobby Boyd, an All-Pro in 1968, and Lenny Lyles provided a combined 20 years of NFL experience at cornerback, and the safety positions were headed by another All-Pro, hard-hitting Rick Volk, and the heady Jerry Logan. Boyd thought it was significant that Volk and Logan had both played quarterback before switching to defense. Volk went to Michigan as a quarterback, and Logan played the position at West Texas State and led the nation in scoring. The fact that Volk and Logan knew the quarterback position so well helped them recognize what the offense was doing.

Boyd had played the quarterback position, as well. He had gone to Oklahoma as a halfback but moved to quarterback and took the Sooners to two bowl games. Boyd wasn't highly regarded as a pro prospect, since at 5'10" and 190 pounds, he wasn't big enough to be a pro halfback and couldn't throw well enough to be an NFL quarterback. He lingered in the NFL draft until the 10th round when Baltimore selected him. The Colts knew about his physical limitations, but they also knew about his background. Boyd was tough, and he was a winner. He had gone unbeaten in more than 20 bouts as a Golden Gloves boxer in Garland, Texas, where he grew up. And when he arrived in the camp of a Colts team that had just claimed its second straight NFL championship, Boyd impressed head coach Weeb Ewbank enough that he earned the starting left cornerback position.

Opposing offenses routinely challenged Boyd, who was shorter than many NFL defensive backs. But his intensity and mental agility would result in him intercepting 57 passes in his nine NFL seasons to rank third all time at the time of his retirement. He was named All-Pro four times and played in two Pro Bowls.

To the fans in the stands, Big Bubba was the most visible member of the Colts defense. The towering presence of the 6'7", 295-pound Smith inspired chants of "Kill, Bubba Kill!" from fans as well as prose from Baltimore poet Ogden Nash:

> *When hearing tales of Bubba Smith*
> *You wonder is he man or myth.*
> *He's like a hoodoo, like a hex,*
> *He's like Tyrannosaurus Rex.*
> *Few manage to topple in a tussle*
> *Three hundred pounds of hustle and muscle.*
> *He won't complain if double-teamed;*
> *It isn't Bubba who gets creamed.*

Bubba, the name, is a southern derivative of "brother," became a terror during the 1968 season, his first as the starting left end. But it hadn't always been that way for Smith. He had been drafted No. 1 by Baltimore in 1967 even though his teammate at Michigan State, George Webster, had been considered the best player on the Spartans awesome defense. The big stud type of player comes along only once in a lifetime, Shula said, and when he does, you've got to get him. Smith had started at end for Spartans squads that had gone undefeated during the 1965 and '66 regular seasons and fought Notre Dame to the famous 10–10 tie in East Lansing in the 1966 Game of the Century.

When the College All-Stars played the NFL champion Green Bay Packers in the annual College All-Star game, a banner in Chicago's Soldier Field read "Watch Bubba Hit Bart." Bubba did hit Bart. Going against Green Bay star guard Jerry Kramer—whose omission from the Pro Football Hall of Fame remains a mystery—Smith was being handled until he surprised Kramer with his quickness on a pass play. Bubba broke inside of Kramer and sacked Starr for a 10-yard loss. "All night, old man, all night long," Smith told Starr. "Big Bubba's gonna be right here on top of you." Smith didn't get past Kramer again, as the Packer veteran adjusted to the rookie's startling speed. But he left Kramer impressed with his quickness. Bubba was voted the All-Stars' most valuable player in a 27–0 loss, and he went on to impress the Colts in his first training camp. In a one-on-one drill against offensive lineman Dan Sullivan, Bubba flattened the veteran. "The kid really showed me something," Sullivan said.

Perhaps thinking that they had in their midst another "Big Daddy" Lipscomb—the giant defensive tackle who had starred on their 1950s title teams—the Colts tried Bubba at defensive tackle. Despite his immense size and strength, the big rookie failed to gain regular starts. He found himself being cut-blocked at the knees regularly by "those little guys at guard" who he said were afraid to challenge him where he was strongest—his upper body. One such cut block injured his knee, and he went to the bench for the rest of the season. "It messed up my mind," he said. "It was the first time I'd ever been on the bench in my life."

Line coach John Sandusky was put in charge of Smith's development. He found that inside that massive frame was a young man who was emotionally vulnerable. Teammates found him highly superstitious. When Smith got into uniform, the first thing he put on was his left shoe and then his pants. Sports columnist Elinor Kane compared it to a woman putting on her high heels *before* she pulled on her girdle. Baltimore's other Smith on the defensive front, Billy Ray, was usually the first Colts player to arrive at the stadium and so observed Bubba trying to pull his form-fitting uniform pants over his size 14½ cleat. "You never heard such groaning and grunting," Billy Ray said.

Teamed on the left side of the line, the two Smiths had an interesting relationship. Everything one man was, the other wasn't. Bubba stormed into the locker room one afternoon and confronted Billy Ray.

"Billy Ray, what's this I hear? Someone told me that you're in favor of segregation."

Billy Ray jumped to his feet. "Whoever told you that is a damn liar," he exclaimed. "I don't want segregation. What I'm in favor of is slavery."

Bubba was momentarily stunned, and then both men broke up laughing.

Sandusky also cultivated a relationship with Bubba. He called him by his given name, Charles. He praised his effort, flattered him, and encouraged him to lead the team in exercises. Sandusky also moved Bubba back to defensive end, where he had dominated at Michigan State. Relieved, Smith said it was like going home. Big Bubba had been rejuvenated and his confidence restored. "If I'm in the right frame of mind," he said, "I can handle anybody."

Smith's physical presence alone on Baltimore's front four inspired the defense, and the Colts surged into the final regular season game, a rematch against the Rams in the Los Angeles Memorial Coliseum. Baltimore had clinched the Coastal Division title the week before, but when it came to facing their rivals, the Colts defense rarely rested.

> O'Donnell: "Third down and seven yards to go... [Bernie] Casey to the far side, Jack Snow to the near side... Long counting is Gabriel. Back to pass, he's being rushed, he's hit, throws anyway... Intercepted by the Colts at the 30! Curtis, 25, 20, 15, 10, 5... Touchdown! And Mr. Gabriel got burned that time, the second time he's tried to throw the ball while being hit. He did and Curtis had a wide-open field..."

Baltimore won 28–24 to clinch a franchise-best 13–1 mark. The Colts joined the 1962 Packers and '67 Raiders as the only pro football teams in the 1960s to record 13 victories in the regular season.

Baltimore's success was due in large part to a record-setting defense that was No. 1 in the NFL against the pass and confused opposing offenses with complex zone coverages buttressed by an eight-man maximum blitz. At a time when most NFL teams were following the lead of Green Bay's Vince Lombardi and were relying on man-to-man coverage, Shula bucked the trend. He had been raised in the zone in Cleveland under Paul Brown and then in Baltimore under Weeb Ewbank and defensive backfield coach Charlie Winner. The Colts would roll their zones to the strongside or weakside, depending on the formation of the offense. Baltimore also used combination man-to-man and zone coverages.

"In a zone," Logan said, "you give up a few things but you make a team work for what it gets." The Colts might not stop a back from catching a pass out of the backfield, he said, but they could hold the play to minimum yardage.

At the heart of Baltimore's system, however, was a simple philosophy espoused by Arnsparger: "You control the blocker, and you find the football. And tackle. That's defensive football."

The Colts bought into Arnsparger's theory; no one more so, perhaps, than Billy Ray Smith. "Football," he said, "is a very simple game for me. It's like two bulldogs in a pit. It's a fight, that's all, just a matter of who is going to lick who."

Smith's partner at defensive tackle took a different approach. "You don't have to want to kill," Miller said. "You don't have to whip yourself into a nasty mood on Sunday mornings. If I did that, I'd probably make more mistakes."

Ends Braase and Bubba Smith were both schooled to get to the ball carrier by employing a pull-and-reach technique known as the "swim." The maneuver requires the defensive end to pull his arm over his opponent and then bring his elbow back into his man to catapult him to the ball carrier. As employed by Braase and Bubba, the move almost guaranteed them a complete break from the blocker.

Unitas had been part of the championship Colts teams in 1958-59 that featured outstanding defenders in Gino Marchetti, Artie "Fatso" Donovan, Eugene "Big Daddy" Lipscomb, Bill Pellington, et al. But he was just as impressed with their 1968 successors.

"I think our defense has kept us in the game all year long with its tremendous play," Unitas said at the time. "Bobby Boyd, Billy Ray Smith, Bubba Smith...pulling together and doing a heck of a job."

The Colts stampede through the NFL proved to be a healing balm of sorts for a city that just months before was ravaged by riots. What is now remembered as the Baltimore Riot began two days after the April 4 assassination of Dr. Martin Luther King Jr. Baltimore was one of 125 cities that was suddenly engulfed in violence and flames. Maryland governor Spiro Agnew sought to stop the uprising in the black ghettos of East and West Baltimore by calling out thousands of National Guard troops and 500 Maryland State Police. It soon became apparent, however, that state forces could not control the situation, and Agnew was forced to request Federal troops from President Lyndon Johnson. Extensive property damage and looting ensued; businesses were destroyed, many of them belonging to whites who were of Jewish background.

By Sunday evening, the second day of the civil disturbance, the streets of Baltimore resembled a war zone. Mixed with rioters were 5,000 paratroopers, artillerymen, and combat engineers from the XVIII Airborne Corps in Fort Bragg, North Carolina. Specially trained in riot control tactics, they hit the streets equipped with fixed bayonets and chemical disperser backpacks. Two days later, a Light Infantry Brigade from Fort Benning, Georgia, joined them. Martial Law was enforced, and a general curfew of 6:00 PM was set inside Baltimore City limits. Airborne units arrested more than 3,000 people, yet rioting continued. More than 1,000 fires were set, and more than 1,000 businesses had been looted or burned. Some never reopened. Eventually, African-American plainclothes officers and community leaders were sent to the ghettos to prevent further rioting.

By the time the riot ended, six people died, 700 were injured, and 4,500 had been arrested. Property damage was estimated at $13.5 million.

Members of the Colts witnessed the rioting on TV and struggled to understand what they were seeing.

"The riots were stupid," Curtis said. "They were tearing up their own neighborhoods. We never had any problems with race on the Colts. Our black guys were men, with wives and kids and families."

Pearson, whose fiancée at the time was white, remembered the summer of '68 as a racially charged time.

"It was a tumultuous year for blacks," Pearson said. "I had not been in Baltimore long, and my fiancée and I walked right into the middle of [the turbulence]."

Pearson agreed that the racial problems that were leading to rioting in Baltimore and across the country at the time were not a problem within the Colts organization. Geraldine Young, the widow of former Colts player Buddy Young, thought the Colts and her late husband played a "major role" in civil rights in the city of Baltimore. Pearson remembered having just one incident with a teammate concerning race. But he added that most blacks at that times stayed in "our own area" when it came to visiting nightclubs and restaurants.

Volk credits the relative lack of racial tension on the team to the organization's desire to draft players who had not only talent but character as well. "More so than the best athletes, the Colts were looking for people who could fit in," Volk said. "The guys in Baltimore were classy; they didn't care if you were white or black. There were no ill feelings at all. We were all there to help each other."

For the most part, Colts players were treated by Baltimore's football fans as part of their extended family. "You would walk downtown, people would recognize you, and you would be treated like a king," Boyd said. "People would come up and say hello, and they might ask why you did a certain thing in the game. They'd see you, holler, and say 'hello.' Baltimore people still hold a special place in my heart."

To Volk, Baltimore was a great football town. "If you were a Baltimore Colt," he said, "you were accepted automatically."

Matte said fans routinely called him on his home phone. "They would either chew my ass out or praise me," he said. "The only other place like that in the NFL was Green Bay."

"They cared," Gaubatz said. "In other cities, I would've just been No. 53. Not in Baltimore. I would be out someplace, and they would see me and yell, 'Hey Gaubatz,' and invite me over to their table to talk."

"We were part of the community," Logan said, "and we were out with the people all the time. We were like a big family. It made football fun, knowing they were going to live or die with you, win or lose. Fortunately, we won."

In a year when an instrumental song titled "The Horse" by Cliff Nobles & Co. climbed the pop charts, the Colts had the horses necessary to make a run at an NFL championship.

6

Heidi: The Greatest
Finish Never Seen

While Baltimore rode its destructive defense to an NFL-best 13-1 regular-season record, the New York Jets relied on their high-octane offense to carry them through the second half of their AFL campaign.

The Jets scored 31 or more points in four of their last five games and finished the season with a club record 419 points, second-best in their league. New York went 4-1 in that span, losing only to the Oakland Raiders in one of the most controversial and memorable games in pro football history. It's a game that lives in lore as the Heidi Bowl.

The November 17 matchup of AFL powers brought together East and West; two teams that were 7-2 on the season and two quarterbacks, "Broadway" Joe Namath and "Mad Bomber" Daryle Lamonica, who were both renowned for their big-play passing arms. A victory would give the Jets the Eastern Division title and clinch the first playoff berth in franchise history.

A year earlier, the Jets had upset the Raiders at Shea Stadium, giving Oakland its only loss of the season until a 33-14 defeat to Green Bay in Super Bowl II. The Raiders exacted revenge on the Jets later in the season. Defensive maulers "Big" Ben Davidson and Ike Lassiter took turns smashing Namath to the Oakland-Alameda Coliseum turf. A Davidson forearm decked Broadway Joe and sent his helmet spinning from his head. The moment was caught on camera, and the photo was blown up and displayed in Raiders headquarters. Lassiter fractured the right side of Namath's jaw with a blow to the exposed area beneath his double-bar facemask. One week later, Namath adopted the half-cage facemask that became one his trademarks.

Namath called the Raiders the "dirtiest team in the league." Asked if he thought Oakland's defense would be gunning for him, Namath grinned. "If they want to win," he said, "they'd better be."

Two Jim Turner field goals gave New York an early 6-0 lead. Oakland responded with Lamonica touchdown passes of 9 and 48 yards to Warren Wells and Billy Cannon, respectively. Namath caught the Raiders, their fans, and a national television audience off-guard by scoring on a 1-yard keeper, and the Jets headed into halftime trailing by two, 14-12. The battle between AFL division leaders raged back and forth. "We took it to the Raiders hard," Namath said, "and they fought right back." Namath would be sacked four times, Lamonica twice. Both the tempo and physicality of the game were brutal; these were two teams with a short but bloody history. Broadway Joe re-injured his right thumb; backup fullback Billy Joe blew out his knee.

The lead changed hands six times during the game as Namath and Lamonica lived up to their reputations as the AFL's top gunslingers. One observer declared that Broadway Joe and the Mad Bomber had come to play "with six-shooters drawn and firing right at the start of the game."

As many games as he had worked, Jets radio announcer Merle Harmon had a feeling even before the opening kickoff that this one was going to be special. "I could sense it was going to be a very entertaining afternoon," he said. Indeed, it was. Harmon captured the breathless pace for his listeners:

> *"Third down and 9 on the 29-yard line... Back to pass is Namath, fading way back, throwing to the goal line for [Pete] Lammons... He's got the ball at the 8, he's down to the 5 and he is knocked down on the 4... It is first and goal-to-go*

on the Raider 4... Namath hands off to Mathis, coming back
to the left side behind Herman, swinging wide at the 5, the
3... Touchdown! Bill Mathis, running behind the fine block
of Dave Herman and Mathis goes in to put the Jets in the
lead by the score of 18–14.

"Third-and-goal, the running backs are split... Lamonica
calls the play, gives off to Charlie Smith... Smith tripped up
behind the line, fumbles the ball, and the Jets cover it! The
Jets recover the ball at the 3-yard line... The tackler on the
play was Paul Crane... He turned Smith upside down and
[Gerry] Philbin fell on the loose football.

"Namath back to pass, Namath in the end zone, throwing long for Don Maynard... It is caught by Maynard on the
40, and he is up near the midfield stripe and out of bounds...
First-and-10 at the midfield stripe for New York. Namath
goes back to pass, Joe Willie looking, throwing long down the
sideline for Maynard... He's at the 15, the 10, falls down,
gets up, the 5... Touchdown! On two pass plays of 47 and
50 yards, both to Don Maynard, the Jets are back in front
again, 25–22."

Broadway Joe and the Mad Bomber combined to launch 71
passes, and the stoppages of the game clock that resulted from 29
incompletions, 19 penalties and 75 points extended the game beyond
its scheduled three hours. The fourth quarter alone took 45 minutes
to complete.

From his home in Greenwich, Connecticut, Scotty Connal, the
executive director of NBC Sports, had placed a call at 6:30 PM (EST)
to the president of NBC Sports, Carl Lindemann. "We're in trouble,"
said Connal, who was the link between the mobile unit in Oakland
and Broadcast Operations Control in New York. Lindemann called
network president Julian Goodman. At 6:50 PM, Lindemann called
Connal back with a message. "Mr. Goodman says the game will run to
conclusion."

Connal contacted Broadcast Operations Control to relay the
directive, but despite re-dialing the number six times, he couldn't get

through. All lines within a six-block radius of NBC headquarters, including police and hospital, were dead. The Circle 7 telephone exchange in Manhattan had been overloaded by thousands of calls from fans demanding that the Jets-Raiders game be shown in its entirety and parents who were demanding with equal vigor that the children's special *Heidi* planned for that Sunday evening at 7:00 PM be shown on time. NBC executive Chet Simmons remembered people calling as the 7:00 PM hour approached and asking, "What are you going to do about *Heidi?*" The high volume of calls, Simmons said, "literally blew out the switchboard."

With the game tied at 29 in the fourth quarter, Namath engineered a drive that ended with Turner making his fourth field goal of the day, a 26-yarder with 65 seconds left. The Jets led 32–29 as clocks in the east crept toward 7:00 PM. The Jets kicked off, and the Raiders drove the ball to their own 22-yard line. Lamonica found Smith for a 20-yard gain, and a facemask penalty put Oakland on the New York 43.

NBC cut away to a commercial, and network executives were faced with a momentous decision. Dare they cut away from the game and begin the children's movie *Heidi* at its scheduled starting time? Or do they stay with the game until it's over? Like millions of Americans, Connal was watching the wild west shootout unfolding in Oakland. As the top of the hour approached, he went into near-panic mode. A hurried phone call was placed to the mobile unit in Oakland and producer Don Ellis. Since the TV feed of the game was controlled by the NBC studio in Burbank, Connal told Ellis that Goodman had ordered the game be shown in its entirety. "Call Burbank," Connal told Ellis, "and tell them verbatim what I tell you."

Ellis relayed the message, then told Burbank studio operatives to call Broadcast Operations Control supervisor Dick Cline in New York. Cline got the message, but it failed to include Goodman's directive that the game be broadcast to its conclusion. Instead, Cline is informed that a "suggestion" had been made to keep the game on the air. Earlier in the week, it had been determined that if the game ran long, the network would switch to *Heidi*. "If football wasn't over, we would still go to *Heidi* at 7:00," Cline said. "So I waited and waited and waited and heard nothing." Since Broadcast Operations Control needed direct orders to deviate from its programming schedule, the decision was made to stick with the original plan. The "magic hour," as Cline called it, arrived and still no counterorder had been sent. "I've got to do what we agreed to do," he thought.

At 7:00 PM, millions of football fans sat slack-jawed as the final, tense moments of the Jets-Raiders game was suddenly replaced by the opening scenes of Johanna Spyri's children's classic. "A guy pushes the button at 7:00, and away they went," Simmons said. "And here's the game going right down the crapper."

The fateful switch had been thrown in Burbank, and viewers had been instantly transported from the tumultuous Oakland Coliseum to serene alpine glades, from Broadway Joe and the Mad Bomber to a pastoral pixie.

"Oh my god," Connal thought.

NBC's switchboard in New York lit up like the Rockefeller Center Christmas tree as an estimated 10,000 irate callers jammed the lines. As Klara, Heidi's paralyzed cousin, appeared on the screen, Jets fans scrambled to their radios to tune in Harmon and Sam DeLuca. What followed was one of the most frantic and fantastic finishes in pro football history:

> Harmon: *"Fifty seconds remaining... Lamonica goes back to throw, Lamonica looking, Lamonica throwing, he's got Charlie Smith on the 20, down to the 15, the 10, the 5... Touchdown!*
>
> *"Mike Eischeid to kick off... Downfield comes the football, he boots it on the ground... It's going to be fielded by [Earl] Christy on the 10, Christy is shaken, fumbles the ball! It is recovered by Oakland for a touchdown! The ball bounced into the end zone and was recovered by Preston Ridlehuber for a touchdown... Now listen to this crowd... Thirty-two seconds left, and Oakland has scored two touchdowns in nine seconds... [George] Blanda for the extra point, it's good... The score: Oakland 43, New York 32... An unbelievable finish."*

In millions of living rooms, Jets fans seethed as they watched Jennifer Edwards, in the role of Heidi, strolling along an Alpine hillside with her grandfather, played by Michael Redgrave. The NBC switchboard was so flooded with phone calls it shorted out; over the next several hours, fuses were frantically replaced 26 times. Irate phone callers blew out the NYPD switchboard as well. What was described as the "most elaborate emergency call system in the world" had been incapacitated by the televised image of a little Swiss miss.

Goodman tried to call Cline to get the faulty orders reversed and the game reconnected, but even he couldn't get through. Fans demanding an explanation called the telephone company, local newspapers, and even the police. A resigned Connal called the production truck in Oakland. "Okay guys," he said. "No way we can ever go back to that game. Let's run a crawl."

It took another 90 minutes before NBC ran a crawl across the bottom of its screen reporting the Raiders shocking comeback victory. It read "Sports Bulletin: Raiders Defeat Jets 43–32" and appeared just as Klara was struggling from her wheelchair in a courageous effort to walk. One writer called NBC's skimpy crawl a "scrawny olive branch" and said the Peacock Network should be replaced by an ostrich.

Not everyone was upset with NBC's decision. *Heidi* director Delbert Mann breathed a big sigh of relief when his movie started on time. He thought it would have been a "disaster" for the movie if they hadn't shown it in its entirety since the opening scenes contained a considerable amount of plot information. The first few minutes of the movie were essential. "If you came into the show in progress," Mann said, "you wouldn't know what was going on."

Like most viewers, Mann had a problem with the scrawl NBC ran across the bottom of the screen. But his problem was that it occurred when Klara was rising from her wheelchair in an attempt to walk, an intense and dramatic moment in the movie. "I jumped up and screamed," Mann said.

A beleaguered Goodman released a statement at 8:30 PM (EST) declaring the incident a "forgivable error committed by humans who were concerned about children expecting to see *Heidi*."

NBC news anchor David Brinkley addressed the issue in his "Huntley-Brinkley Report":

"NBC apologized for the error. But by then, Oakland had scored two touchdowns in the last minute, had beaten New York. The game was over, but fans who missed it could not be consoled."

Nonetheless, NBC tried. The next night, Brinkley went on the air to further explain the situation:

"Somebody, in the vast reaches of the NBC Network, didn't get the word.... The result was that football fans by the thousands were roused to a cold fury and some probably haven't cooled down yet. Here is the last minute as it would have been seen last night if somebody at NBC had got the word...."

The final minute was replayed, complete with the original play-by-play of sportscaster Curt Gowdy:

> "*Lamonica to Charlie Smith and... He scores!*
> "*He [Eischied] squibbed this one to prevent a runback... Earl Christy fumbling it around... He fumbled the ball and Oakland has it for a touchdown! Oakland has scored two touchdowns in nine seconds.*"

Syndicated columnist Art Buchwald wrote that "all hell broke loose" when NBC cut off the end of the game in favor of the *Heidi* movie. "Men who wouldn't get out of their chairs during an earthquake rushed to the phones to scream obscenities at the man responsible for cutting off the game," Buchwald wrote.

Cline maintained his innocence. He didn't do anything wrong, he said. He only did what he was supposed to do. "Joe Namath and Co. didn't get the game over in time," he said, "so I went to *Heidi*."

Cline also took exception to Brinkley labeling him "the faceless button-pusher in the bowels of NBC." He wasn't a button-pusher, Cline said, and if he had done the logical thing and preempted the start of the movie, "I would have been fired the next day."

CBS poked fun at its rival network by "revealing" the final minute of the movie: Heidi married the goat keeper, and they lived happily ever after.

The actress playing Heidi, 11-year-old Jennifer Edwards, had a difficult time in the immediate aftermath. The step-daughter of singer-actress Julie Andrews was living in England at the time and unaware of the furor until a Hollywood publicist began sending her manila envelopes stuffed with fan mail, hate mail, and clippings of venomous newspaper editorials calling her the "little brat in white stockings."

She was stunned by the uproar. She couldn't understand, she said, why she was being personally attacked. Years later, Edwards was at Howie Mandel's house for a pool party when Mandel came sprinting toward her. "You're a great moment in sports!" he exclaimed.

Several ironies emerged from the Heidi Bowl. Because of its controversial ending, it remains one of the most memorable regular season games in pro football history. Strangely, earlier that same day, Lindemann had ordered that the end of the San Diego-Buffalo game be preempted in order to begin the Jets-Raiders broadcast precisely at 4:00 PM.

NBC's gaffe was the result of a breakdown in communication, ironic because the network was owned by RCA, the nation's leading communications conglomerate. On a day of poor timing by NBC executives, the *Heidi* movie was being sponsored by, of all things, Timex watches.

The final irony was that for all its controversy, or perhaps because of it, the Heidi Bowl was the best promotion the AFL, and the movie, could have asked for. "People still talk about it," Mann said. "The infamous *Heidi* game." The most infamous gaffe in television history was played up on the front page of the next day's *New York Times* and *New York Daily News*. The headline in the latter read, "Jets 32, Raiders 29, Heidi 14."

Nationally syndicated writer Ed Schuyler wrote, "The most controversial block of the football season is the one thrown by Heidi, the little Swiss girl of storybook lore. Hit by the block were millions of irate football fans and caught in the middle was NBC-TV."

The Associated Press ran a next-day story that captured the contradiction that confronted NBC:

"Thousands of children settled happily in their chairs to watch *Heidi* last night, moments after their fuming football-loving fathers leaped to their feet in outrage and reached for the telephone."

In the years that followed, a red telephone was installed in NBC that served as a direct line to Broadcast Operations Control. It was called the *Heidi* phone. Probably the most significant factor to come out of the Heidi Bowl, said Val Pinchbeck, the NFL's former senior vice president of broadcasting, was this: whatever you do, you'd better not leave a pro football game. In the years that followed, Cline never ceased to be amazed by the number of people who still talk about the *Heidi* game. People, he said, who weren't even born when the game was played.

NBC took out a full-page ad in the *New York Times* and *Los Angeles Times*. It was titled "Huzzahs For Heidi" and contained flattering quotes from critics. The last quote in the last column read: "I didn't get a chance to see it, but I heard it was great." It was signed, "Joe Namath." Years later, Namath worked with Cline. When Cline said he was sorry for the *Heidi* debacle, Namath shrugged it off. "Don't be, we lost."

The immediate aftermath of the game, however, found the Jets seething. Tempers had flared during the game, then raged. Jets coach Weeb Ewbank knew his team was edgy before they even took the field. He tried to calm them with platitudes. "Be intense, not tense," he said. "Play football. Don't fight."

Still, New York was hit with a personal foul on the opening kickoff. Strong safety Jim Hudson was later whistled for unsportsman-like conduct. Hudson protested and was ordered from the field by officials. His replacement, Mike D'Amato, was beaten for the go-ahead score in the final minute when he was outrun to the end zone on a circle pattern by halfback Charlie Smith. "I would've outrun Hudson, too," Smith said.

The Jets suffered their second ejection when defensive tackle John Elliott was sent to the sidelines following Smith's score. Ewbank ranted about the officiating in his postgame conference. Mathis, speaking with color analyst Sam DeLuca on the Jets radio show, called it a "sickening" defeat. "We're just all heartbroken now," Mathis said.

Still on edge, Ewbank took a phone call from his wife, Lucy, who, like many people watching in the tri-state area, thought New York had won.

"Congratulations," she said.

"For what?"

"On winning," she said.

"We lost."

The *Heidi* game has been called the most memorable regular-season game in pro football history. The end result, however, still haunts some of the Jets. New York had control of the game, halfback Emerson Boozer said, and then lost it at the end. Center John Schmitt calls it the "most bitter defeat" he has ever suffered on the football field.

The Jets bounced back by winning their next four games, beginning with a 37–15 victory over the Chargers in sunny San Diego. Ewbank's team was not without its problems, however. Namath had re-injured his right thumb against the Raiders and also had a sore foot. Fullback Billy Joe was lost for the season after tearing knee ligaments in Oakland. Linebacker Larry Grantham had a neck injury; cornerback Johnny Sample, who had played the previous three games with a slightly pulled hamstring, had a temperature close to 102 degrees.

As if their assorted injuries and illnesses weren't aggravation enough, the Jets white road uniforms had disappeared on the trip from Oakland to San Diego. And they were hit with one of the largest fines in pro football history to that point–$2,000–by commissioner Pete Rozelle for criticizing officials. Hudson and defensive coordinator Walt Michaels were fined $150 each, and Hudson and Elliott were each fined $50.

By game day in San Diego, things were looking up for the Jets. Their white road uniforms arrived that morning, and the Jets shook off the loss to the Raiders and played brilliantly before a standing-room-only crowd of 51,175. Among the players at the forefront of New York's surge was Maynard. His explosive performance in the Heidi Bowl—10 catches for a club record 228 yards and one touchdown—was typical of his Hall of Fame career. In San Diego, Maynard wrote his name in the Jets record book again when he hauled in an 87-yard touchdown pass from Namath that was the longest in team history and the AFL's longest scoring reception in 1968. The score highlighted what Harmon described as a "spectacular show of offense" as New York improved to 8–3 and clinched at least a tie for the Eastern Division title.

> Harmon: *"Namath fakes the draw, drops back to pass, he throws long for Maynard down the far side... Don's got the ball at midfield, he's down to the 40, down to the 30, into the clear at the 20, the 15, the 10, the 5... Touchdown!"*

An original member of the Titans, Maynard's game-breaking speed and glue-like hands helped establish a wide-open playing style that became the fledging league's identity. A native of Crosbyton, Texas, Maynard was nicknamed Sunshine or Shine for short. After graduating from Texas Western College, he signed with the New York Giants in 1958 and saw limited playing time as a backup to flanker Frank Gifford in assistant coach Vince Lombardi's offense. Maynard was cut from the Giants in 1959 after Lombardi had left to take the head coaching job in Green Bay and was replaced by Allie Sherman.

"Lombardi was a great coach," Maynard said. "He was a disciplinarian, he wouldn't tolerate mistakes. That was nothing new to me because I grew up that way."

Maynard thought less of Giants head coach Jim Lee Howell. "I was never impressed with Jim Lee," he said. "I don't know how he got the job."

Maynard clashed with Sherman, who couldn't get used to the sight of his receiver running a pass route with long, loping strides. "Run!" Sherman would yell. "This isn't a track meet!"

Angered, Maynard would shout back. "I can cover more ground than any two backs you have here!"

The Giants cut Maynard, and he spent the 1959 season playing football in the Canadian League. Lombardi sought to sign him to the Packers in 1960, but Maynard joined the Titans when the AFL opened operations that same year.

"The only people who went to Titans games were Giants fans who couldn't get tickets to Yankee Stadium," Maynard said. The wiry, 6'1" and 185-pound Maynard wore cutoff sleeves, and had white cleats before Namath. His dark sideburns were long, almost as long as his strides when running routes. His swift feet and sure hands allowed him to flourish in the pass-happy AFL, and by 1968, he had set 14 team records.

When Jets coaches criticized him for running what they felt were undisciplined patterns, Maynard merely shrugged. "My job is to get loose, and I'll get loose whatever way I can figure," he said. "After I get loose, it's up to the quarterback to find me."

Jets quarterbacks, Namath included, found it difficult at first to connect with Maynard. Namath said Maynard's square-out patterns looked more like round-outs. "He doesn't run pass patterns with the perfect precision of a George Sauer," Namath said at the time in comparing his two wide receivers.

Maynard and Sauer were sharp contrasts. Maynard wasn't an all-out, 100-percent practice player, Namath said, because Maynard liked to pace himself. He had enough confidence in his ability to monitor his progress. Sauer, on the other hand, would stay after practice and work constantly on his footwork and catching the ball. He paid strict attention to his coaches; Maynard, at times, didn't. Sauer ran tight patterns; the free-spirited Maynard was known to free-lance. Ewbank benched Maynard several times through the years for blowing pass patterns. Sauer, who started at split end for New York, said Maynard had his own style when it came to running routes. "It's just Maynard," he said.

The animosity between the free-spirited Maynard and Jets coaches reached the boiling point in 1965. After Maynard turned in the opposite direction of a Namath pass and the ball fell incomplete, coaches were waiting for him on the sideline.

"Trade me or shut up!" Maynard shouted. "How am I going to concentrate on catching passes when I have to worry about being yelled at all the time?"

His outburst stunned the team, and the coaches eased up. Finally left alone, Maynard began to get in sync with Namath. Though he worked with 26 different quarterbacks during his 15-year pro career, Maynard's relationship with Namath allowed the two to become one of the game's all-time great pass-catch combinations.

In a 35–17 win over Miami on December 1, 1968, Maynard passed retired Colt Raymond Berry as pro football's all-time career leader in receiving yards with 9,275. Harmon noted the feat during the game, and on the next play, Maynard hauled in a 25-yard touchdown pass from backup quarterback Vito "Babe" Parilli. It marked Maynard's third touchdown of the game—tying a club record shared by several players—and brought a standing ovation from the Shea Stadium crowd of 61,766. Harmon's announcement of Maynard's pro record on WABC caused DeLuca to deadpan, "And I don't think Weeb cares if he wears sideburns or not."

Maynard and Namath both wore white cleats, but that's where their similarities in clothes ended. While Namath favored mink coats, Maynard wore cowboy hats. Still, they shared a desire to live their lives as they saw fit.

"I just like to be different," Maynard said. "I think I'm a colorful type."

Hours of practice helped Namath and Maynard develop a sixth sense between them. Maynard would signal with his hand when he broke a pass pattern and Namath would adjust his reads and look for him. Along with San Diego's Lance Alworth and Oakland's Warren Wells, Maynard was one of the AFL's most feared deep threats. Against the Raiders, the Jets were on their own 3-yard line when Namath found Maynard for a 47-yard completion. When Maynard came back to the huddle, Namath had a question for him.

"Hey Don, how you feeling?"

"Shoot, Joe. I'm just fine."

"Think we can do it again?"

"You go ahead and lay it out there. And I'll go get it."

Namath did, launching a 50-yard bomb that Maynard gathered in for the score. Two plays, 97 yards. Touchdown Jets.

That sequence, coming against one of the AFL's top defenses, spoke volumes about New York's high-powered, high-profile offense. Maynard and Sauer proved the perfect complement to one another. Defenses had to respect Maynard's speed or he would beat them deep; Sauer didn't have great speed, but he ran precision routes. The result was that the Jets devastated defenses not only with the bomb but also with square-outs, slants, hooks, and turn-ins. Each of those patterns was a key component in the Jets quick-strike offense.

"Shoot, we were running things back then that they're not even running today," Maynard said. "One thing about Joe: If we needed 10 yards to get a first down, he'd throw the ball 10 yards, not seven yards like you see quarterbacks do today. And Joe, shoot, he could throw the ball like nobody's ever seen."

Yet over a span of six straight games in the 1968 season, Namath did not throw a touchdown pass. The New York media took to writing "What's wrong with Namath?" stories. But what was overlooked by some was that Namath's strategic passing had helped the Jets win five of those six games.

"What the hell's the difference how you score?" an angry Namath asked reporters. "I don't care how many touchdown passes I've thrown. People are making a big thing out of it."

The Jets made a habit of winning close games with late drives in 1968. Against San Diego in New York's home opener, the Jets trailed by four with 5 minutes left. Mark Smolinski and Emerson Boozer made key gains as the clock wound down, and Boozer scored the game-winning touchdown with a minute remaining.

For the second time in four weeks, the Jets had used a ball-control offense to defeat one of the AFL's top teams. New York's front line had been bolstered by the addition of Bob Talamini. The All-Pro guard who had been a member of the Houston Oilers title teams during the league's early years brought skill and savvy to the Jets line. Talamini started next to Winston Hill, a 6'4", 280-pound tackle who was considered one of the best blocking linemen in AFL history.

The combination of Talamini and Hill gave New York one of the top guard-tackle tandems on the left side of the line in the AFL and one of the best weakside rushing attacks in football. Center John Schmitt served as the linchpin of the line. The right side was fronted by guard Randy Rasmussen and tackle Dave Herman, who would replace Sam Walton and turn in a strong performance despite having previously played guard.

The offensive line's performance paved the way for Boozer and fullback Matt Snell, both of whom had recovered from injuries suffered the season before, to rush for a combined 1,188 yards and 11 touchdowns. New York's ground game was deep and versatile, and it led the league in rushing touchdowns. Boozer flowed through defenses like a trotting horse, pirouetting away from would-be tacklers with a distinctive high-knee style. Columnist Elinor Kaine described him as having "bounce to the ounce."

Boozer's hit-and-spin style stemmed from his playing days at Lucey Laney High School in Augusta, Georgia. Lucey Laney coach David Dupree made his players hit a tackling dummy and spin off. In Boozer's case, it created a running style in which he would hit the primary hole but under control, in case there was no opening. If the hole was closed, Boozer would veer outside and look for another hole, spinning into the open area. Tacklers didn't expect the extra spin move, he said. They didn't expect him to go right in on them and bounce off.

When Boozer first got to the Jets, he had difficulties with his blocking. Ewbank wasn't about to allow an incompetent blocker line up in front of his $427,000 quarterback, so Boozer had to learn to pass block. He learned well enough to eventually be considered the best pass blocker among Jets backs, and he and Snell formed a devastating blocking duo.

Boozer initially had another problem aside from his pass blocking. He developed painful bunions on the side of each foot off the big toe. Boozer balked at having the bunions removed. He remembered the curious case of Billy Joe, his teammate on the Jets in 1968 and the former Denver Broncos and Buffalo Bills running back who was named AFL Rookie of the Year in 1963. Joe had bunions removed following his rookie campaign and afterward had problems maintaining his balance when he ran. Boozer didn't want that to happen to him. "Balance," he said, "let's you twist and turn."

Boozer compensated by buying extra large shoes—size EEE. His feet swam in them, but he lined the shoes with foam rubber and extra soles. Boozer, however, never stopped running with pain. After games he had to soak his feet sometimes for up to an hour before the pain subsided. Ewbank thought his halfback displayed "tremendous courage."

Snell was a plow horse, and he dished out as much punishment as he took. He led the team in rushing, and game films show him lowering his helmet and shoulders into defenders as he exploded into them. Snell and Boozer were solid receivers, and both were adept at blocking for both the run and pass. Mathis, a solid blocker, scored a combined five touchdowns running and receiving, and Billy Joe was one of the strongest inside runners in the league.

New York's solid ground attack provided balance for an offense known primarily for its passing game. Maynard, Sauer, and Lammons comprised a trio of Texans that ranked as one of pro football's top receiving corps.

Against the defending division champion Oilers in the Houston Astrodome, Namath called on all facets of his formidable offense in the closing minutes of a tight contest. Trailing 14–13 with four minutes remaining, the Jets took over on their own 20. Namath gunned completions of 14, 9, and 13 yards to Sauer. His fourth straight completion came courtesy of a shoestring catch by Boozer, who carried to the Oilers 27-yard line for the Jets third first down in four plays. Having moved New York in range of a possible game-winning field-goal attempt by Turner, Namath switched gears and called upon his time-consuming ground game. Boozer and Snell carried twice each, and it was left to Snell to power his way into the end zone on an off-tackle slant behind Hill with 45 seconds to play.

In the Jets radio booth, personnel director George Sauer Sr. told his audience, "You won't see many drives better than that one."

New York's late march capped a 20–14 win and re-established the Jets control of the Eastern Division race. One month later, on a cold and rainy November 10, before 60,242 soaked fans at Shea Stadium, the Jets all but ended the Oilers reign as division champs with a 26–7 win. Mathis slogged through Shea's icy mud puddles to score two touchdowns, and Turner drilled four field goals.

Two weeks later, New York clinched a tie for the division title with three games remaining when it rebounded from the Heidi loss to the Raiders and downed San Diego. The Jets title-clinching became official the following Thursday when Kansas City eliminated Houston from contention with a 24–10 win on Thanksgiving Day.

With the division title secured, the Jets primed themselves for the postseason by winning their final three regular-season games to finish 11–3. Against the Dolphins in the Miami Orange Bowl in the season finale, Jim Turner drilled a field goal and four extra points to lift his point total for the season to 145, the fifth highest mark in pro football history at the time.

Earlier in the season, Jets players had dedicated themselves to winning a title and vowed not to cut their hair until they had accomplished their goal. By December 1968, the Jets shaggy appearance made them look like extras from the musical *Hair*:

> "Gimme a head with hair, long beautiful hair
> Shining, gleaming, streaming, flaxen, waxen
> Give me down to there, hair
> Shoulder length, longer, hair!"

The players' unshorn appearance helped the club achieve a swaggering esprit de corps and created an identity with New York's younger fans, many of whom would show up at Shea Stadium on game days as if they were arriving for a love-in. Their Love Bugs and minibuses were decorated in splashy, Peter Max–style day-glo colors. On the bumpers were stickers that read, among other things, "Question Authority."

In the AFL, 1968 was, indeed, the year of the Jets. As the Concorde supersonic passenger jet prepared to make its first test flight, the Jets were preparing to make some noise of their own in the postseason.

The AFL and NFL playoffs were at hand.

7

The March to Miami

All the leaves were brown and the sky was gray as the 1968 NFL play-offs began with bruising intensity in Cleveland's Municipal Stadium. Saturday, December 21, saw the skies over Ohio threatening an after-noon snowfall. By 1:00 PM (EST), the cavernous Olympic-style stadium that sat hard on the bank of Lake Erie was filled with 81,497 fans for the Eastern Conference final between the Cleveland Browns and Dallas Cowboys.

Officially dedicated on July 1, 1931, the massive steel-and-concrete structure was home to both the Browns and baseball's Indians. Gray and dingy, with rusting steel pillars supporting its upper tiers, players and fans alike referred to Municipal Stadium as the "mistake by the lake." By December, its bluegrass turf was worn and brown. The field ran northeast to southwest, with end zones located in center field and behind home plate. Inclement weather turned the baseball infield slick, and the off-track conditions varied from November mud to December frost. The front of the stadium carried a sign that read, "Home of the Cleveland Browns" in large brown-and-orange lettering accompanied by the team logo, a grinning elfin figure holding a football.

The Cowboys entered the conference playoff as prohibitive favor-ites to reach the NFL Championship Game for the third consecutive year. Dallas had defeated Cleveland four straight times dating to 1966, including a 52–14 victory on Christmas Eve in the 1967 playoffs. Only a pair of last-minute victories by the Green Bay Packers in the title games the past two seasons had prevented head coach Tom Landry's team from representing the NFL in the first two Super Bowls. In Week 2 of the 1968 regular season, the Cowboys converted Browns turnovers into points in a 28–7 win at the Cotton Bowl. Dallas and Cleveland were the dominant powers in the Eastern Conference, so much so that Gib Shanley, who broadcast Browns games on WHK Radio, predicted at the close of the 1967 season that Landry and Cleveland coach Blanton Collier "could very easily meet again next year in Cleveland for the Eastern Conference championship."

Shanley proved prophetic. The Cowboys cruised to the Capitol Division crown with a 12-2 record that was the best in the nine-year history of the franchise. Avoiding major injuries, they won their first six games by outscoring opponents by an average of 36–11 and closed their campaign with five straight victories. Dallas put together an awesome statistical season. Their flashy, multiple I-formation offense produced an NFL-best 431 points. Landry's Doomsday defense and its imaginative Flex formation, which featured two down linemen offset, surrendered just 186 points, second in the league to Baltimore.

The Browns road to the Century Division title was not as smooth. They started slow en route to a 10-4 finish and underwent a change at the quarterback position early in the season when Bill Nelsen, recently acquired from Pittsburgh, replaced Frank Ryan as the starter. Cleveland's strength, as it had for years, lay in its ground game. Running in the footsteps of Marion Motley and Jim Brown, halfback Leroy Kelly led the NFL in rushing for the second straight season. In the process, Kelly joined Brown and former Green Bay fullback Jim Taylor as one of just three men in NFL history to that point to rush for more than 1,000 yards in three consecutive years. Receivers Paul Warfield and Gary Collins helped balance the Browns ground game. While Cleveland's offense was impressive, however, its defense was less so. The Browns had allowed 273 points during the regular season, the most of any playoff team from either league in 1968. Still, Landry warned his squad not to take the Browns lightly.

"In a championship game like this," Landry said, "there aren't 2 inches separating the teams."

His players listened, but the feeling inside the organization was that the Doomsday defense could control Kelly and Co., and that the Cowboys offense, led by quarterback "Dandy" Don Meredith, backs Don Perkins and Dan Reeves, and game-breaking receiver "Bullet" Bob Hayes would roll up points on Cleveland's suspect defense. To some, the Browns were seen as a mere speed bump on the road to Dallas' highly-anticipated showdown with Baltimore in the NFL championship game.

Dressed in royal blue jerseys and silver metallic pants, the Cowboys quieted Cleveland's howling fans early. Linebacker Chuck Howley decked Nelsen on a blitz that forced a fumble, and he scooped the ball from the turf and returned it 44 yards for a score. To Browns fans, Howley's touchdown was eerily similar to their team's September 22 loss at Dallas. In that game, Cowboys defensive tackle Bob Lilly had forced a fumble that was recovered by end Willie Townes and returned for a score. Doomsday struck again later in the first half. Linebacker Dave Edwards picked off a Nelsen pass intended for Warfield to set up a Mike Clark field goal for a 10–3 lead.

With time running out in the opening half, the Browns finally brought the big crowd to its feet. Slipping out of the backfield on a pass play, Kelly got behind Howley on a deep route and was wide open when he gathered in Nelsen's pass at the 15-yard line. The 45-yard touchdown play not only tied the game at halftime, it gave the Browns a needed boost.

Wearing their classic white uniforms trimmed in burnt orange and brown, Cleveland carried its momentum into the second half. On the first play from scrimmage, Meredith's sideline pass to Hayes was batted in the air and intercepted by linebacker Dale Lindsey, who returned it 27 yards to the end zone. The Cowboys quickly collapsed. On Dallas' next series, Meredith's pass to Lance Rentzel bounced off the receiver's hands and into the grasp of cornerback Ben Davis. The turnover set up the game-breaking score by Kelly. Veering right on the Browns famous sweep, Kelly burst through an attempted tackle by cornerback Cornell

Green and followed center Fred Hoaglin and tackle Dick Schafrath for a 35-yard touchdown and a 24-10 lead.

Snow fell from darkening skies as the final seconds melted away in the Browns 31-20 upset victory. As the white veil of flakes swirled beneath the bright stadium lights, it was clear that the catalysts for Cleveland's victory were the four turnovers committed by the Cowboys offense. Nelsen, interviewed by CBS-TV sportscaster Tom Brookshier after the game, praised his team's defense. "When the defense gives us the ball that many times," he said, smiling and squinting under the bright television lights, "we're going to score some points."

Having stunned the rival Cowboys, the Browns settled back on Sunday to watch the CBS broadcast of the Western Conference championship between the Colts and Minnesota Vikings in Baltimore. Guided by icy-cool coach Harold "Bud" Grant and his fiery quarterback, "Injun'" Joe Kapp, the Vikings rode this Canadian Football League combination to an 8-6 record that proved good enough to win the Central Division title.

The Colts-Vikings playoff not only offered a rematch of their regular-season meeting in late November which was won by Baltimore 21-9, it also matched up two of pro football's most physical defensive units. Game day in Baltimore was miserable. A steady mix of cold rain and sleet pelted Memorial Stadium and turned the stadium floor, already winter-brown and sparse in some areas, into an icy mud bowl. The temperature at kickoff was 30 degrees; 14-mph winds dropped the wind chill into the low 20s. Colts fans, more than 60,000 strong, bundled against the elements in winter coats and rain gear, cheered wildly as stadium announcer Rex Barney introduced the Baltimore offense:

> "At quarterback, No. 15, from Michigan State, Earl Morrall..."

Despite the dreary elements, Morrall took a certain amount of comfort from playing at home in Memorial Stadium. There was something comfortable about being in his stadium, in his town, in front of his fans. And he always seemed to play better among friends. To him, playing a game at home was like being in a room in his house. There was something secure about it; a feeling of comfort he never got anywhere else, even in the home of a close friend. The house could be the same, but it was still different; it wasn't his.

Morrall knew he was going to need as much good karma as possible facing the Vikings. Baltimore had beaten Minnesota 21-9 on November 24 and Jimmy "the Greek" Snyder had installed them as 11-point favorites in the rematch. Morrall, though, remembered how Minnesota's rugged defense had succeeded in shutting out the Colts offense in the second half. The Vikings featured a rugged front four. Ends Jim Marshall and Carl Eller teamed with tackles Alan Page and Gary Larsen to form the famed Purple People Eaters. They were also called the Purple Gang and the Four Norsemen.

Whatever name they went by, Morrall knew the Viking defense posed a lot of problems. Minnesota had replaced Green Bay as the most physical team in the NFL, but the Central Division champions weren't just about muscle. Minnesota played mental games with opposing offenses, as well. During the 1968 season, the Vikings had confused quarterbacks with an array of defensive schemes. They would replace a linebacker with an extra defensive back in an early version of the "nickel" defense, but in the Vikings scheme, they would stunt with the extra defensive back or use him to double up on outside receivers. In a game against Washington on November 3, Minnesota surprised Redskins quarterback Sonny Jurgensen by replacing all three starting linebackers with defensive backs. Jurgensen found himself with plenty of time to throw but no one to throw to. His passing routes flooded with defenders, Jurgensen was forced to hold the ball longer than usual and was overwhelmed by a wave of purple. He was sacked eight times for minus-49 yards in a 27-14 Viking victory.

A showdown of great defensive units was anticipated, and Minnesota's Purple People Eaters proved dominant in the early going. With the stadium lights flaring on their glistening purple helmets and illuminating uniforms that were white in the early going, the Vikings quickly shook off whatever nervousness might have afflicted them in the first playoff game in franchise history. Eller drove his helmet into Earl Morrall's midsection on a first-quarter sack, and Larsen and Page combined to trap Morrall for another loss.

CBS-TV sportscaster Jack Whitaker later called the first quarter a "defensive spectacular," and the defense continued to dominate throughout the first 27 minutes of scoreless play. Minnesota's Purple Gang sacked Morrall three times in the first quarter alone; defensive tackle Fred Miller responded with a great first half for the Colts. As halftime approached, Baltimore's offense finally broke on top. Morrall had beaten the Vikings deep in their November encounter and found flanker Willie Richardson for a 39-yard scoring pass in the second quarter.

For the rematch, the Colts installed a new sideline pattern that called for the receiver—in this case, Richardson—to break down and then in toward the sideline. Film study had revealed that Minnesota made extensive use of linebackers Roy Winston, Wally Hilgenberg, and Lonnie Warwick in pass coverage. Baltimore figured the down-and-out move would move pull the covering linebacker out of position. To thwart the rush of the Purple Gang, Morrall would fake to the fullback and roll out behind him.

Chuck Thompson made the call on the Colts radio broadcast:

> "First-and-10 from the Baltimore 25, no score... Morrall at quarterback, eyeing the defense, rolls out to his left side, Morrall rolling to his left, setting up, now fires... Willie Richardson makes the grab at the 50! The Viking 40, Viking 30, the Viking 25, Richardson to the Viking 15 and out of bounds, and they ruled that he stepped out of bounds upfield at about the 36-yard line of the Minnesota Vikings... Morrall, rolling out to offset that tremendous pressure developed by the Minnesota front four.
>
> "First-and-10 from the Viking 36... Morrall, looking at the defense, rolls off to the right side this time, Morrall rolling out, setting up, firing deep... And racing down at the 1-yard line, a diving grab and out of bounds at about the 3-yard line, a beautiful, beautiful catch by Willie Richardson."

Breathing clouds of steam as he shouted signals at the line of scrimmage, Morrall dropped back, looked left, and found tight end Tom Mitchell in the end zone for the game's first score. The touchdown came from a double tight-end alignment that Baltimore head coach

Don Shula had used on occasion during the regular season. The alignment seemed to confuse the Vikings, who blitzed right cornerback Ed Sharockman and left Mitchell wide open in the end zone.

> Thompson: "Morrall, looking for a receiver, Morrall throws into the end zone... Touchdown, Baltimore! Tom Mitchell on the receiving end of the pass from Earl Morrall and Baltimore scores first."

The Colts clung to their 7–0 lead at the close of the first half. A gray fog stretched like gauze over Memorial Stadium at the start of the third quarter and all but obscured the poplar trees beyond the north end zone. An icy rain intensified the playing conditions. On the Colts sideline, defensive tackle Billy Ray Smith exhaled small clouds of frosty air as he exhorted the offense through his mud-caked facemask. Facing second-and-9 from the Vikings 49-yard line, Morrall took a short drop and lofted a pass to tight end John Mackey. The ball barely slipped past the outstretched fingers of Winston. Mackey hauled it in at the 35, used his 225-pound bulk to run over safety Paul Krause, and then used speed uncommon for a big man to outrun cornerback Earsell Mackbee to the end zone.

> Thompson: "Still huddled back at their own 40, the Colts roll out of it now led by Bill Curry, their offensive center, with [Glenn] Ressler on the left side, [Dan] Sullivan on the right side, Sam Ball the right side tackle, and Bob Vogel the left side tackle... Morrall back to throw, sets up, fires down the middle... It is going to be complete! Mackey has it in the clear, Mackey 20, Mackey 15, Mackey 10, Mackey 5, Mackey scores!"

For frenzied Colts fans, the play was typical Mackey. A 1992 inductee into the Pro Football Hall of Fame in Canton, Ohio, Mackey was named in 1969 as the best tight end in the NFL's first 50 years. In 1993, he was named pro football's greatest tight end by a panel of NFL writers and historians. His peers recognized him as the best, as well. Hall of Famer Mike Ditka, a contemporary of Mackey's, was the first tight end to be enshrined in Canton. "I'm thrilled beyond words,"

Ditka said at the time. "But you guys have to get John Mackey into the Hall. He belongs more than anybody."

A product of Syracuse University, Mackey was selected by Baltimore in the second round of the 1963 draft. Like teammate Mike Curtis, Mackey's rare blend of size and skill had Colts coaches experimenting with him at running back. "We weren't sure what to do with him because he was such a great talent," Shula said. "We weren't sure whether he should be a running back or a tight end."

Mackey had played running back at Hempstead High School in New York before switching to tight end at Syracuse University. As a member of the Orangemen's offense, he was a teammate to halfbacks Ernie Davis and Floyd Little and fullbacks Larry Csonka and Jim Nance. "Can you believe that [talent]?" he asked. "That's why I knew how to block."

Recruited as a fullback, Mackey knew his playing time would be limited when Syracuse head coach Ben Schwartzwalder told him as a freshman that he would wear the team's most coveted jersey number: 44. It was a number that had been worn by Jim Brown and was being worn by Davis. Since Davis was still a sophomore at the time, Mackey knew what his coach was implying. "That means," he thought, "I'm going to have to sit on the bench."

Mackey spent his freshman season practicing with the second string, and then he told Schwartzwalder he didn't want to sit any longer. Schwartzwalder told Mackey he could switch to tight end. Mackey agreed and asked for uniform No. 88. Later, he jokingly told Davis that he had been given that number for a simple reason. "I'm twice as good as 44."

Mackey wore No. 88 throughout his Colts career, which lasted from 1963-71. Little known is the fact that Mackey almost played for the AFL's New York franchise. He was drafted by the Jets as well as the Colts, and he could have signed with a team located in the same state in which he had played his high school and college ball. But he was never contacted by anyone in the Jets organization, and he eventually signed with Baltimore.

Colts coaches may have been uncertain where to play him early in his pro career, but Mackey had little doubt. When Shula asked him in training camp what his career goals were, Mackey stated, "I want to be your starting tight end."

Shula brought former Baltimore tight end Jim Mutscheller to camp to tutor Mackey, and Mackey said later that the most important thing he learned from Mutscheller was to get off the line of scrimmage quickly on the snap count. "If you get off on the count," Mutscheller told him, "you can block a 300-pounder because you'll hit him before he moves."

Mackey made it a point to explode off the line, and he used his size and speed to perfect two passing plays that became his signature routes—Tight End Out and Tight End Option.

Pro football in the 1960s was a less complicated game, evidenced by the fact that if Mackey got down into his stance on the right side of the line, his play call was prefaced by an "R." If he was on the left, it was an "L." Regardless of which side of the line Mackey placed himself, he terrorized NFL defenses. His blocking skills, honed at Syracuse, made him the equivalent of a third tackle on running plays. "My job," he said, "was to wipe out the defensive end and go get the linebacker. That's what I loved. I wiped out a lot of those guys."

A devastating blocker on running plays, Mackey was even more dangerous to defenses when turned loose in the open field on a pass play. "Once he catches the ball," Colts tight end coach Dick Bielski said, "the great adventure begins." Defenders would climb all over Mackey in an attempt to bring him down. "The lucky ones," Bielski said, "fall off."

Mackey could overpower linebackers and outrun defensive backs. In 1966, he scored six touchdowns on plays that covered 50 or more yards and had a long gain of 89 yards. He used his padded elbows in a fashion that Marciano might have envied. "He could catch a 6-yard pass," Rams coach George Allen said, "and run 60 yards with it, just bowling over opponents."

Mackey would eventually make 331 career catches and average 15.8 yards per reception. Throughout his career, he played with the words of Baltimore equipment manager Freddie Schubach burned into his memory:

"I shine your shoes every day. I polish and clean your helmet every day. I press your practice uniform. And I demand that you play the way I make you look."

Mackey did play as well as Schubach made him look, and in time he became the prototype modern tight end, the forerunner to the greats that followed him at his position—Dave Casper, Kellen Winslow, Ozzie Newsome, Shannon Sharpe, etc.

Mackey's touchdown against Minnesota gave Baltimore a 14-0 lead, and NFL Films cameras caught halfback Tom Matte, standing in ankle-deep mud on the sidelines, calling on the Colts defense to go out and win it.

"C'mon Shinnick, get 'em goin'," Matte yelled, and the Baltimore defense did get going. Sending nine men storming in on Kapp in a variation of their maximum blitz, the Colts caught him in a pincer between defensive ends Bubba Smith and Ordell Braase. Smith's high hit forced Kapp to lose his grip on the ice-slicked ball, and it squirted straight up into the frosty air. Linebacker Mike Curtis pulled it in and, clutching it against his muddied blue jersey, the former Duke fullback covered 60 yards to the end zone for Baltimore's second score in less than two minutes.

> Thompson: "Second down and eight at the Baltimore 30... Kapp snapping his count, barking his count... Takes it away without a fake, rolling to his left side, sets up and is going to be swarmed under... The ball is free! Baltimore's got it! Racing for the goal line is Mike Curtis... He's to the 15, 10, 5... Curtis scores! Go to war, Miss Agnes! Baltimore's defense just took the ball away from Kapp, left Kapp in the mud of Memorial Stadium, and Curtis raced it home and the Colts defensive unit has struck again."

Jack Whitaker later called Curtis' thunderous touchdown run the play that completely shocked and demoralized the Vikings. As the skies over fog-shrouded Memorial Stadium darkened and the cold rain continued to fall, the Colts raucous fans might have recalled the words of Ray Bradbury:

> "Their hoofmarks fill with rain
> As thunders close and shut the end of day"

Colt hoofmarks covered Kapp, who appeared to Morrall to be battered, bruised, and beaten—but not broken. Baltimore's ferocious rush had seemingly gotten a piece of Kapp on every play, but Injun' Joe remained defiant to the end. Knocked to the mud by Braase late in the game, Kapp was trying to get up when he saw Braase extend his hand. Kapp refused it. "Why should I have taken his hand?" he asked later. "The Colts are not nice people. Hey, neither are we. That's the game."

The Colts 24-14 victory clinched their first Western Conference title in four years and gave them a long-awaited rematch with the Browns, the only team to have beaten them in 1968 and the squad that had shut them out in the 1964 NFL Championship Game. The victory over the Vikings also served to give Morrall a measure of success that had eluded him during his gypsy-like travels from one NFL team to another. Morrall had pierced the Purple Gang for 280 yards passing and two touchdowns, and his performance prompted praise from Mackey in the Colts steamy locker room.

Speaking with *New York Post* columnist Milton Gross, Mackey said, "I can't say enough about Earl's ability to grasp things quickly, control our attack, and strike fast."

Matte recalled marveling at how far Morrall had come in one short season. "His numbering system was so screwed up when he got to Baltimore he couldn't even call plays," Matte said. "I called them for him. But he's such a class guy; we all wanted to help him. Earl was a veteran, and he learned. He got the MVP that season, and he deserved it."

New York Daily News sportswriter Norm Miller, who covered the Jets, reported on the Colts impressive showing. "If the Jets and the Browns, and maybe even the Chiefs and the Raiders were watching on TV today, these Super Bowl hopefuls could not have derived much encouragement from the sight of the Colts dismantling the Vikings 24-14 to win the NFL's Western Division title in muddy Memorial Stadium."

Christmas had come three days early to Baltimore, and holiday festivities were about to be heightened in Oakland, as well. As a Santa Claus look-alike strode the sidelines of the Oakland-Alameda County Coliseum, the Raiders hosted the Kansas City Chiefs in a special Western Division playoff game. The divisional playoff was just the second one in the AFL's nine-year existence and added another chapter to the storied rivalry that was one of the fiercest in football.

By 1968, the blood feud that existed between the Raiders and Chiefs was unparalleled in AFL history. In their 18 prior meetings, the teams had achieved a near-even split; Oakland had won 10 games to Kansas City's eight. They split their regular-season meetings in 1968, the Chiefs winning 24–10 in Kansas City in October and the Raiders claiming the rematch, 38–21, in Oakland in November. The total point differential from the two games favored the Raiders by a mere three points, 48–45.

The playoff featured intriguing matchups on both a team and individual level. Oakland led the AFL in scoring with 453 points; Kansas City led the league in defense with 170 points allowed. The Raiders quarterback was Daryle Lamonica, who was known as the Mad Bomber for a reason. The Chiefs countered with the conservative short-range passing game of Len Dawson. There were battles of all-league linemen to look forward to as well: Raiders left guard Gene Upshaw against Chiefs tackle Buck Buchanan; K.C.'s left offensive tackle Jim Tyrer opposite Oakland defensive end Ben Davidson.

A silver-and-black clad crowd of 53,605 filed into the Coliseum on an overcast afternoon. Surrounded by a picturesque green ivy slope, the Coliseum sits on San Leandro Street near the Nimitz Freeway. A national audience tuned in for the 4:00 PM kickoff, but the expected grudge match never materialized. Scoring on three of their first four series, the Raiders posted 21 points in just 18 minutes. True to his nickname, Lamonica fire-bombed the Chiefs secondary, sandwiching touchdown passes of 24 and 44 yards to Fred Biletnikoff around a 23-yard scoring pass to Warren Wells. Biletnikoff devastated Kansas City, gliding his way through the secondary to grab seven passes for 180 yards and three touchdowns.

Dressed in his black Raiders jersey with the silver No. 25 and trademark cutoff sleeves, Biletnikoff continually burned the Chiefs with big plays. He scored on a 54-yard pass 28 seconds before the half to make it 28–6, and Oakland put an exclamation point on its overwhelming win by scoring 13 points in the fourth quarter en route to a 41–6 final.

Lamonica launched five touchdowns of 23 yards or more, and the Raiders rolled up 454 yards of offense against the AFL's stingiest defense. Oakland's defense, nicknamed the Angry Eleven, pirated four Dawson passes and held coach Hank Stram's imaginative offense without a touchdown, the first time the high-powered Chiefs had failed to reach the end zone since 1963.

The Raiders won the wild, wild West, and would head east for a championship showdown with Broadway Joe and the Jets.

8

Prelude to Destiny

Asked once to explain a preseason loss, New York Jets quarterback Joe Namath paused to consider the question. Following a moment's hesitation, Broadway Joe issued a rakish grin.

"Booze," he said, "and broads."

Namath was the dark-haired darling of the mini-skirt set, and they sang his praises with a teeny-bopper song that hit record stores as a 45-rpm single in 1968:

> *He's a hero, he's a pro*
> *He's something else our Broadway Joe.*
> *He's a groovy, super guy*
> *He can throw a football through a needle's eye.*
> *What a feeling, what a sight*
> *When we see that Number 12 in green and white.*

The roguish Namath was cut from the same colorful cloth that produced Bobby Layne, whose love of the nightlife did not stop him from leading the Detroit Lions to NFL titles in the 1950s. Like the street-corner harmonists of his era, Layne let the good times roll, and so did Namath. If Layne's celebrated "Rock Around the Clock" attitude could be characterized by Bill Haley and The Comets, Namath's style was reflected best by Steppenwolf's "Born To Be Wild" song that ranked among the top rock 'n roll hits of 1968.

When teammates thanked wives and families for their support at a team party in Shea Stadium's Diamond Club, Namath offered thanks of his own. Dressed in a gray-striped double-breasted suit, he told his audience, "Wives must be wonderful. But personally, in appreciation for what they did for me this year, I want to thank all the broads of New York."

Two days before the AFL title game against Oakland, the *New York Daily News* proclaimed Namath "A-1 for the Big One." Staff writer Norm Miller led off his story by stating, "The Big Man is ready." Namath spent the eve of the championship game in his Manhattan apartment alternating, it was said later, between a beautiful blonde and his white leather bar. The next morning, the swinging quarterback bid his date farewell with a pat on her backside and slipped into his mink coat.

Sunday, December 29, saw gray clouds dominate the northeast. It had snowed that week, and brutally cold winds from nearby Flushing Bay dropped the temperature to 12 degrees and prompted a Christmas Day headline in the *New York Daily News* that read, "Jets Dread Shea Winds." By noon (EST) on game day, a half hour before the scheduled start of the AFL title game at Shea Stadium, the temperature in New York stood at 35 degrees. Icy winds whipped in at 30 to 50 miles per hour, and made it feel much colder.

Fans clutching tickets to the game in their gloved hands encountered vendors selling game programs, pennants, and woolen white-and-green Jets hats. Scalpers hawked $12 game tickets for $50 and found willing takers. Inside Shea's cavernous horseshoed tiers, an AFL Championship Game record crowd of 62,627 howled louder than the wind that whistled through the open end of the stadium. The 400-member squad of ticket-handlers, ushers, and grounds crew pulled their green-and-white winter jackets tighter as they braced against the razor-like gusts. On the sidelines, a motorized miniature jet plane skirted the edges of the frozen field.

The 1968 AFL championship was pro football's first title game in New York since 1962, when the Giants lost to Green Bay, 16–7, at Yankee Stadium on Jerry Kramer's three field goals. That game, too, had been

128

marked by high winds and intense cold. Some of the Packers thought the conditions in Yankee Stadium that day were worse than those they would encounter in the Ice Bowl classic at Lambeau Field in 1967.

As the Jets and Raiders ran through their pregame drills, strong gusts stirred loose dirt from the infield into sudden swirls. In his press-box seat at the stadium, *New York Daily News* sportswriter Larry Fox looked down on the wind-swept playing surface. Studying the field, he thought it resembled a frozen wasteland. "A snowless version," he said later, "of the Russian Front." The grass in the west end of the field, where center field was located, was frozen and faded. The infield in the east end, which dipped three feet and caused uneven footing, was spongy with mud. Puddles of icy water made the sideline areas treacherous. The middle of the field was splotched with a white chemical drying agent designed to provide traction on the slippery surface.

"Of all the fields I played on, Shea Stadium was one of the worst," Jets receiver Don Maynard said. "The wind factor, the field conditions, all of it. It wasn't a field for football. When it rained, it was a mud bowl. The tarp only covered part of the field, and when they would take the tarp up, you would have water running up and down the field."

Jets offensive tackle Dave Herman thought game-time conditions were brutal. "That wasn't a breezy wind," he said. "They were gusts. And the field was hard and had no grass on it."

On NBC television and radio, commentators Curt Gowdy, Charlie Jones, Al DeRogatis, and Jim Simpson previewed the showdown between the AFL's top two quarterbacks—Broadway Joe and Daryle Lamonica. Taking the field to test the gusting wind, Namath noted the conditions. "Nasty cold," he thought. It felt, he recalled, like Ice Station Zebra. The field, sparse and wind-blown, looked like something from an old Western movie. Some grass, Namath remembered, and a lot of dust.

In the Jets radio booth, announcers Merle Harmon and Sam DeLuca prepared for what was then the biggest game in team history. A native of Illinois, the silver-haired Harmon brought a sense of middle America to Gotham. He began his professional career in 1949 calling baseball games for Class C Topeka and reached the major leagues in 1955 as the play-by-play man for the Kansas City Athletics. Four years later, Harmon was in Yankee Stadium broadcasting the first football game between Army and Air Force.

Harmon looked out at the windswept conditions at Shea Stadium. "The weather was brutal," he said. "One thing about Shea Stadium at that time of year was the wind blowing in off the water."

On NBC Radio, Simpson told listeners of the arctic weather conditions. "The wind," he said, "is whipping through the stadium."

In another radio booth inside Shea Stadium sat Bill King, the voice of the Raiders. King had spent the night before the game having dinner with Oakland general manager Al Davis. Davis was just 39 years old at the time but had already amassed an impressive resume: assistant to San Diego Chargers coach Sid Gillman; head coach of the Raiders; AFL Coach of the Year; AFL commissioner; Oakland GM. Davis had popularized the phrase "Commitment to Excellence" and made it a Raiders slogan. He took over a team that had won one game in 1962 and coached them to 10 wins in 1963, at the time the greatest single-season turnaround in pro football history. A native New Yorker, Davis designed Oakland's silver-and-black uniforms using the Black Knights of the Hudson as a model. The rebellious GM encouraged the Raiders miscreant attitude and take-no-prisoners approach—"Just win, baby!" he told them—and cloaked himself and his organization in intrigue and mystery.

Born on July 4, Davis thought of himself as the All-American (Football League) boy. When he was named AFL commissioner in April 1966, Davis, who studied military tactics, immediately began a blitzkrieg campaign against the NFL. He signed NFL stars to lucrative contracts and encouraged AFL owners to do the same. With total war looming, AFL and NFL owners huddled in private meetings. Davis was not included, and when the merger was announced, he called it the "biggest betrayal since Yalta."

The slick Davis, who favored long sideburns and a pompadour, returned to boss the Raiders and used shrewd trades and skillful drafting to build the silver and black into the AFL's most feared team. They set a league record for wins in a season in 1967 with 13 and won the AFL Championship Game with a 40-7 destruction of Houston. Two weeks later, in Super Bowl II, the Raiders ran into a Green Bay Packers team playing its last game for legendary head coach Vince Lombardi. The Packers were aging but still had an aura of greatness about them. "It was like playing our fathers," halfback Pete Banaszak said. The Packers won easily.

The Raiders returned to prominence in the 1968 AFL season, and their one-sided win over rival Kansas City the week before in the divisional playoff game allowed Oakland to reach the 13-win plateau for the second straight season. With two straight Western Division titles in hand and a second consecutive trip to the Super Bowl just a victory away, Davis told King at dinner that if the Raiders could beat the Jets, they could become pro football's next dynasty.

Still, there was the matter of beating the Jets first. Davis had great respect for Namath and his abilities. "He tips the field," he said, a reference to the idea that Broadway Joe always seemed to be throwing the ball downhill. To help aid his team in its quest to repeat as AFL champions, Davis had a makeshift structure built on the Raiders sideline to protect players from the harsh cold and wind. When Jets coach Weeb Ewbank saw the protective tarp that had been constructed on the Oakland side of the field the day of the game, he exploded in anger.

"Al was a New Yorker," Herman said. "So when his team played in New York, he always saw it as a homecoming. That added to the intensity of the game."

The high stakes of the game, fierceness of the rivalry, the frenzy of the sellout crowd, the energy of New York fans, the brutal cold and wind, and the talent on both teams all combined to ensure that this championship would be played on a level higher than any other AFL title game. The Jets offense opened with the wind at its back, and less than 3 minutes in, Namath, wearing a long-sleeved white thermal shirt beneath his green Jets jersey, fired a 14-yard touchdown pass to Maynard, who was conspicuous for playing in cutoff sleeves that exposed his bare, thin arms to the elements. On their first drive, the Jets had already scored more against Oakland than Kansas City had in 60 minutes the week before and as much as Houston had managed in being mauled by the Raiders 40–7 in the 1967 AFL title game.

Fans in the stands holding small transistor radios to their frozen ears heard Harmon call the key plays on New York's opening drive:

"The Jets come out with a wide spread and a slant-in pass goes to Maynard on the 30-yard line...

"Here's a handoff to Matt Snell. He bombs his way through the middle to the 15, down to the 14...

"Namath back to pass on second down, throws for the end zone... Touchdown to Maynard!"

The Jets touchdown was the result of Ewbank's strategy to isolate Maynard, a 10-year veteran, on Raiders rookie George Atkinson. Maynard had scored two touchdowns in the Heidi Bowl the month before and had torched Atkinson for 228 yards on 10 catches. Namath said the Jets knew that in time Atkinson was going to be a good player. But this was 1968, and the Jets had a veteran going against a rookie. "We felt," Namath said, "we could take advantage of [Atkinson's] inexperience."

Switching Maynard to the split-end side of the field rather than his normal flanker position, the Jets not only locked Atkinson in single coverage on a corner pattern, they forced him to negotiate the uneven footing of the infield.

Because of Maynard's success against him in the Heidi Bowl, Atkinson knew the Jets would waste little time testing him again. He tried to prepare by borrowing one of the team's film projectors and studying the *Heidi* game until he had Maynard's moves almost memorized. "I knew they'd come at me," he said, and the Jets did. With his cutoff sleeves flapping in the wind, Maynard drove Atkinson back and then cut to the left corner of the end zone. Unfamiliar with the nuances of Shea's tricky surface, Akinson lost his footing as Maynard made his cut on the muddy turf. Film of the game shows Maynard was wide open for the score.

Oakland's bump-and-run coverage proved difficult for many AFL quarterbacks to solve, but it was tailor-made for Namath. The Jets quarterback could speed-read defenses and was a marksman with his passes. New York's offense was also highly flexible. Jets receivers were experienced enough to run variations of their passing routes, and they sometimes lined up in exotic formations that would see halfback

Emerson Boozer at wide receiver and Maynard in the slot alongside
end George Sauer. On their touchdown drive, the Jets succeeded in
confusing the Raider defense by lining up in a double wing formation
that had Boozer and tight end Pete Lammons lined up wide on either
side and Maynard and Sauer in the slot.

It was a formation New York had not used before. But as
Namath pointed out, the Jets were 1–4–2 against the Raiders in
their last seven games; they had to do something different. So they
went to four wideouts. Even with the wind howling through the
stadium, the Jets believed they could beat Oakland by passing. Their
strategy was designed to encourage the Raiders to play man-to-man
defense. Oakland didn't need much encouragement. Raiders corner-
men Willie Brown and Atkinson prided themselves on aggressive
bump-and-run coverage. Namath respected Brown, one of the best
defensive backs in the game and a future Hall of Famer.

Namath said Brown would give opponents one thing, the deep
pattern. The 6'1", 190-pound Brown took away short patterns by lining
up almost nose-to-nose with the receiver at the line of scrimmage and
challenging him to run by. Brown would bump the receiver, then bump
him again. Namath believed his receivers could get a half-step on the
deep patterns. "But if it's not a perfect pass," Namath said, "you can't
complete it. He's the best."

Still, the Jets felt Maynard and Sauer could beat Atkinson and
Brown one-on-one and that their offensive line could hold off the
fierce Raiders rush. New York planned to vary its attack by pounding
the Raiders defense with its hammer, power back Matt Snell.

Jim Turner's 33-yard field goal late in the first quarter gave New
York a 10-0 lead. Lamonica, who had struggled to connect with his
receivers early and hit on just three of his first 15 passes, got the Raiders
on the scoreboard in the second quarter with a 29-yard post pass to
Fred Biletnikoff. On the Jets sideline, Ewbank was furious. Biletnikoff
had burned Sample a month earlier when he made seven catches for
190 yards. Prior to the title game, Ewbank took Sample aside. "Don't
let him run a post pattern. The first one he runs, you're coming out
and we're going with [Cornell] Gordon."

Less than a minute into the second quarter, Biletnikoff ran a post, hauled in Lamonica's pass, and broke a weak tackle attempt by Sample en route to the end zone.

As Sample trotted off the field, Ewbank was waiting.

"What happened?"

"I don't know, Weeb. I just missed that tackle. I don't know."

"Well, I'm going to let Cornell go in."

Sample had never felt so disgusted. It was the first time in his 11-year career that he had been taken out of a game.

Ewbank had other concerns. Namath trotted to the sideline in the second quarter, his left hand limp in front of him. The ring finger had been dislocated courtesy of a hit by Dan Birdwell and was now pointing in different directions. "Oh, Joe," Hill cried. "Joe, look at it, man. That's hideous." Namath glanced at the grotesquely twisted digit and quickly turned away. Birdwell saw the mangled finger and began to jump up and down with excitement. "Hey, Joe, you broke your finger! You broke your finger!" Team trainer Jeff Snedeker popped the finger back into place and asked Broadway Joe if he wanted a painkiller. Namath shook his head. "No, not my hands. I have to have feel in my hands."

Namath's afternoon of pain was not over. Herman, an All-AFL guard, had been moved to tackle to neutralize end Ike Lassiter, the Raiders pass rush specialist who had given tackle Sam Walton problems in the Heidi Bowl. To accommodate the switch, Ewbank further revamped his offensive line for the title game by moving Randy Rasmussen to right guard and Bob Talamini to left guard.

"Weeb came to me before the game and said, 'Dave, Sam's been making some mental errors, and we can't afford to let that happen in this game.' I said, 'Coach, whatever it takes to win, I'm all for it.' We go into a team meeting and Weeb says, 'Dave is going to switch to left tackle.' Well, here I am, 250, 255 pounds, and I'm playing a different position and I'm going against Ike Lassiter. [Lassiter was listed at 270 pounds but Herman believed he was closer to 300.] I said, 'Weeb, I don't want the job anymore.'"

Since the Raiders had a Western Conference playoff game against Kansas City, the Jets had two weeks to practice. Herman worked on his footwork. The biggest difference between playing guard and tackle, he said, was that as a guard, he usually had a defender right in front of him or offset just a few inches left or right. At tackle, the defender playing opposite him could be lined up several feet outside of Herman's right shoulder, meaning there was much more ground for him to cover.

"I decided I was going to block Lassiter the way I always blocked, and that was right down the middle of him. I would explode into him," Herman said.

Herman decided he would challenge Lassiter, "make him go through me and not around me," he said. He told Namath, "The first play goes over me."

Herman said he hit Lassiter as "hard as I ever hit anybody. I got into him on every play. He forgot about the white-shoed quarterback, forgot about everybody, and wanted to get back at this little guy in front of him."

Herman had an outstanding day against Lassiter. Leaning on the teachings and technique he learned from Ewbank—"Weeb could have been an excellent line coach," he said—and former Jets line boss Chuck Knox, Herman helped build an iron pocket around the fragile-kneed Namath. But on this play, as Broadway Joe dropped back into the pocket, Lassiter beat Herman for the only time all afternoon. "Look out, Joe," Herman shouted. Namath's buggy-whip release allowed him to get the pass off but Lassiter and Ben Davidson converged on Broadway Joe. Namath stuck out his left hand to ward off Big Ben before the three men tangled and fell hard to the frozen ground. *New York Post* sportswriter Paul Zimmerman said Lassiter stood over the downed quarterback like a "gladiator waiting for Nero to give the thumbs-down sign." Namath staggered to his feet, blinking. He had suffered a concussion.

The teams then traded field goals, with Jim Turner hitting a 36-yarder for the Jets and a 26-yard field goal by the game's elder statesman, 41-year-old George Blanda, that allowed the Raiders to cut the lead to 13–10 at the half.

The game had become great theatre. Despite the swirling winds, Namath and Lamonica would combine to throw 96 passes and gain a startling 649 yards through the air. The 1968 Championship Game was

AFL football at its best; a combined 10 future Hall of Famers were on the field that day. Edwin Shrake, writing for *Sports Illustrated*, thought there were enough big plays in the second half alone to fill a highlight film. Jim Simpson told his NBC Radio audience, "This has been quite a championship football game." His broadcast partner, DeRogatis, whom Simpson referred to throughout the afternoon as "DeRo," was equally impressed. "If you had to ask for a championship game to be played better, Jim, I just don't know how you get one."

In the Raiders broadcast booth, King thought he was watching one of the greatest games he had seen. "Namath and Lamonica put on a show that day," he said. So, too, did their primary receivers, Maynard and Biletnikoff. Maynard moved through the thicket of elbows in the Oakland secondary to snare six passes for 118 yards and two touchdowns; Biletnikoff burned the Jets for seven catches for 190 yards and one score.

The intensity of the game rocked Shea Stadium's massive structure. Both teams, Schmitt said, were "trying to kill each other." Jets defensive coordinator Walt Michaels thought the intensity was unreal. Sideline cameras caught Jets linebacker Larry Grantham shouting at his teammates. "Keep your poise!" A Jets fan was shown on film screaming for his team to "Play with your heart!"

In the muddy trenches, Jets left tackle Winston Hill hand-fought Davidson to a standstill. Known for his elaborate handlebar mustache and huge frame, Big Ben had drawn the ire of the Jets the year before when he leveled Namath and knocked his helmet flying from his head. The Jets accused Davidson and the Raiders of illegal tactics. Ewbank showed New York sportswriters game films of Namath being punched in the groin by defensive tackle Dan Birdwell. Namath also had his jaw fractured in 1967 by a blow to the face from Lassiter. The Raiders responded by accusing New York's offensive linemen of holding and Namath of receiving preferential treatment by the league's officials.

Jets center John Schmitt knew the quickest way to beat the Jets was to physically hurt Namath. The Raiders rough treatment of Namath angered the Jets because, as Schmitt said, he and his teammates had a love for Namath they had for no one else on the team. Schmitt's linemate, Herman, remembers the Jets as a "great bunch of guys who really got along with each other." Schmitt said Oakland was the only team the Jets ever hated, and their targeting Namath was a big reason why. The hard memory of the *Heidi* game was another.

When Namath named Birdwell and Davidson as two of the dirtiest players in the AFL, Ben Ben smiled and stroked his waxed handlebar mustache as he downplayed the accusations. "He just does that because it's New York and he knows it will be big publicity," Davidson said. "I'm no cheap-shot artist."

The title game reflected the raging nature of the Jets-Raiders rivalry. Namath thought it was one of the toughest physical and mental trials he had ever endured. At times he wasn't sure if he could continue; he contemplated quitting. Early in the second half, Lamonica moved the Raiders to Blanda's game-tying field goal, a 9-yarder. That Oakland had settled for a field goal was balm for the bruised Jets defense. The Raiders had reached the Jets 6-yard line, but three straight tackles by safety Jim Hudson, including a combined stop with middle linebacker Al Atkinson on 230-pound running back Hewritt Dixon on the 1, stopped the drive and forced Blanda's field goal.

Namath regrouped and drove the Jets 80 yards in seven minutes. Snell, who posted game-high numbers with 19 carries and 71 yards, did much of the heavy lifting.

> Harmon: "Third down and 11 for New York... Namath calling signals, Namath drops back to pass, Birdwell after him... Namath throws to Boozer and he's got at the 25 and he's out of bounds right there...
>
> "Snell and Boozer in the backfield...The handoff goes to Matt Snell, Snell belts his way into the left side, goes for about 10 as Rodger Bird from the secondary pulls him down...
>
> "A big, big third-down play for New York... Here's a handoff to Snell, Snell blasts his way for the first down getting six yards...

> *"Namath fakes, throws, slant-in to Sauer, jumping catch*
> *on the 41-yard line of Oakland and down he goes, Willie*
> *Brown making the tackle...*
>
> *"Namath fakes the handoff, drops back to pass, he*
> *throws for Maynard... Great catch on the 21 by Don*
> *Maynard! Down-and-in and Atkinson pulls him down on the*
> *21-yard line of the Raiders."*

Namath converted crucial third-down situations four times on the drive. As New York moved into scoring position, Ewbank told an assistant, "Let's run a 'Q' [pattern] into that soft stuff." Namath rolled away from a Raiders pass rush and fired a pass to Pete Lammons. The big tight end caught the ball in the mushy infield and scored to complete a 20-yard touchdown pass. Namath had been hit as he released the ball, but his arm was so strong he still managed to throw the pass with so much velocity that Lammons swore he could hear it whistling as it approached.

> *Harmon: "Third and 10 for New York on the Oakland*
> *21... Fake handoff to Mathis, Namath in trouble, throw-*
> *ing... Caught by Lammons on the 10, the 5... Touchdown!*
> *Namath, hit very hard as he threw the ball but Lammons*
> *caught it and it's a touchdown for New York."*

Namath was putting on a remarkable display of quarterbacking skills, but his rifle right arm backfired midway through the fourth quarter. Atkinson was again tested on an out pattern, but the Raiders cornerback finally exacted a measure of revenge against his tormentors. Namath hung his pass and Atkinson, stepping in front of Maynard, picked off the ball as it seemed to hang suspended on a cold current. He returned it to the Jets 5-yard line before being knocked out of bounds by Namath.

"You son of a bitch," Atkinson screamed. "I'm gonna kill you."

Namath yelled back. "Hey man, lighten up. Play the damn game right. Keep your damn mouth shut."

Two plays later, Pete Banaszak burrowed through the middle of the line to give Oakland its first lead of the game, 23–20.

Harmon: "Namath back to pass on a first down, Namath throwing for Don Maynard... It is intercepted by Atkinson at the 30, down to the 25, the 20, he's down to the 10, the 5 and he is knocked out of bounds...

"Here's Lamonica handing to Banaszak... Banaszak to the 1, to the goal line... Touchdown! Banaszak goes in."

The Jets were jolted. The sight of the sun fading behind gray clouds symbolized their situation. The Raiders were on the verge of returning to the Super Bowl. The Jets were trailing, and they had eight minutes to reclaim their destiny.

New York's comeback would take just 68 seconds.

On first down at New York's 32, Namath called "74," a quick sideline pattern, and found Sauer for 12 yards and a first down. On the next play, Namath called "60 G," a go-route to Maynard. His green-and-white uniform muddied, Broadway Joe dropped deep and launched a long strike that cut through swirling currents and was cradled by Maynard in a great over-the-shoulder catch. Atkinson, who provided blanket coverage of Maynard on the play, thought the ball moved crosswind toward the near sideline and that the Jets receiver had adjusted by gathering it in over his right shoulder rather than his left, which would have been the case under normal circumstances.

"On the sideline earlier, Don told me he might be able to get by Atkinson deep," Namath said.

"I had told Joe, 'Joseph, I got a deep one when you need it,'" Maynard said. "He said, 'Alright, we're going to go for it.'

"He dropped back and let it go. I'm going toward the closed end of the field and I'm looking to catch the ball at 10 or 11 o'clock [position-wise]. But the wind caught it, and now I have to catch it at 2 o'clock. Greatest catch I ever made."

Namath calls it one of the great catches anyone has ever made. Atkinson agrees. "A hell of a catch," he said. "I didn't think he could come up with it. We were both looking up at the ball while we were running. We both could see it fine. Then all of a sudden it moved crosswind toward the right sideline. He adjusted from the inside to the outside, took it way over his right shoulder."

> *Harmon: "Namath dropping back to pass... He is looking, he is going to throw long for Don Maynard and... Maynard makes the catch at the 10, and he is dumped out of bounds at the 8-yard line! A great over-the-shoulder catch, Don Maynard against George Atkinson... It is first-and-goal to go, the ball now spotted at the 6-yard line."*

John Madden was Oakland's linebacker coach in 1968 and had spent the week before the game devising schemes to break down the Jets passing game. As he felt the lashing of the wind, Madden figured he had an ally in the weather. "He can't throw against that wind," Madden said as he watched Namath drop back, but the sight of the ball knifing through the leaden sky shocked the Raiders coach. Figuring the distance from where Namath threw the ball on his own 30 to where Maynard caught it on the Oakland 10, Madden estimated the pass had traveled some 75 yards in the air. Namath, Madden concluded, never worried about the wind at Shea. He just threw the ball right through it.

On NBC Radio, Simpson and DeRogatis sounded stunned by what they saw.

> *Simpson: "Namath back to throw, Namath with lots of time, going with the wind... For Maynard and he's got it! Dragged down from behind by Atkinson at the 9-yard line!"*
>
> *DeRogatis: "What an absolutely brilliant call, and what a sensational catch. Atkinson was right there and Don Maynard, who has just been superb all year, put his hands up, held onto that football... A brilliant play, Jim."*

Shrake thought it was brilliant, as well. In his *Sports Illustrated* article, he described it as "an amazingly perfect play."

Striding to his place behind Schmitt, Namath put his arms up to silence the raucous crowd. Facing him from across the line of scrimmage was linebacker Dan Conners. Both were products of Pennsylvania, and just as Namath was part of a royal line of great quarterbacks—Unitas, Joe Montana, Dan Marino—from the western part of the state, Conners was linked to Chuck Bednarik, Joe Schmidt, and Jack Ham as linebackers forged in the region's steel mills and coal towns.

At the snap, Namath faked to Snell and rolled left on a play called "9-Option." It was designed as a play-action pass to Mathis, who was running a short arrow route to the left front flag of the end zone. Mathis was covered, so Namath looked instead for Sauer, who was running a post pattern from left to right. Sauer was blanketed by Brown. Given time by a crucial and often-overlooked block by Snell on blitzing linebacker Gus Otto, Namath looked for his third option, Lammons, who was running a crossing pattern right to left. He, too, was covered.

Amid a swirl of green-and-white and silver-and-black uniforms, Namath looked for his fourth option on the play, Maynard, who was running a square-in from the right side of the end zone to left. As Joe Willie's white shoes slipped on a loose chunk of infield dirt, Birdwell, Davidson, and Lassiter closed in. Namath stopped, swung suddenly to his right, and spotted Maynard. Having looked to four receivers in a span of five seconds, Namath settled himself and unfurled a frozen rope of a pass that zipped past three Raiders and into Maynard's midsection three yards deep in the end zone. Namath estimates the ball traveled no higher than three feet off the ground. Either Maynard would catch it, he thought, or no one would.

The sequence of the play left many startled, including Sauer. How many quarterbacks, he thought, can go through four different options in five seconds? From the sideline, Jets defensive end Gerry Philbin watched his quarterback operate. Namath was unbelievable, he thought.

"Joe had that ability," Herman said. "A lot of what he had was more than ability. It was instinctive."

Harmon and broadcast partner Sam DeLuca called the decisive play of the AFL title game:

> Harmon: "Here's a fake handoff to Matt Snell... Namath looking for the end zone, throwing... Touchdown to Maynard! Joe Namath throwing to Don Maynard... He was not the intended original receiver..."
>
> DeLuca: "Namath was looking to his left, saw George Sauer, and you've got to give the offensive line credit for that one, Merle, because he had all the time in the world. If he

didn't have that good pass protection, he would have never had time to change, look completely across the field to Don Maynard, see him open in the end zone and throw for a touchdown."

On NBC Radio, DeRogatis and Simpson analyzed the play for their listeners above the background of deafening noise from the Shea Stadium crowd:

DeRogatis: "[Namath] was in trouble as Jim Simpson called it. He was looking out to the left side to No. 31 Bill Mathis, but Mathis was covered very well. Joe very smartly turned around, tossed back to Don Maynard, who made another brilliant catch."

Maynard's path to paydirt was not an easy one. He was bumped at the line of scrimmage by Atkinson, then rolled away from the corner-back before finding some open space in front of him. At the same time, Namath raised his right arm to a cocked position behind the earhole on his helmet, then cut loose with a laser beam of a pass that flared like a tracer in a diagonal direction across the field.

"I threw the ball as hard as I've ever thrown a ball in my life," Namath said. Maynard remembers it as an "unbelievable throw." Though Atkinson was guarding him closely, Namath led Maynard two to three yards away from the Raiders cornerback and drilled the ball so low and fast that Maynard had to lower his body to catch it and then fell to his knees and rolled over.

In lightning-like fashion, Namath had moved his team nearly 70 yards in three plays against one of pro football's best defensive units. Atkinson's earlier interception had only served to ignite Namath's competitive fire. Prior to taking the field on the Jets scoring drive, Namath approached Ewbank. "Don't worry," he said. "I'll get it back."

NBC sportscaster Charlie Jones thought Namath and Maynard had proved themselves to be "as poised a combination under pressure as the AFL has ever seen." Namath finished the game with 19 completions in 49 attempts for 266 yards, three touchdowns, and one interception.

His counterpart, Lamonica, completed 20-of-47 attempts for 401 yards and one touchdown.

The Jets had taken a 27–23 lead, but 7:47 still remained on the game clock and memories of Heidi and the Raiders fantastic comeback the month before were never far from the minds of either team. Snell could feel a sense of foreboding on the Jets sideline. Oakland had beaten New York late in so many games. The Jets, Snell said, were almost waiting for the Raiders to come back again.

New York's defense had already made some spectacular plays, including Hudson's heroics in the second quarter. Given a four-point lead, New York's No. 1-ranked defense went out to win it.

The week of the game, Jets defensive coordinator Walt Michaels told reporters the name of the game was "Get Lamonica." Pressure on the quarterback, Michaels said, was the best defense against Oakland's passing attack. If the Jets could get to Lamonica early, New York wouldn't have to play catch-up. The problem was, Michaels added, that Lamonica threw so quickly. Once Daryle found his rhythm, he could get hot very quickly. Even if you can't tackle him, Michaels told his linemen, try to distract him; "get your hands in his face," he said. Still, the best way to ground the Raiders' passing game was to beat its Mad Bomber. "We've got to keep him on his back," Michaels said.

With six minutes to go and Lamonica marching his team into Jets territory, All-AFL defensive end Verlon Biggs took Michaels' words to heart. Making an inside move on tackle Bob Svihus, Biggs blindsided Lamonica for a big fourth-down sack.

> Harmon: "Almost 63,000 fans standing as Oakland is going to go for it... Fourth-and-10 on the 26... Lamonica calling the play, goes back to pass, he looks... He is hit by Biggs and brought down on the 34! Biggs got him blindside... Daryle never saw him coming."

Four minutes later, the Raiders were again driving toward the potential winning touchdown. In its film study, Oakland found what it felt was a weakness in the New York defense and looked to take advantage of it with a quick swing pass to fleet halfback Charlie Smith, one of the heroes of the Heidi Bowl. The Raiders had practiced the play all week. "We thought it would be a big play for us," Lamonica said.

> Harmon: "First-and-10 at the New York 13... Lamonica back to pass, looking, throwing a swing pass behind... He threw the ball behind Charlie Smith... It's recovered by the Jets! That was a lateral pass, it was not a forward pass... That pass was thrown behind the receiver, Charlie Smith, in the right flat, Ralph Baker picked it up."

There were two minutes left when Lamonica floated the ball into the right flat. Smith thought a current of wind caught it and carried it backward. "The ball just took off in the wind," Smith said. By the time the ball reached Smith, it was behind him. In the somber Oakland locker room after the game, Smith, a rookie, said that since he didn't think the pass was a lateral, he didn't bother to chase it. Michaels credited Baker, his veteran outside linebacker who was responsible for covering Smith, for being prepared and alert. Realizing it was a lateral and not a forward pass, Baker scooped up the loose ball. "I started running, and I thought I had a touchdown," he said. "But as it was, we got the ball, and that was important at that point."

Lamonica said he recognized right away that it was a lateral and tried to get to the live ball. "Baker got there ahead of me," he said. Raiders coach John Rauch said it was simply a bad throw by Lamonica, but Rauch had left himself open to criticism, as well. Earlier, he had run a big risk by rolling the dice and going for it all on fourth down rather than calling on the reliable Blanda to boot a field goal that would have cut Oakland's deficit to a point with 6 minutes still remaining. He had thought about the field goal, Rauch said. "But I wanted seven [points]," he added. Lamonica would throw for more than 400 yards on the afternoon, but Rauch said he still had doubts whether his offense could get into position again to kick a potential game-winning field goal.

Harmon thought the turnover was critical to the Jets keeping a date with destiny. "I think Oakland would have scored," he said.

On NBC Radio, Simpson and DeRo sorted out a play that had left many players, coaches, and fans confused.

Simpson: "By throwing the ball the way he did, Lamonica threw it behind Smith, it became a lateral not a forward pass. It's New York's football."

DeRogatis: "And Lamonica knew it all the way because he started downfield. He knew what he had done, and the football now goes over to the New York Jets. Two minutes and eight seconds to go."

As the sun set behind the stadium's west wall, it was clear Heidi would not reappear this day. The final second in the Jets exhausting 27-23 victory melted from the clock at approximately 3:30 PM (EST).

Harmon: "Four seconds, three seconds, two seconds, one second, and there it is! The Jets have won the American Football League championship, beating the defending champion Oakland Raiders 27–23... And bedlam breaks loose at Shea Stadium..."

Simpson: "Listen to this crowd... The Jets have won the championship! Two seconds, one second, it's over! The Jets win and go to the Super Bowl!"

Ewbank, whose leg was twisted by an overzealous fan as the coach was carried from the field, became the only man to win championships in both the AFL and NFL. NBC's late-night talk show host Johnny Carson, a Jets fan, was doused with champagne in a clubhouse so overflowing with people that a security guard at the main entrance was moved to shout, "Please, let the players in the locker room!"

Simpson: "Weeb Ewbank, former coach of the Baltimore Colts and in recent years the coach and general manager of the New York Jets, has won his first American Football League championship and now he will go back, presumably, to face Baltimore, which is out in front of Cleveland 17 to nothing. His old team, the Baltimore Colts, look like they're going to win the National Football League championship."

As he stood cradling the game ball during a postgame interview with NBC-TV, Ewbank was told by Charlie Jones, "Baltimore is leading in the NFL." Above the din, Namath shouted to Maynard.

"Are you ready for Baltimore?"

"I'm always ready," Maynard said.

Across the crowded room, Hill was being interviewed on the radio by DeLuca. Not many realize or remember, but it was Hill, not Namath, who made the first public guarantee of a Jets victory in Super Bowl III. When DeLuca asked if the Jets were going to win, Hill responded without hesitation.

"Yes we are."

9

The Revenge of '64

High in the rafters of Cleveland's Municipal Stadium, a crowd of 200 people gathered at noon in the Wigwam Club to watch the start of the AFL Championship Game in New York. Two color televisions were installed for the occasion, allowing the media and league executives to tune in NBC and watch the Raiders and Jets until the 2:30 PM start of the NFL title game on CBS between Baltimore and Cleveland.

The Wigwam Club overlooked Lakeside Avenue and downtown Cleveland, which was shrouded by a cold, gray mist. NFL loyalists inside the warmly lit club stared with contempt at the TV sets as Joe Namath and Daryle Lamonica launched a series of deep passes that forced the first quarter to drag on for 45 minutes.

"What you are watching," Harry McClelland of the *Cleveland Press* said dismissively, "is known as Mickey Mouse football."

Inside Cleveland Municipal Stadium, a crowd that would eventually number 78,410 began filing in. The banks of stadium lights had been turned on, providing a glaring white backdrop against skies already darkening. Snow was piled on the sidelines and behind the end zones, and 12 heaters had been positioned near the team benches to deal with game-time temperatures that had fallen well below freezing.

Four years earlier, on this same frozen field and in this same game, the Browns had shocked the favored Colts 27–0. Baltimore had not beaten Cleveland since 1962, but the Colts entered the rematch as prohibitive favorites. Baltimore fans hung a banner from a railing calling for the "Revenge of '64."

Pro football experts saw the rematch as a collision between Browns superstar running back Leroy Kelly, the NFL's leading rusher in 1968, and the Colts record-setting defense. Baltimore's brain trust of head coach Don Shula and defensive coaches Bill Arnsparger and Chuck Noll studied film of Kelly in the week leading up to the title game and saw the Browns halfback devastating defenses with his signature plays—quick openers through the middle and sweeps to the flanks.

Kelly's running style, his change of pace and direction, and his explosive first step helped him lead the league in rushing with a career-best 1,239 yards and 16 touchdowns. He was instrumental in the Browns 30–20 win over the Colts in Baltimore in October, carrying 30 times for 130 yards. On the eve of the title game, Shula reminded reporters that Kelly's performance in Baltimore was better than any two backs, much less one, had had against the Colts all season.

All-Pro linebacker Mike Curtis thought the message from his coaching staff was clear: stop Kelly and you stop Cleveland. Even though Curtis had not been with the Colts when they were humiliated by the Browns in 1964, he joined in as the team geared up for the rematch with revenge on its mind. The Colts were concentrating on Kelly, but they were also aware of Browns quarterback Bill Nelsen. Baltimore quarterback Earl Morrall thought "Admiral" Nelsen, as he was called by some, loomed as a larger obstacle than Kelly. Nelsen had picked apart the Colts defense earlier in the season, and Morrall noted that the Cleveland quarterback seldom set up in conventional fashion. Instead, he would take the snap from center Fred Hoaglin, dart back a step or two, raise his passing arm, and fire. It was Nelsen's way of beating the rush, and it worked well enough to allow him to throw for 19 touchdowns in 1968, including three against the Colts.

Shula, coaching against his former team, the Browns, and against his former coach, Blanton Collier, installed a few new wrinkles for the rematch. Colts coaches had noticed from game films that Cleveland strong safety Ernie Kellerman always lined up on the same side of the formation as Baltimore tight end John Mackey, while free safety Mike Howell went to the other side. The Colts designed a set which put Mackey in the backfield directly behind Morrall in a variation of the I formation. Baltimore also planned to align flanker Willie Richardson and split end Jimmy Orr to split wide left in a formation titled "wing left opposite." Mackey would line up on the right side. From that set, the Colts planned to send halfback Tom Matte sweeping to the right side behind the bullish Mackey, an excellent blocker who would be taking on defensive end Ron Snidow.

The game plan also emphasized a series of draw plays. One such draw featured an innovative trap-blocking scheme. Center Bill Curry would angle-block Browns left tackle Walter Johnson, while right guard Dan Sullivan trapped Cleveland right tackle Jim Kanicki. Left guard Glenn Ressler would fire out and drive-block middle linebacker Bob Matheson. Morrall would turn and hand off to either Matte or fullback Jerry Hill, who would follow the convoy in a hard sprint. The altered blocking scheme was designed to confuse Cleveland, since the center usually blocks the middle linebacker on a draw.

Field conditions the day of the game seemed to favor the Browns. The grassy centerfield area in the northeast end zone was soft and moist; the southwest end of the field was frozen mud. The rest of the field contained little grass and thus promised inconsistent footing. Perfect playing conditions, it seemed, for an off-track runner like Kelly. He was a "mudder," a back whose deceptive moves could make defenders slip and slide on slick surfaces. CBS Radio sportscaster Bob Reynolds, who was working the game with Andy Musser, thought the field resembled a dry river basin. "It's pretty loose down there," he told his listening audience. Colts equipment man Freddy Schubach had anticipated Cleveland's winter weather and packed accordingly. The players had various types of footwear to choose from—conventional cleats, ripple soles, tennis shoes, and soccer shoes.

When the Colts took their field in their waist-length blue warmup jackets and white-and-blue woolen caps, they saw the leaden skies and felt the cold air. Morrall, breathing steam, felt the stiff wind blowing in from Lake Erie and thought it made the temperature feel like zero.

Baltimore was favored by six points, but privately, the Colts had doubts. "We were scared going into Cleveland," cornerback Bobby Boyd said. "We knew we were going to be in a dog fight. But sometimes that can be good for a team. That was the 'revenge' game, the game we geared up for."

Cleveland Stadium was archaic and rats roamed its catacombs, but the Browns loved their old haunt. They knew the old stadium's rabid fans and steel-and-concrete appearance made it one of the league's toughest places to visit. Writer Bob Sudyk thought Municipal Stadium had all the cheery warmth of a fog-shrouded castle in Transylvania. As the Browns assembled in the tunnel beneath the stands for pregame introductions, they could feel the vibrations of the fans. Cleveland wide receiver Paul Warfield said the stadium was shaking as the Browns took the field in their white uniforms trimmed in burnt orange and dark brown.

Nelsen got the Browns off to a fast start. Mixing the run and the pass, he moved his team into field-goal range. "The great Baltimore defense is being tested," Musser told his CBS Radio audience. His words were nearly drowned out by the almost breathless chant of "Go! Go! Go!" of close to 80,000 Browns fans. But the big crowd fell silent when Don Cockroft's 41-yard field goal attempt was blocked by the upraised left arm of Bubba Smith, who played defensive tackle rather than his customary end position on field-goal attempts. It was, Collier said later, the turning point of the game.

The first quarter ended in a scoreless tie, but the Colts seized control in the second. Game films show Morrall finding Orr on the left side for a 14-yard gain, then following two plays later with a 13-yard pass to Richardson. With Cleveland's defense conscious of the passing game, Morrall switched to the run. Matte slanted for six yards and then for 12, and Hill ground out three hard yards through the middle.

Colts offensive tackle Sam Ball loved the transition to the ground game. If the defense is allowed to anticipate the passing game, Ball said, things get turned around and the offense becomes the defense because the pass rusher gets to make the first move. Emphasizing the running game allowed the Colts offensive line to become more aggressive. "We could really play football," Ball said.

Baltimore's drive finally stalled, but a 28-yard field goal by left-footed kicker Lou Michaels made it 3–0. Morrall looked up and thought it felt good to get that zero off the Colts side of the scoreboard.

When he got the ball back, Morrall directed a 10-play, 60-yard drive. Baltimore's bewildering variety of alignments was causing confusion and hesitation within the Cleveland defense. With Orr and Richardson lined up on the left, Morrall sent Mackey to their side on a running play, and the big tight end thundered for 10 yards. Hill followed Ressler for four yards, then Morrall hit on three straight passes—the last a 19-yarder to Orr. We're rolling, Morrall thought. The march ended with Matte driving in from the 1-yard line after he had rolled off a thunderous hit by the 6'4", 265-pound Johnson.

Bill O'Donnell made the call on Colts radio:

> *"Second down and goal to go... Here's Earl Morrall, calling signals. Handoff to Matte, he's in! Matte is in for the touchdown... And the score is Colts 10, the Browns nothing."*

Baltimore's battering defense, meanwhile, was breaking down the Browns blocking and putting extreme pressure on Nelsen, whose surgically scarred knees made him virtually immobile in the pocket. Bubba Smith did the most damage. Working against outstanding right tackle Monte Clark, Bubba muddied Nelsen's uniform No. 16 several times with knockdowns and made seven unassisted tackles. Smith succeeded in part because Baltimore's front four was running a series of stunts and loops that allowed Bubba to crash the pocket by taking an inside route from his end position. The Colts strategies were also stuffing Cleveland's vaunted ground attack. Baltimore's secondary had been instructed to key tight end Milt Morin. The instant Colts defensive backs recognized Morin was not releasing for a pass but was instead staying back to block for Kelly and Co., Baltimore read it as a running play and stormed the line of scrimmage.

Colts return specialist Preston Pearson felt his team was sky-high and playing with a controlled ferocity. Safety Rick Volk's interception of a Nelsen pass intended for tight end Milt Morin gave Baltimore the ball at the Browns 42. Morrall drove the Colts deep into Cleveland territory before Mackey fumbled and cornerback Erich Barnes recovered at the

14. With time running out in the opening half, Nelsen tried to rally the Browns. He was hit as he released a pass, and the ball fluttered— "like a wingshot duck," Tex Maule wrote in *Sports Illustrated*—until it was plucked from the air by Curtis, who made a juggling interception along the Colts sideline at the Browns 33. Musser called the key play on CBS Radio:

> *"Here is a near interception and... Did he keep it? He did! The Colts have it right back on a sideline juggling act by Mike Curtis."*

Matte ran for 12 yards on first down, and Hill ground out an additional nine. The Colts were driving, and fans back in Baltimore listening on the radio heard O'Donnell's lively calls:

> *"From the Browns 33-yard line, Morrall calls signals, drops back, delay handoff to Matte up the middle, to the 30, at the 25, to the 21-yard line... Tommy Matte breaking over the middle... He got great blocking up the middle and was knocked down by Dale Lindsey, the right linebacker.*
>
> *"First-and-10, Colts at the 21. Again, they break that huddle. The time remaining 1:34 in the first half. Colts by 10, 10 to nothing... Morrall calling signals, Morrall drops back, delay handoff to Hill, he breaks over the middle to the 15, to about the 12-yard line... The clock ticks away."*

With the ball at the 12, Matte veered left behind Ressler and tackle Bob Vogel and on a play called "Flow-39."

> Musser: *"A minute and five seconds is all that remains here in the first half of play... Matte, sweeping to the left, inside the 10, to the 5, he's gonna go! A touchdown for Tom Matte! He swept to the left side, used his blockers perfectly, and got the score."*

For Matte, the title game represented a homecoming. He grew up on 93rd and Hough in Cleveland, which at the time was the No. 1 crime district in the city. He played at Shaw High School in East Cleveland, then at Ohio State University. Browns fans, however, weren't interested in Matte's Ohio roots. His momentum on his second scoring run carried him up a short grassy embankment that separated the end zone from the lower stands. As Matte turned away from the crowd and began heading back to the field, a hail of snowballs were thrown in his direction. One fan leaned over the lower railing and hurled something other than snowballs—a few well-chosen words—at the Colts star.

"I was catching a little hell," Matte said. "I was up on the embankment, and they're throwing snowballs at me. I said, 'Take this football, and shove it up your ass.'"

Just as they had devastated the Vikings the week before by scoring two touchdowns in the third quarter to break open a tight game, the Colts had all but buried the Browns by scoring 17 unanswered points before halftime. Hill thought Baltimore's second touchdown had succeeded in taking Cleveland out of its game plan. The Browns had hoped to spring Kelly for consistent gains on sweeps and draws and have Nelsen hit Warfield, Morin, and Gary Collins on medium-range passes. But a series of offside penalties and a 17-point deficit took the Browns out of their ball-control mindset. The Browns, Hill said, were now forced to play catch-up. "It made them play our game," he said.

By halftime, Cleveland's running game had been held to 37 yards. Municipal Stadium's huge throng sat in chilled silence as the Colts dominated the first two quarters.

"It was win or go home," Baltimore safety Jerry Logan said. "In the back of my mind, I was thinking that we had to leave it all out there on the field. If they're good enough to beat us, then they beat us. We knew what we had to do defensively."

The Colts were in control, but few thought they had the game won. Shula warned against a letdown in the locker room at halftime. "We're not going to sit on this lead," he said. "We're going to add to it. Play like the score is nothing-nothing."

Both defenses dominated early in the third quarter, and the Colts were looking at a second-and-17 when Morrall and Richardson connected for a big play. Chuck Thompson had taken over the second-half radio play-by-play for O'Donnell, and he called the series of plays that clinched a title for the Colts:

> "Second down and about 17 for Baltimore from the Cleveland 43-yard line... Morrall, looking at the defense, takes it away and fakes, rolls back deeper, sets up, under pressure, now fires for the end zone... Willie Richardson and Erich Barnes... Willie Richardson makes the catch at the Cleveland 5! Morrall's pass to Willie Richardson sets up a first-and-goal Baltimore at the Cleveland 5...
>
> "Morrall, snapping signals, still barking, turns, hands to Matte... Down the middle goes Matte, weaves his way for a couple of tough yards near the Cleveland 2-yard line...
>
> "Second-and-goal Baltimore at the Cleveland 2. Morrall turns, gives to Matte off the right side... Touchdown, Baltimore! Matte dove over the right side for a score, his third touchdown of the afternoon, and the Baltimore Colts run it up over the Cleveland Browns. The Cleveland Kid, Tom Matte, having a great afternoon in his hometown."

Matte tied an NFL Championship Game record in the third quarter when he scored his third touchdown, a 2-yard burst behind Sullivan and Hill. Sideline cameras showed Matte celebrating with a teammate. "I just dove over," Matte said. "It was the biggest hole you ever saw."

Matte had tied a record set four years earlier by Collins on the same field and in a game involving the same two teams and head coaches. "I would have had a fourth touchdown," Matte said. "But I got a concussion in the second half. I got hit in the spine, and it sent shock waves up to my brain."

Richardson's sensational grab and Matte's slamming into the end zone for his third score sealed the deal for the Colts. It was late in the third quarter and the Baltimore defense, playing with confident abandon, wasn't about to surrender the lead. "We knew we had them," Morrall said. "We knew we had it won."

Trailing 24–0, the Browns continued to search for answers to the Colts riddle. Collier instructed wide receivers Warfield and Collins to take wider splits at the line of scrimmage to spread out the Colts and find the seams in their suffocating zone. But all it did was make it more difficult for Warfield and Collins to hear the snap count, thus contributing to Cleveland's rash of penalties. Nelsen tried attacking the Baltimore zone with deep passes, but this tactic failed, as well. Baltimore defensive tackle Billy Ray Smith thought the Browns became desperate when they learned they couldn't run on the Colts. Once Baltimore realized it, Billy Ray said, they put more pressure on Nelsen and shut off his passing game. Their resources taken away one by one, the Browns were left without hope and without points.

Seldom in the long history of NFL Championship Games, Maule wrote in *Sports Illustrated*, has one team so thoroughly dominated the other.

"It all came together on that day," Volk said. "Cleveland was a good team, and anything can happen in a game. But when you get up on a team by 20 points or so, it's hard for them."

The Colts added 10 more points in the final quarter on a 10-yard field goal by Michaels and a four-yard run by halfback Timmy Brown, who followed Ressler into the end zone. Icing on the cake, Morrall thought. On the Baltimore sideline, players were flashing wide grins and confident nods. Their satisfaction stemmed not only from playing like champions, but from playing an almost flawless brand of football.

"We were well-prepared," Ressler said. "We had a good game plan, and we executed. Sometimes you have days where everything goes right, and that was one of those days."

When Morrall came off the field after the Colts had scored their last touchdown, he found John Unitas waiting for him. "Congratulations, Earl," Unitas said, smiling. "It was a great season for you, and you deserved it."

The final gun in the Colts 34–0 victory sounded at 5:20 PM (EST), and Thompson provided the exclamation point for Baltimore fans:

> *"This ballgame is history as the gun sounds, and it's been a very gloomy, gloomy Sunday in Cleveland. But in that great city of Baltimore, ain't the beer cold!"*

On CBS Radio, Musser and Reynolds closed their radio broadcast by praising Baltimore's team effort.

> Reynolds: *"The Baltimore Colts, with a superb defensive job and a fine attack directed by their Most Valuable Player, Earl Morrall, have moved into the Super Bowl."*
>
> Musser: *"Earl Morrall had it in clutch situations, and Tom Matte was one of the big heroes here today with three touchdowns... A magnificent job turned in by the Baltimore defense."*

The shutout was the fourth of the year for Baltimore's brilliant defense, and it marked the 11th time in 16 games an opponent had been held to a touchdown or less. Nelsen told CBS sportscaster Pat Summerall afterward that the Colts had confused the Browns by showing zone coverage and then switching to man-to-man. The shifting alignments, Nelsen said, forced him to hold the ball a split second longer than usual, allowing the Colts pressure to succeed. He was sacked four times for minus-34 yards and intercepted twice before being replaced by Frank Ryan, one of the heroes of Cleveland's 1964 championship.

Kelly fared no better. Like Motown's Martha and the Vandellas, the NFL's leading rusher had no place to run to, no place to hide. He finished with 28 yards on 13 carries. Kelly, Charlie Harraway, and Ernie Green combined to manage 56 yards on 20 carries. The Browns' offense crossed midfield just twice and penetrated no deeper than the Baltimore 33. CBS-TV sportscaster Jack Whitaker remarked that the Colts had won because a defense he labeled as "incomparable" shut out an offense that averaged 28 points a game during the regular season and scored 31 points the week before against the Dallas Doomsday defense.

The Colts offense, meanwhile, ground out yardage in methodical fashion. Matte rushed for a game-high 88 yards on 17 carries, and Hill carried 11 times for 60 yards. Fronted by their offensive line—Curry, Ressler, Sullivan, Ball, Vogel—Baltimore produced 22 first downs to Cleveland's 12 and outgained the Browns 353–173 yards.

Shula thought his team played a perfect blend of offense and defense; "real machinelike execution," he said. He also gained a measure of personal redemption in the win. Members of Shula's family shared his satisfaction. He later found out that near the end of the game, when the score was still 27-0—the same as it was when the

The quarterbacks of Super Bowl III stood in stark contrast on and off the field. For the Baltimore Colts (above), Johnny Unitas (19) and Earl Morrall (15) preferred buzz-cuts and business suits, while the New York Jets "Broadway" Joe Namath (left) opted for long hair and a mink coat.

(PHOTOS COURTESY AP IMAGES)

Even under pressure from the blitzing Colts, Namath managed to complete his passes in Super Bowl III.

Jets fullback Matt Snell is hit by a Colts defender but stays on his feet in Super Bowl III. Snell rushed for a then-Super Bowl record 121 yards. (PHOTO COURTESY AP IMAGES)

Pete Lammons (87) dives to catch a Joe Namath pass in Super Bowl III. (PHOTO COURTESY AP IMAGES)

In an attempt to get the sluggish Colts offense on the scoreboard, quarterback Earl Morrall sets up to pass in *Super Bowl III.*

(PHOTO COURTESY AP IMAGES)

The Jets made good use of their running game in Super Bowl III as Joe Namath (12) hands off to running back Bill Mathis (31). Guard Bob Talamini (61) leads interference. (PHOTO COURTESY AP IMAGES)

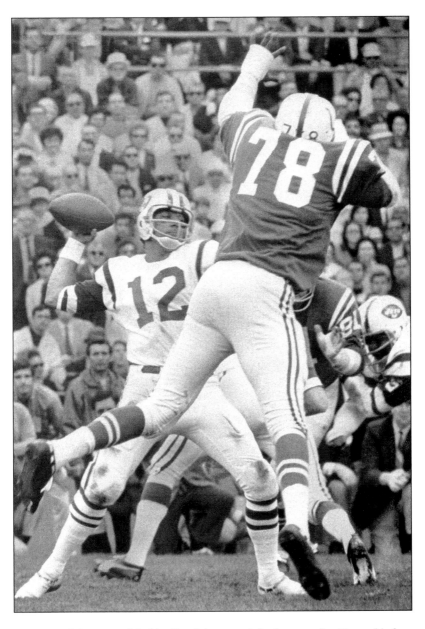

Colts star defensive end Bubba Smith leaps to defend against Joe Namath's deep pass to Don Maynard. Smith altered Namath's pass enough to cost the Jets an early touchdown. (PHOTO COURTESY AP IMAGES)

Coach Weeb Ewbank congratulates Joe Namath during the final seconds of the Jets 16–7 victory over the Colts in Super Bowl III. It was an emotional moment for Ewbank, who was formerly the coach of the Baltimore Colts and quarterback Johnny Unitas.

Browns won in 1964—his mother jumped from her seat. "Get one more touchdown!" she shouted. "We want to beat the Browns worse than they beat us."

"That was a special day," Matte said. "I played pretty good, but you have to give credit where it's due. Our offensive line did a great job."

Amid the celebration in the Baltimore locker room, Morrall held court for crowds of reporters. "After so many ups and downs," he said, "it's nice to win." Colts owner Carroll Rosenbloom told a CBS national television audience that the 1968 Colts were the equal of Baltimore's great 1958-59 squads.

The Colts were one win away from being celebrated as the greatest team in pro football history. All they had to do was beat the champions of the AFL, the New York Jets. It didn't seem, Shula said later, as if it would be difficult.

Norm Miller of the *New York Daily News* provided an early preview in his report on Baltimore's victory:

"The Colts, with their colorless but methodically destructive efficiency, clobbered the Browns, 34-0, today to win the NFL championship and set up a beaut of a Super Bowl matchup with the Jets at Miami on January 12.

"It will be a matchup of the brainy experience of ex-Giant Earl Morrall against the glamour-tossing of Joe Namath, and it will pit Weeb Ewbank, in his year of comeback triumph, against Don Shula, whom he once coached, plus at least 10 of the Colts who played for Weeb at Baltimore."

10

A Heated Rivalry
in the Sunshine State

The phone in Johnny Sample's room in the Galt Ocean Mile Hotel rang loudly as it sat cradled in its receiver. It was early in the afternoon on Sunday, January 5, 1969, one week before Super Bowl III, and Sample was resting in his room after attending the 9:30 AM mass at St. Pius X, a Catholic Church located a few miles down Route A1A.

Sample had been waiting for this call since he heard the Baltimore Colts had arrived by charter jet the day before. As the Colts disembarked at Fort Lauderdale International Airport, they were greeted by a crowd of some 250 fans, many of whom waved autograph books in one hand and pens in the other. Threading their way through the mob, the players boarded two buses that were waiting to take them to the Statler Hilton Hotel, which was less than one mile away from the Jets residence.

Sample had been a member of Baltimore's 1958 and '59 title teams and had remained friends with some of his former teammates, including cornerback Lenny Lyles. The two were roommates in 1958 and had vacationed together with their wives and children in the offseason.

When Sample's phone rang that Sunday, the defensive captain of the American Football League champions knew who was calling. Picking up the receiver, he heard a familiar voice.

"John," Lyles said, "the champions of the National Football League have arrived."

Perhaps more than any other player on the Jets, Sample understood the deep meaning of the AFL-NFL rivalry. The war between the leagues had been raging since 1959, when Lamar Hunt and seven other owners founded the AFL. Because of the daunting challenge of succeeding where past challengers to the NFL had failed, Boston Patriots owner Billy Sullivan jokingly referred to the AFL's executive committee as The Foolish Club. NFL owners called their latest challenger The Other League, refusing to even refer to the AFL by name.

Jets receiver Don Maynard was one of several AFL stars who had started their pro careers in the NFL. "We had a lot of quality people in the AFL," he said. "I couldn't understand why the press didn't help this new league more. It meant new jobs and new teams for people to support. The AFL gave 400 jobs to players, 50 jobs to coaches, 50 to 60 jobs to personnel in the front office, and it gave teams to cities that couldn't get NFL teams."

Jets linebacker Larry Grantham, who had been drafted by the Colts before signing with New York, knew that the NFL would receive more favorable press because it was the older, more established league. "But the thing that really hurt," he said, "was the disparity between players, the way we were perceived. A Jets player would get $50 to make an appearance somewhere. A Giants player would get $500."

From 1960–68, AFL players, coaches, owners, fans, and media bristled at the unfavorable comparisons with the NFL. "For a long time, we had to listen to a lot of talk about how much better the NFL was than the AFL," said former San Diego Chargers coach Sid Gillman, who had coached the Los Angeles Rams before joining the AFL. When AFL and NFL players met at league meetings, AFL players like Buffalo's Jack Kemp and San Diego's Ron Mix felt NFL players looked down on them, and thought them "minor leaguers" who were in an inferior league. Chicago Bears owner and coach George Halas referred to the AFL as "that damn Mickey Mouse league" and sent a telegram to Green Bay coach Vince Lombardi prior to Super Bowl I imploring him to, in effect, "show those clowns who's boss." Lombardi told his Packers it would be a "disgrace" to lose to the upstarts. "He hated the AFL," Packers wideout Max McGee said. AFL players remembered Packers center Ken Bowman acting like they shouldn't even talk to him at player rep meetings.

The rivalry spurred constant debate over which league was superior—the innovative AFL or the tradition-bound NFL. Joe Namath had signed with the AFL in part because he had been impressed with the wide-open style of play of teams like the Chargers and because the younger league was more non-conformist. The NFL had great players, Namath thought, but everybody in that league seemed to wear their hair short and live by an arbitrary code of conduct. Namath saw the AFL as a maverick league. He would be able to wear his trademark white leather cleats and his hair long. To Namath, the AFL was fresh; the NFL staid. The AFL represented freedom; the NFL conformity.

"Variety is our style," innovative Kansas City Chiefs coach Hank Stram boasted. Gillman said AFL coaches realized early on they weren't going to attract many new fans by playing the same brand of power football favored by the NFL. Since many of the AFL's coaches had recently coached in college, they brought college thinking into pro football.

"These people brought with them different concepts," Gillman said. "You have to have fresh thinking all the time and then adjust new ideas to the pro concept."

Along with future Hall of Famers Gillman and Stram, the AFL provided the first pro coaching opportunity for Bill Walsh, John Madden, Chuck Noll, and Al Davis. They would combine to win 12 Super Bowl titles.

As the AFL matured, teams developed their own playing styles. Gillman created the original West Coast Offense and Fearsome Foursome defense. The Chargers burned up the track with blistering speed at running back and wide receiver. "El Sid" owned an armada of talent—Lance Alworth, Paul Lowe, Keith Lincoln, John Hadl, Ron Mix, Tobin Rote, Walt Sweeney, Earl Faison, Ernie "Big Cat" Ladd—and in 1963 became the first AFL champion to draw serious comparison with its NFL counterpart, Halas' Monsters of the Midway, the Chicago Bears.

"If the Chargers could play the best in the NFL," former Cleveland Browns star quarterback Otto Graham said in a shocking statement, "I'd have to pick the Chargers."

In Oakland, the Raiders developed a devastating deep passing attack—a "vertical" game that utilized the talents of pass-catching tight ends like Billy Cannon along with wideouts Fred Biletnikoff, Bill Miller, and Warren Wells, plus running backs Hewritt Dixon and Charlie Smith.

In New York, Weeb Ewbank built a balanced attack around Namath's ability to read defenses.

In Kansas City, Stram created flashy and imaginative offensive and defensive strategies—the Moving Pocket; the Mini-Backfield; the Tight-end I; the Stack and Triple Stack defenses; and Odd fronts.

In Buffalo, the Bills became the first AFL team to win a league championship with a style built on a punishing ball-control offense featuring 250-pound fullback Carlton "Cookie" Gilchrist and an even-more punishing defense, headed by Ron McDole, Tom Sestak, Mike Stratton, and George Saimes.

The AFL saw these diverse styles as proof that its league was more progressive and colorful than the conservative NFL.

"The AFL featured a wide-open style," Jets radio announcer Merle Harmon said. "The NFL was power, power, power."

The NFL, however, didn't believe its brand of ball was one-dimensional. In 1966, at the midpoint of the AFL's colorful 10-year history and the height of the war between the leagues, former New York Giant Kye Rote wrote a book titled, *The Language of Pro Football*. In it, Rote described the varying team personalities of each NFL team. The Baltimore Colts were the Strategists, the Cleveland Browns the Stylists, the Dallas Cowboys the Tacticians, the Detroit Lions the Defenders, and the Green Bay Packers the Fundamentalists.

Tex Maule, who covered the NFL in the 1960s for *Sports Illustrated*, thought the verbal war between the leagues polarized fans across the country. Maule was an outspoken supporter of the superiority of the NFL, and never hesitated to say so in his magazine stories. In December 1964, he wrote a piece for the magazine imagining what would happen if Baltimore, who was considered to be the best team in the NFL prior to their championship game loss to Cleveland, played AFL powerhouse Buffalo. Maule predicted that dream game would end with Colts backup quarterback Gary Cuozzo finding second-string receiver Willie Richardson for a touchdown and the final score in Baltimore's 48–7 romp.

Maule's story infuriated the AFL. Gillman spent several minutes of a postgame interview telling the media how little he thought of Maule's football expertise. AFL writers chided Maule as the "high priest of the NFL." Larry Felser, who covered the Bills in the 1960s for the *Buffalo Evening News*, believed that if the Super Bowl had started earlier in the decade, the 1963 Chargers and '64 Bills might have become the first AFL champions to beat the NFL in a title game.

Maule scoffed at the notion. San Diego and Buffalo were still in the league in 1966, he argued, the season that led to the first AFL-NFL Championship Game. The Chargers and Bills were both beaten by eventual league champion Kansas City, which was in turn beaten by the NFL's Green Bay Packers, 35–10, in the first meeting between the leagues. Lombardi took pride in the Packers 25-point victory but refused at first to comment in the postgame as to whether the lopsided score was proof of NFL superiority. Under constant badgering by the press, Lombardi relented and said there were three or four teams in the NFL that were better than Kansas City. It was a statement, he said later, that he regretted as soon as he had made it.

Lombardi and the Packers returned to represent the NFL in Super Bowl II, and their opponent was an Oakland Raiders team that was considered to be one of the best in AFL history. Lombardi and his Packers were at the end of their dynastic run—Green Bay won a record five NFL championships in the 1960s, including an unprecedented and still unmatched three straight—but they were aging and had spent themselves physically, emotionally, and mentally in their epic Ice Bowl win over Dallas that wasn't decided until quarterback Bart Starr's 1-yard sneak in the final seconds.

Still, the Packers handled the Raiders and made it look easy. Raiders general manager Al Davis believed Green Bay's victories in the first two Super Bowls didn't prove the superiority of the NFL over the AFL, just the superiority of Lombardi and his Packers over pro football. Davis' statement would prove to be closer to the truth than anyone could have realized at the time. By 1968, the AFL-NFL rivalry was the hottest in pro sports, some would argue the hottest in sports history, and proved to be the perfect backdrop of an era in which young upstarts everywhere were challenging the authority of the establishment.

From 1960-66, the two leagues competed hotly for college players, and stories of "baby-sitting" campaigns in that era are legendary. Blue-chip athletes were signed to contracts on the field after bowl games; some "bonus babies" were taken by league reps to remote spots and hidden away from the rival league until contracts were finalized. Lawsuits between the leagues were filed and counter-filed. When someone asked NFL commissioner Pete Rozelle if, to satisfy public demand, the NFL champion would play its AFL counterpart in an interleague title game, Rozelle declined. "We don't play," he said, "with people who sue us."

The signing wars were escalating into a financial bloodbath. Finally, both sides realized in 1966 that they were on the road to ruin unless a compromise could be worked out. Even after the merger of the two leagues in the summer of 1966, a family feud atmosphere still pervaded pro football. Stram and the Chiefs, still stinging from their loss to Green Bay and Lombardi's unkind words the previous January, took their frustrations out on the next NFL team they played, Halas' Bears, and humiliated one of the NFL's flagship franchises, 66-24, when interleague preseason games began in 1967. Fans, players, owners, and media kept track of the number of preseason games won by each league. The NFL won 13-of-16 interleague games in 1967; the AFL 13-of-23 in '68; the NFL 19-of-33, with one tie, in '69. All told, the NFL won the preseason war, 42-29-1. But the AFL captured the two most memorable games—Kansas City over Chicago in '67 and the Jets over the Giants 37-14 in their celebrated Yale Bowl encounter in '69.

But it was between the Jets and Colts, the two teams that would meet in Super Bowl III, that the AFL-NFL rivalry was most pronounced. Several Jets—including Ewbank, Sample, Winston Hill, Billy Baird, Curley Johnson, Bake Turner, and Mark Smolinski—had been with the Colts prior to joining the AFL. Baltimore's Tom Matte and Bob Vogel played on the same Ohio State football team with the Jets Matt Snell. The two head coaches, New York's Weeb Ewbank and Baltimore's Don Shula, also had a history together dating back to their years as coach and player, respectively, on Paul Brown's Cleveland Browns. Their defensive assistants, Walt Michaels of the Jets and Chuck Noll of the Colts, had also played for Brown in Cleveland. Ewbank and Colts defensive coordinator Bill Arnsparger both came from Miami University in Oxford, Ohio, a school whose fertile coaching ground has earned for it the nickname "Cradle of Coaches."

Ewbank, Arnsparger, Brown, Gillman, Red Blaik, Ara Parseghian, Woody Hayes, Bo Schembechler, and Jim Tressel are among the outstanding coaches who have come out of Miami (Ohio) University. Ewbank joined Brown's staff in Cleveland as a scout and offensive line coach, and he helped Brown popularize the notion of "pocket passing," which saw offensive linemen form a semi-circular cup around the quarterback to protect him from opposing pass rushers.

Ewbank taught the Browns linemen to vary their styles of blocking depending on the type of pass. At a time when many NFL coaches believed that offensive linemen should block aggressively from the snap of the ball, Ewbank realized that such a tactic gave defensive linemen an opportunity to recover quickly and get their hands in the air to deflect a pass. Cleveland linemen were taught by Ewbank to cut-block or block low on the man opposite them, cutting them down, in effect, to create passing lanes for quarterback Otto Graham.

Ewbank put such emphasis on pass protection that when Browns linemen spun from their huddle, they would shout in unison, "No one touches Graham." Ewbank took this emphasis with him to Baltimore and then New York, and he built the same protective walls around quarterbacks John Unitas and Joe Namath. Buddy Ryan, the Jets linebacker coach under Ewbank in 1968, was so impressed by his boss' emphasis on protecting the quarterback that he came to believe that the best defense was one that could break down the protective pocket and pressure the quarterback. When he became defensive coordinator for the Chicago Bears in the 1980s, Ryan designed the ferocious "46" defense that terrorized the NFL and led to the Bears remarkable 1985 Super Bowl season.

Ewbank's other chief duty with the Browns was scouting, and it was on a 1951 trip to John Carroll University that he discovered a young player named Shula. Upon Ewbank's recommendation, Brown took Shula in the ninth round of the 1951 NFL draft. Ewbank left the Browns three years later when he was hired by team owner Carroll Rosenbloom to coach the Colts. Announcing a five-year plan to turn the franchise around, Ewbank worked his plan to near-perfection, winning the NFL title in overtime against the Giants in the 1958 Sudden Death classic at Yankee Stadium. Rosenbloom would later joke that Ewbank's five-year plan had actually taken five years and eight minutes, the latter being the elapsed time of the extra quarter.

Shula, who had been traded to the Colts in 1953, was reunited with Ewbank through the 1956 season. Shula played one season with the Washington Redskins and then began his NFL coaching career as a defensive assistant under Detroit Lions head coach George Wilson. The Lions of the early 1960s featured one of pro football's most ferocious defenses, and they annually engaged in mud-and-blood battles with their Western Conference rivals. Their fiercest rivalry was with the Lombardi Packers, and when Shula was promoted to defensive coordinator in Detroit, he parried Lombardi's power offenses. Their most famous confrontation occurred on Thanksgiving Day in 1962. Detroit had dropped a 9–7 decision at defending league champion Green Bay in October, and the loss infuriated members of the Lions defense, who pinned the defeat on a late interception thrown by Detroit quarterback Milt Plum that led to the Packers winning score. By Thanksgiving Day, the Packers were 10–0 and being labeled by some observers as the greatest team in NFL history. The Lions were 8–2 and represented the last major obstacle between Green Bay and an undefeated season.

Shula designed a series of stunts and blitzes aimed at making the most of the Lions pent-up aggression toward the Packers. Defensive tackle Roger Brown led a charge that sacked Green Bay quarterback Bart Starr 11 times in a 26–14 win. The Packers recovered and did not lose another game that season en route to repeating as NFL champions, but Shula and the Lions had prevented Lombardi and Co. from achieving perfection. Ten years later, Shula, as coach of the Miami Dolphins, did achieve the perfect season when he guided his team to a 17–0 record.

The Ewbank-Shula connection continued in 1963 when Rosenbloom fired Ewbank as coach of the Colts and replaced him with Shula. The 33-year-old Shula was the youngest head coach in the NFL, but it took him just one season to restore the Colts to glory. Baltimore went 12–2 in 1964 to win the Western Conference before falling to Cleveland in the title game, but Shula kept the Colts competitive for the next several years with shrewd trades that brought in veterans like quarterback Earl Morrall and middle linebacker Dennis Gaubatz, and solid drafts that yielded young stars in Bubba Smith, Mike Curtis, and Rick Volk.

At the same time that Shula was retooling the established Colts, Ewbank was building up the young Jets. "I've seen sicker cows than this one get well," he announced at the time of his hiring. "I had a five-year plan in Baltimore, and I don't see why we can't build a winner here in five years."

Backed by a wealthy syndicate that had purchased the bankrupt Titans franchise in 1963, the team's new ownership dedicated itself to making New York the flagship franchise of the AFL. Team uniforms were changed from drab blue and gold to bright green and white, and old battered helmets and shoulder pads were replaced by first-class equipment.

In 1964, the renamed Jets relocated from the crumbling Polo Grounds to sparkling new Shea Stadium, a 64,000-seat, state-of-the-art structure that became one of the AFL's top facilities. One of the team's new owners was David A. Werblin, an aggressive and likeable show business agent who knew star quality sold and wasn't afraid to go out and buy it.

AFL founder and Chiefs owner Lamar Hunt thought that Werblin's taking over the Jets was one of the two most important turning points in AFL history. The other, he said, was the NBC contract in 1964 that guaranteed the AFL's financial solvency.

"The television contract," Hunt said in a later interview, "gave the league the stability and financial ability to compete for players."

Werblin's nickname was "Sonny," as in money, and he and his partners spared no expense in bringing blue chip college players to the Big Apple. In 1964, the Jets signed bruising Matt Snell away from their city rivals, the Giants. In 1965, Werblin and Co. shook the sports world by luring Joe Namath away from the NFL with a golden carrot worth $427,000.

Original Titans like Maynard and Grantham were ecstatic with the changes being made.

"Sonny was a marketing man, and he developed interest in the team, even from women," Maynard said. "He got a lot of publicity when he signed Joe Namath." Grantham thought Werblin did a "great job selling the Jets to the people of New York."

Bolstered by talented young players like Snell and Namath, established veterans like Grantham and Maynard, and free agents like Sample and Hill, the Jets reached contender status in 1967. Knee injuries to Snell and halfback Emerson Boozer decimated New York's running game and forced Namath to carry the offense. He responded by passing for 4,007 yards, the first man in pro football history to surpass the 4,000-yard mark in a season, but New York finished a game behind first-place Houston in the Eastern Division standings. Had the Jets not been riddled with injuries, they might have won the division and played Oakland for the AFL championship and a berth in Super Bowl II opposite the Lombardi Packers.

Still, Ewbank's job was in jeopardy. Jets ownership had spent lavishly to rebuild the franchise and wanted a return on its investment. New managing partner Donald Lillis tried to lure Lombardi into taking Ewbank's job. But Lombardi had just retired as head coach of the Packers following his third straight NFL title and wanted at least a year away from the sidelines. Lillis died of a heart attack just as training camp was beginning at the Jets new headquarters at Hofstra University, and Phil Iselin took over as managing partner.

Iselin agreed to allow Ewbank to remain as head coach, but he warned that if the Jets didn't at least win the East in 1968, there would be a coaching change at the end of the season. The offseason recovery of Snell and Boozer, the acquisition of All-AFL guard Bob Talamini in a trade with the Oilers, and the maturity of players like Namath and split end George Sauer contributed to New York's 1968 championship season. Grantham credited Ewbank for the Jets success. "Weeb came in with a five-year plan and worked it to perfection," he said.

It had actually taken Ewbank six years to bring an AFL title to New York; yet had it not been for a series of injuries that devastated his running game in 1967, the Jets might have given him at least an

Eastern Division title within his five-year time frame. Now, his AFL title brought him face-to-face with his former player, Shula, and former team, the Colts.

Surprisingly, Shula's job was also said to have been on the line in 1968. He had been named the NFL's Coach of the Year twice, but postseason losses to the Browns in 1964 and to the Packers in '65, along with missing the playoffs in 1966 and '67, had reportedly left Rosenbloom impatient with the Colts inability to win the big game.

The link between Ewbank and Shula was one of the many between the AFL and NFL champions. Namath and Unitas, both products of western Pennylvania, had a chance meeting the week before the game. Unitas and his wife Dorothy were paying a courtesy call on Ewbank at the Galt Hotel when Namath arrived, as well. Two generations of quarterbacks stood face-to-face in an unexpected encounter, and their differences were apparent in their appearance and dress. Unitas wore a crewcut and gray business suit with white shirt and dark tie. Namath wore a black turtleneck whose high collar was covered by his long locks.

"How's your arm?" Namath asked.

"How's your knees?" Unitas countered.

Neither man received an answer.

The feuding atmosphere surrounding the Jets and Colts was evidenced most by long-simmering relationships on the offensive and defensive lines. Winston Hill, New York's power offensive tackle, was preparing to face Baltimore defensive end Ordell Braase. The two had more than a nodding acquaintance. When Hill was drafted by Baltimore in 1963, he had been cut from the team largely because of his failure to handle Braase in scrimmages.

"Braase was my undoing," Hill said. He had been told that Braase had been to war. He thought they meant Vietnam. Hill was startled to learn Braase had been in the *Korean War*.

A graduate of Texas Southern, Hill had been selected on the 11th round of the draft by Ewbank when the latter was still coaching the Colts. Baltimore's '63 draft had brought in a number of top college players, including Ohio State tackle Bob Vogel. In the interim between the draft and training camp, Ewbank was fired. Because Baltimore was a veteran team, Shula planned to keep only one rookie offensive line-man. Vogel was the Colts top pick in the draft, and when Hill looked bad against Braase, Shula made a decision.

"Winston, I'm sorry we're going to have to let you go," he said. "If you're interested in the AFL, try the Jets."

Hill instead tried the Denver Broncos, who had expressed interest in him. But when the Broncos failed to return his call, Hill headed to the Jets training camp. The Jets initially tried to persuade Hill to play center, but he insisted on the tackle position and asked the team's premier pass blocker at the time, Sherman Plunkett, for help. Hill made measurable progress, but Ewbank still cut him. Hill startled the Jets coach by refusing to leave camp, and even offered to stay at his own expense to prove he could make the team. He simply wasn't ready, Hill said, "to accept the fact that I had found something I couldn't conquer."

Hill's persistence paid off. He made the team and spent the 1963 season on the special teams squad. By 1964 he had worked himself into the starting lineup. By 1968 he was one of the top linemen in pro football. From 1963 through '76, Hill played in 195 straight games—a testament to his talent, toughness, and desire.

The fact that Hill struggled to deal with Braase in Colts camp said more about Braase than it did about Hill. The two men shared a common background. Like Hill, Braase was a low pick in the draft, not chosen until Baltimore selected him in the 14th round of the 1954 draft. Like Hill, Braase was a product of a southwestern school in Braase's case, South Dakota. He saw active duty in the armed forces and returned to the Colts in 1957. He was considered a long shot to make the team; line coach John Bridgers was told by a colleague that Braase would be the first lineman cut from the squad that summer. The book on the 6'4", 245-pound Braase at the time was that he wasn't big enough for his position and didn't have the ability to play in the NFL.

Braase was still in camp prior to the final cut, but Ewbank favored keeping Luke Owens, a third-round selection, over Braase. Bridgers, however, was impressed by Braase's intelligent play and defended him vigorously at a coaches' meeting. "Braase," he argued, "is too good a player to cut."

Ewbank relented, and Braase made the Colts as a backup defensive end to starters Gino Marchetti and Don Joyce. Though undersized for his position, Braase made up for his lack of mass with hard work. He was one of the first NFL players known to lift weights, and he studied Marchetti, a future Hall of Famer, to learn technique. Braase also sharpened his skills in scrimmage battles with Colts great Jim Parker, who was considered the premier offensive left tackle in pro football in the late 1950s.

When Marchetti broke his leg late in the 1958 title game, Braase took his place at defensive end. The Colts traded Joyce after the 1960 season, and Braase earned the starting position at right end. He continued to work to improve and earned NFL Pro Bowl honors in 1966 and '67. Yet it was his performance during the 1968 season that led longtime Colts radio announcer Chuck Thompson to describe Braase's play that year as good as at any time in his career.

Braase's strongest attribute had always been rushing the passer, but by 1968 he was an 11-year veteran who had become adept at reading the run and playing off blocks. Braase and defensive right tackle Billy Ray Smith, a 10-year vet whose quickness off the ball earned him the nickname Rabbit, played alongside one another through the 1960s, and they excelled at end-tackle games that saw them looping and stunting behind one another as they exchanged rush lanes to the quarterback. Braase also varied his technique on running plays. He would take on the left tackle opposite him when the offense went into an alignment that indicated an off-tackle run but take an inside charge if the alignment indicted a power sweep. No matter which move he made on his rush upfield, Braase knew his success or failure hinged on timing and technique. "You want to get off the ball quick before the offensive tackle has time to set up on you," he said. "It's a battle of balance."

The battle between Hill and Braase loomed large for both sides as game day neared. Hill took great pride in his pass-blocking skills; he liked the challenge of matching his agility against that of a man who usually weighed 20 or even 30 pounds less than Hill's 280 pounds. Hill was surprisingly agile for a man his size; he had been a tennis champion in college and still played the game in the offseason. He used his footwork to ride defenders away from Namath. Some of his pass blocks were so pretty, he once said, he would have liked to have framed them and hung them on a wall to admire.

In Braase, Hill would not only be facing an excellent pass rusher but the man who had run him out of Colts training camp five years earlier.

Other personal battles loomed as well, but the pairing that drew the most publicity was on the right side of the Jets offensive line. Tackle Dave Herman was not only a guard playing out of position—he had supplanted starter Sam Walton—but Herman was also expected to contain the awesome charge of Bubba Smith. The matchup was viewed as one of the keys to the game. If Herman failed to handle the 6'7", 295-pound Colts giant, big Bubba would be able to draw a bead on Broadway Joe.

Smith had terrorized NFL quarterbacks in 1968, and the sight of this massive man bearing down on enemy ball carriers struck a responsive chord with Colts fans. Home games in Baltimore soon reverberated with chants of "Kill, Bubba, Kill!" Following their devastating win over the Browns in the NFL Championship Game, the Colts were mobbed by fans upon their return to Friendship International Airport. None more so than Bubba who, despite his immense presence, needed a police escort to get through the crowd.

Like Hill and Braase, Herman and Smith had a history together. Herman was a senior lineman for Michigan State when Smith arrived as a heralded freshman out of Beaumont, Texas. Located in southeast Texas, Beaumont boasted two high schools—Charlton-Pollard and Hebert—that developed so many pro football players they came to be known as the Boys of Beaumont. Mel and Miller Farr, Jerry LeVias, Warren Wells, and Smith were among those who graduated from one of the two schools.

"Nobody awed us," LeVias once said. "I don't care if Jim Brown himself stepped in there. They were nobody until they got tested by the Boys of Beaumont."

A product of Edon, Ohio, Herman came from a rural high school so poor that it couldn't afford game films to show college recruits. Michigan State teammates noted his country background and called him Haystack after Haystack Calhoun, a gargantuan professional wrestler of the era who was said to weigh 600 pounds and was known for appearing in the ring sporting blue overalls and bare feet. Off the field, Herman was quiet and introspective, given to perusing the *Wall Street Journal* through horn-rimmed glasses. Unknowing sportswriters who wanted to talk football were caught off-guard by Herman's in-depth knowledge of the stock market. "IBM lost nine points," he would say, "the biggest drop of the day."

With his scholarly manner, Herman might have passed for a businessman. But a calcium ridge in the middle of his forehead, the result of years of butting helmets with enemy defensive tackles, gave away his trade. Herman's head was huge, and it sat atop a columnar-like 18½-inch neck; he wore the biggest helmet on the team, a size 7⅞. Jets resident sports artist LeRoy Neiman loved to sketch the expressive Herman; his head, Neiman said, was a "beautiful head, magnificent."

Herman's head may have been beautiful to Neiman, but opponents saw it as something else—a battering ram. His helmet-first blocking style could be directly attributed to the teachings of former Jets line coach Chuck Knox. When Browns coach Blanton Collier was the head man at the University of Kentucky in the 1950s, Knox was one of his assistants. Shula and Arnsparger were on the same stellar staff. When Ewbank was hired as Jets head coach in 1963, he was looking for an offensive line coach. Collier, who knew Ewbank from their years together with the Browns, recommended Knox.

"I told Weeb there was no better coach in college at teaching pass protection," Collier said. "Chuck was an artist at it."

Herman, Hill, and center John Schmitt all broke in with the Jets under Knox and thus learned his system of pass protection, which was described as "spear blocking." Knox taught his linemen to target an opponent's body and then drive the defender where he wants to go. Sam DeLuca, who was a guard for the Jets and San Diego Chargers before becoming a color analyst for the Jets on WABC Radio, said Knox was the finest line coach he had ever played for. DeLuca had always played his position in a cool, detached manner, but when he tried to impart this patient attitude to Herman when both men were on the Jets, he failed. Sportswriter Paul Zimmerman, who observed the process, said it was like trying to teach a wild stallion the moves of a Tennessee walking horse.

No one on the Jets incorporated Knox's aggressive blocking techniques as well as Herman; they were a perfect fit for both his head and temperament, both of which were outsized. "My head is my number one weapon," Herman said at the time. "That's where my strength is."

Herman used his head with such shattering force he routinely cracked two or three of his helmets per season. Namath compared Herman's piston-like head movements to a machine gun. Like many of the Jets, Namath was looking forward to the Herman-Smith showdown. Big Bubba, Namath said, was going to find a machine gun in his chest all afternoon.

NFL linemen weren't so sure. The consensus among them was that Bubba was a load, a guy who could beat you with his size and strength or with speed surprising for such a big man.

As he prepared to face Smith, Herman told Jets defensive end Verlon Biggs to imitate the Colts star. "Try to grab hold of me and throw me," Herman said, "like Bubba tries to do."

In the Colts camp, Smith was prepping for the coming battle, as well. Huddling with quarterback Johnny Unitas, the two men watched film of Joe Willie taking deep drops in the pocket before setting up to pass.

"Willie Boy," Smith observed in the darkened room, "uses a 10-yard drop." With that much room to work, big Bubba figured Broadway Joe might provide an inviting target come Super Sunday.

11

Super Sunday

Al DeRogatis sat in the NBC-TV broadcast booth high above the manicured floor of the Miami Orange Bowl, watching the television camera and awaiting the flashing red light that would signal the start of the pregame player introductions of the Baltimore Colts.

One by one, the starting members of the Colts defensive unit trotted through the blue-painted turf at the west end of the stadium. Despite the fact that the New York Jets were AFL champions and that Miami was a city that played host to the AFL's Miami Dolphins, the 75,377 fans in attendance greeted the celebrated champions of the National Football League with a sustained ovation.

As the red camera light flashed, millions of viewers saw and heard DeRogatis, who provided the color analysis for play-by-play man Curt Gowdy as the Peacock Network's lead broadcast team for this game, analyze the NFL champs as the stadium announcer introduced them:

> "At left end, from Michigan State, Number 78, Bubba Smith..."
>
> "At left linebacker, from Duke University, Number 32, Mike Curtis..."
>
> Derogatis: "And now as the Baltimore Colts come on the football field, this is a team that in 1968 had one theme, and that was 'All the way in '68.' And they have one more to go."

AFL writers covering the Super Bowl trained their sights on the men they had read about all season but not yet seen, the all-conquerors who had set an NFL record in 1968 for shutouts in a season with four and tied another league mark by allowing an average of just 10.3 points per game. Dressed in their royal blue jerseys with the white shoulder loops, white pants, and white helmets with dark blue horseshoe logos on either side, the Colts looked supremely confident. Marty Ralbovsky of the *New York Times* had watched the Baltimore defense trot off the frigid field in Cleveland two weeks prior after shutting out the Browns in the NFL Championship Game and had seen in their stride an unmistakable swagger.

The Colts carried that attitude into their Super Bowl against a Jets outfit that oddsmakers listed as 18-point underdogs. Don Shula's squad arrived in Miami sporting a 15–1 record and a reputation as one of the great teams in NFL history. Baltimore had outscored playoff opponents Minnesota and Cleveland by a combined aggregate of 58–14. To a man, the Colts fully expected the next 60 minutes of playing time would end with them being crowned world champions and ranked as arguably the NFL's best team ever.

"We were confident, no doubt about it," left guard Glenn Ressler said. "Green Bay had handled AFL teams in the first two Super Bowls, and to us, the AFL was really an unknown. Nineteen sixty-eight had been a great season for us, a great year."

In the Baltimore locker room before the game, safety Rick Volk gave Bubba the thumbs-up sign. Smith strode over to tight end John Mackey. "Just give me a little rest between our times on the field," Bubba said, "and we'll whip the hell out of them." Bubba turned and looked at John Unitas. The old master appeared as relaxed as he would be if he was at a boy scout picnic. That Johnny U was suited up, Smith thought, assured the game's outcome.

Colts head coach Don Shula addressed his NFL champions. "Don't wait for them to lose it," he said. "We've got to win it ourselves."

Across the spongy, bright green turf of the Orange Bowl, the Jets could sense the Colts' self-confidence. "The Colts had a lot of arrogance when they showed up on the field," New York linebacker Larry Grantham said. Jets place-kicker Jim Turner thought the same.

He respected the Colts as a "great, great team" but bristled at the lack of respect being shown to the Jets. People didn't believe in the Jets, he thought, because they didn't believe in the AFL. Green Bay had won the first two Super Bowls in convincing fashion, and observers believed Baltimore would continue the NFL's domination of the AFL. How great it would be, Turner thought, to win over "that arrogant NFL bunch from Baltimore."

Namath walked over to fellow team captain Johnny Sample. He could see that Sample was keyed up. "Hey man, don't worry," Namath said, slapping Sample's shoulder pad. "In three hours we'll be the world champions. It's in the bag." Earlier in the day, Namath had sought to break the tension in the locker room by repeating a favorite phrase that circulated within the team: "Chicken ain't nothin' but a bird, and this ain't nothin' but another football game. Let's go out and win."

Before the game, Jets head coach Ewbank was walking the field when he encountered Shula and Colts owner Carroll Rosenbloom. Small talk was exchanged, and Rosenbloom invited Ewbank to Baltimore's victory party that evening.

Ewbank blinked in disbelief, then turned and walked away. Shula heard later that Ewbank related Rosenbloom's insensitive comment to his team. "Let's have a victory party of our own," Ewbank said.

In the Jets locker room, Ewbank told his team this was their chance to show the world how great they were. He again stressed poise and execution. The AFL champions knelt down and recited the Lord's Prayer. Ewbank could feel the emotion of his team, and he liked it. They were ready to play. "One more thing," he said. "When we win, don't pick me up and ruin my other hip. I'll walk."

Because the two teams operated in different orbits, some Baltimore fans might have been concerned that the Colts as an NFL team were not used to playing conditions inside the Orange Bowl. The Colts had played in the Orange Bowl in January 1966 and '67, beating Dallas and then Philadelphia in a postseason game officially known as the Bert Bell Benefit Bowl after the late NFL commissioner. Because it was a matchup between second-place teams from the NFL's Eastern and Western Conferences, the game was more commonly known as the "Runner-Up Bowl." They had also played and beaten the Dolphins in Miami in the 1968 preseason. Meaningless though they were, those games did give the Colts experience with the notoriously tricky cross-winds that coursed through the Orange Bowl and could affect the flight of the football on long passes, field goals, punts, and kickoffs.

As NBC cameras panned the inside of the stadium and showed palm trees behind the west end zone swaying to an 18-mph northerly wind, Gowdy talked to viewers about the weather conditions at game time:

> *"It's going to be very gusty today. It's blowing across the field, and we may have some swirling currents that can do some peculiar things with passes, punts, and kickoffs."*

The Colts spent much of the pregame trying to gauge the unpredictable gusts. Place-kicker Lou Michaels and holder Bobby Boyd practiced field-goal attempts in the west end, the open end, of the stadium. As he went through his drills, Michaels could feel the stare of older brother Walt, defensive coordinator of the Jets. Baltimore return specialist Preston Pearson watched Colts quarterbacks Earl Morrall and John Unitas put extra zip on their passes and thought they were doing it to compensate for the wind. Pearson tested his footing and was surprised at the thickness of the grass in the west end; other Colts noted the sandy texture in the east end. Baltimore realized two other Orange Bowl oddities, as well. The bright white yard stripes that contrasted so sharply with the green field were also gully-like and made for uneven footing. Also, the colorful background inside the stadium made it difficult at times for receivers to see the ball.

Colts center Bill Curry took his attention away from the wind and the field and studied Jets quarterback Joe Namath's passing style. Whether or not one liked Namath from a personal standpoint, Curry saw that the man could throw a football. His style, Curry thought, was beautiful.

Broadway Joe's appearance on the field brought forth a mix of cheers and boos, whistles and insults from the crowd. Gowdy noted that while both Namath and Unitas received loud responses from the audience, it was Johnny U who received the biggest ovation. On an afternoon in which they would prove prescient more than once, Gowdy and DeRogatis predicted that the old master could, and perhaps would, have an impact on the outcome of Super Bowl III:

> Gowdy: *"Don't forget about Unitas today because he was throwing fairly well in practice. His arm has improved, and you never know what will happen. Johnny U, who many consider the greatest quarterback who ever lived, could still be a factor in this game."*
>
> DeRogatis: *"The interesting thing is that in this great classic, the great John Unitas will not be starting. But John is ready, and no one will be surprised if John gets into this game."*

After DeRogatis, a former tackle for the New York Giants, analyzed the Colts, another former Giant and the third man in the booth, Kyle Rote, previewed the Jets:

> *"For the New York Jets, the 1968 season was the one in which for the first time in their nine-year history all the pieces fell into place. The defensive unit was number one in the league... Offensively, the line gave Joe Namath great protection all season long... And, of course, Joe Namath himself—controversial, exciting, but above all, a most talented player, a great passer on whose right arm will be riding the hopes of not only the New York Jets today, but the hopes of the entire AFL."*

Among the numerous signs unfurled from the orange railings in the stadium, one that hung inside the Colts locker room was most succinct: "Can Joe Namath Do What He Says?"

It was the question to which millions were awaiting the answer.

Namath, despite his exterior cool, felt the pressure of the moment when he and Sample headed to midfield to meet Colts captains Unitas, Pearson, and Lenny Lyles for the pregame coin toss. Namath felt like for the first time, he had started to get a grasp of what was at stake. He knew it was work and he had a job to do, but he soaked it all in—the Super Bowl, the Jets, the Colts, AFL vs. NFL, Johnny U. For a moment, even Broadway Joe was wowed by the occasion. There was a vast mix of personalities fighting one another on this day, and the whole thing was coming to a head. He thought how special it was that Sample, the former Colt, NFL reject, and alleged dirty player, and he, Namath, whatever he was perceived as, were New York's team captains. And here they were meeting the legendary Unitas and the champion Colts at midfield on pro football's biggest stage. "I started to get a grasp," Namath said.

Sample had made it a point during the pregame introductions to be the only player to run on the field sans helmet. This was the moment he had been waiting for since being drummed out of the NFL three years earlier; this was his chance for redemption and revenge against the league he believed had blackballed him. He would, Sample thought, show the NFL and the Colts that he could still play.

As Sample approached Unitas and Lyles, his teammates on the Colts 1958 and '59 title teams, he smiled as he turned to look at referee Tommy Bell. "You don't have to introduce us," Sample said in his normally raspy voice. "We're old friends."

The statement brought a grin from Unitas. The Jets had been given the option of calling "heads" or "tails," and Sample called "heads" as Bell flipped the shiny coin into the air. When the Jets won the toss and elected to receive, Sample looked at Lyles and grinned. "We get the first one today," the former Colt said.

Because Bell was an NFL referee, some of Colts felt an extra measure of comfort. Not because Bell would do anything to favor the NFL champions, but because he had a reputation of never allowing his officiating crew to lose control of a game. In one particularly bruising game against the Chicago Bears, the Colts began shouting at the officials that the Bears play had gone beyond physical and that Chicago was taking cheap shots. Curry, for one, screamed at Bell.

"You can't let them get away with this crap!" he yelled. "They've been doing it all day, and they're going to keep on doing it!"

Drawing himself up to his full height of 5'7", Bell calmly looked up at Curry. "Not with Tommy here," he said.

The Colts became more aware of Bell from that moment on. It wasn't any surprise to them that Bell always seemed to be working the NFL's biggest games.

At approximately 3:05 PM (EST), Bell stood at the 40-yard line in front of the Baltimore bench with his right arm raised. Michaels approached the ball, swung his left foot into it, and sent it into an arcing parabola to the accompaniment of a roaring crescendo from the crowd.

Super Bowl III was underway.

The kick sailed two yards deep into the Colts' blue-painted end zone, and Jets return specialist Earl Christy returned it to New York's 23-yard line before being brought down by Alex Hawkins and Jerry Logan. Unlike in today's game, there were few, if any, prima donnas in pro football in the 1960s. Offensive and defensive starters also routinely played on special teams. In Super Bowl III, it was not uncommon that Logan, the Colts starter at strong safety, would make the tackle on a kickoff or that Jets starting fullback Matt Snell would use a rolling body block to stop Pearson from scoring on a punt return later in the game.

As center John Schmitt spun from the huddle and led the Jets offense to the line of scrimmage, fans inside the stadium and across the nation edged forward on their seats for this first confrontation between Broadway Joe, the man who had brazenly guaranteed a Jets victory, and a record-setting Baltimore defense.

The Colts sized up Namath for the first time. Up close, he was physically bigger than many realized. When Namath appeared on the Johnny Carson show one night with Fran Tarkenton of the crosstown rival New York Giants, people were startled to see the size difference between the two quarterbacks. Many didn't realize how strong and powerful Namath was until they saw him in person.

Across the line, Baltimore middle linebacker Dennis Gaubatz prepared himself to match wits with Namath. Wearing a half-cage facemask and with his forearms wrapped in thick padding and tape, Gaubatz stood with hands on hips waiting for New York to show its first offensive alignment. He had been calling signals for the Colts defense since 1965 and doing it so well he was once considered "a hero without headlines," as *Sports Illustrated* tabbed him in 1965. But by December 1968, he was being featured in an action photo on the cover of *Life* magazine and immortalized in verse by Baltimore poet Ogden Nash:

> *Look at Number 53,*
> *Dennis Gaubatz,*
> *That is he,*
> *Looming 10 feet*
> *or taller*
> *above the Steelers'*
> *signal caller...*
> *Since Gaubatz acts like*
> *this on Sunday,*
> *I'll do my*
> *quarterbacking Monday*

Gaubatz was confident and bright; he had learned to be self-sufficient growing up in Needville in East Texas, where he prospered in football and track and field despite the doubts of his high school coaches. He played linebacker at Louisiana State under head coach Paul Dietzel, architect of the famed Chinese Bandits defense that won a national title the year before Gaubatz arrived at LSU. He was taken in the eighth round of the 1963 NFL draft by the Detroit Lions and eventually started at outside linebacker in a crew headed by veteran middle man and future Hall of Famer Joe Schmidt.

Colts general manager Don Klosterman had been impressed watching Gaubatz play against Baltimore. After Schmidt went down with an injury, Gaubatz moved to the middle. When Bill Pellington retired at the end of the 1964 campaign after 12 seasons as their middle linebacker and defensive signal-caller, the Colts had to fill an important spot. Klosterman placed a call to Detroit coach Harry Gilmer and director of player personnel Russ Thomas and, after a bit of haggling, brought Gaubatz to Baltimore.

When Gaubatz arrived in Colts camp in Westminster, Maryland, for the 1965 season, he was given a crash-course in Baltimore's elaborate defensive system. The Colts had a lot of defenses, but the volume and variety suited Gaubatz. The way he figured, defenses needed to give quarterbacks a lot to think about and not much time to think in. Baltimore would show two defensive sets prior to the snap, then change again once the play started. That gave quarterbacks no more than three, possibly four seconds to recognize what defense the Colts were in and then decide how to attack it. "That shouldn't be enough time, we figure," he said.

Gaubatz had the same amount of time prior to the snap to analyze the opponent's offensive set and decide to stay with the call sent in by defensive mastermind Bill Arnsparger or change it. Gaubatz's decision-making was based on the game plan provided by the Colts coaching staff. Shula, Arnsparger, and defensive backs coach Chuck Noll had studied films of New York's offense and given Gaubatz a chart of which plays Namath was likely to call in any down-and-distance situation and from anywhere on the field.

The Colts defense had a wide variety of plays to choose from. Gaubatz would get the signal from the sideline and make the call in the huddle. But like Namath, his opposite on Super Sunday, Gaubatz would be changing plays at the line of scrimmage with an audible. It was his job to figure out what Namath was going to call and then quickly set the Baltimore defense to match it. If the Jets offense came out in a set that was going to hit the Colts where they were weak, Gaubatz had to change the call at the line. If Namath then shouted an audible, Gaubatz would, too. Gaubatz called it a "guessing game" between him and the quarterback, and the high-speed hunches of both men would prove intriguing amid the high-stakes atmosphere.

As Namath bent behind Schmitt in what was to AFL fans a familiar stance—shoulders rolled forward, knees bent, feet spread—he scanned the Colts defense for the first time. Bubba Smith's huge bulk was evident on the left side of the Baltimore line. Namath checked the Colts linebackers and safeties, then called for a shift to an unbalanced line. Left guard Bob Talamini hurried to the right side of the line, and right guard Randy Rasmussen moved outside right tackle Dave Herman. The play gave New York a power look to the right side, but to Namath, the move was more than strategic. He wanted to let the Colts know on the game's first play from scrimmage that they were going to have to adjust to him, that the champions of the AFL were going to act and the NFL champs would have to react. He wanted to let Baltimore know that despite their being heavy favorites, they weren't dealing with kids.

Gaubatz reacted quickly, and the Colts overshifted their line to the strong side of the field. Namath turned and handed off to fullback Matt Snell, who veered instead to the weak side and picked up three yards behind left tackle Winston Hill before being brought down by right side linebacker Don Shinnick and Hill's former tormentor in the Colts camp, end Ordell Braase. The gain wasn't huge, but the play was important to the Jets for two reasons: New York believed it had struck a strategic blow on its first play by going to an unbalanced line, and Hill had delivered a physical blow to Baltimore by driving Braase off the ball.

Confidence was key for the Jets offense since the Colts played defense, one writer NFL declared, "the way textbooks say it should be played." The problems posed to Namath by Baltimore were complex—shifting fronts, rolling zone coverages, maximum blitzes. Cleveland Browns quarterback Bill Nelsen told reporters after the NFL title game that the Colts "seem to blitz everybody on the team—the assistant coaches, the waterboy, everybody."

Minnesota Vikings quarterback Joe Kapp, an acknowledged tough guy who bore a scar on his chin from a barroom brawl with his own teammate, linebacker Wally Hilgenberg, had been impressed by the Colts savage rush in the Western Conference playoff. Tarkenton was forced to scramble away from the Baltimore bullies in a 26-0 shutout loss during the regular season. Their defense, he said, had reached a "fantastic peak of sophistication.... You can't break big plays against the Colts." Providing a brief scouting report, he noted that the Colts ignored the threat of quick passes in front of them because they were willing to give the offense a short gain and gamble that the receiver might fumble the ball following a hard hit or that the quarterback wouldn't have the discipline to sustain a patient passing game. Tarkenton also saw Baltimore defenders as having confidence that their rush line and blitzing linebackers and safeties would eventually break down the pocket and get to the quarterback.

Dallas Cowboys coach Tom Landry noted that the Colts had previously been a predictable defense that did one of three things—roll strong with the zone, roll weak with the zone, or blitz. By 1968, Baltimore was using multiple looks that included various fronts and eight to 10 coverages per game. "You never see them the same way twice," Landry stated. "They're difficult to read."

The Colts were difficult to read because they knew how to disguise their coverages. Cornerbacks Lenny Lyles and Bobby Boyd had a combined 20 years of NFL experience between them. And safeties Logan and Rick Volk had both been college quarterbacks—Logan at West Texas State, and Volk at Michigan.

"We had a lot of coverages, and we tried to disguise whether we were playing man or zone so that the quarterback couldn't anticipate it, he had to read it as he was dropping back," Volk said. "And with our pass rush, quarterbacks didn't have time to read it."

Therein was the intrigue in matching up with the Jets, since Namath had the deepest drop and quickest release in football.

Gowdy and DeRogatis highlighted the showdown between Broadway Joe and the Baltimore defense:

> Gowdy: "We all know that Namath gets back deep, he has one of the quickest releases in pro football. Can Baltimore get a pass rush on him?"
>
> DeRogatis: "Curt, Baltimore has put a pass rush on just about everyone, so I don't think Joe is going to have that easy an afternoon. Obviously, Don Shula has built this great Baltimore defense to stop Joe Namath... And Joe is going to see the very best defense he has seen all year."

The Colts confusing schemes received a doctoral thesis-like review in the Jets seven-page offensive game plan. Typed, mimeographed, and fastened inside folders, it included the following:

Page One—A list of Colts defensive players, including their names and uniform numbers.

Page Two—The three basic formations—flank, slot, and split—from which the Jets offense would work. From these formations, New York could run a combination of 46 different plays.

Page Three—Diagrams of the six primary defenses Baltimore would use.

Page Four—Diagrams of the Colts four stunting defenses.

Pages Five, Six, and Seven—Diagrams of Baltimore's blitzes.

Prior to the game, Ewbank had warned Namath not to run sweeps against the Colts because their linebackers—Gaubatz, Shinnick, and Mike Curtis—were active and moved well. Namath at the time was resting on a trainer's table with his eyes closed and didn't respond. Now, on the second play from scrimmage, he changed his call at the line to "19 Straight," an off-tackle slant to the left side. In the backfield, Snell and halfback Emerson Boozer exchanged glances. Both backs thought Namath had made a mistake. Snell wondered if his quarterback had blacked out but also realized he had to run the play that had been called. Namath faked a handoff to Boozer, who crossed in front of Snell and headed right to influence Gaubatz, and move him out of position. Snell broke clean off left tackle for nine yards before Volk charged up from his safety position to meet him.

In just his second season as a starter, Volk had already achieved All-Pro status in the NFL. The 195-pounder had earned a reputation as a physical and hard-hitting safety. He was so efficient playing the run that the Colts considered him the equivalent of a fourth linebacker. Highlight films of the Colts 1968 season frequently show Volk firing in from his safety position to stop runners cold at the line of scrimmage. "When Rick hits you," Shula boasted during the season, "you might not get up."

Volk bent low to meet the powerful Snell, who churned into the hole coiled for impact, and the two big hitters slammed together at the 35-yard line. All the sound and fury of their respective Michigan and Ohio State backgrounds was evident in their violent meeting. Curry saw the collision from the Baltimore sideline and thought it was a tremendous smash. Smell's momentum and bulk allowed the 212-pound fullback to roll Volk back an extra yard. As Snell rose and strode back to the Jets huddle, Volk lay face down and motionless on the turf.

"Snell was a hard runner," Volk said. "I went in low, ducked my head, and his knee caught my helmet, knocked me out."

Helped to his feet by teammates, Volk was unable to stand straight. Curry thought the Colts safety wobbled unsteadily like Ray Bolger's straw man in *The Wizard of Oz*. If Volk hadn't been hurt so badly, Curry thought, it would have been a comical scene.

Volk was hurt physically, but his pride was wounded, as well. "Snell went to Ohio State," he said, invoking college football's fiercest rivalry, "and I'm a Michigan guy. So I was mad about that."

Volk's injury was pivotal for several reasons. It allowed the Jets to accomplish in just two plays against Baltimore what NFL teams other than the Browns had been unable to do all season—establish a ground game. On another level, the sight of a Colt, not a Jet, being helped off the field proved to the AFL that the NFL was made up of mere mortals. Volk did return to the game despite having suffered a concussion, but his play was sporadic.

The impact of Volk's injury had a ripple effect on the Baltimore defense. From Baltimore's standpoint, holding Snell to short yardage on his previous carry fit in with their theory concerning first-down plays. Arnsparger and Noll used a variety of alignments on first down in an effort to put opposing offenses in second-and-long situations. Believing that the quarterback would then look to pass, the Colts would shift into a zone and blitz. The end result was that NFL offenses found it difficult to maintain long drives against Baltimore.

Volk was a key part of the Colts equation, since his responsibilities at safety were four-fold—help Lyles on inside routes; double-cover the split end, in this case George Sauer; help contain the weak-side running game, which proved to be an integral part of the Jets' game plan; and blitz the quarterback, which he did three or four times per game. Shula called Volk a "big play guy" following a season in which the young star intercepted six passes and returned one for a team-long 90 yards.

Volk said that the most important factors in playing the free safety position were "being able to read plays, read your keys, and know what you have to do." The concussion he suffered following the violent collision with Snell dulled his ability to read the Jets offense and slowed his reaction time to developing plays. Volk was essentially taken out of the flow of each play that New York would run to its weak side. Volk was expected by the Colts to have an impact on running and passing plays that were aimed toward the left side of the Jets offense, but the concussion prevented him from reacting fast enough. Later, he watched game films of Super Bowl III, and when he saw Snell and Boozer grinding out yards off left tackle and Namath hitting Sauer on weak-side passes, Volk kept thinking, "Where am I?"

"I should have been coming up in run support, and I should have been there on the pass plays as well, but I wasn't," he said. "I was a half-step slow because of the concussion. And when you're playing team defense and one guy isn't 100 percent, it hurts the team. I played, but I wasn't playing like I could."

It wasn't just Volk who was below par physically. Braase had played one of his best games of the season in the NFL championship shutout of Cleveland, but he was nursing a sore back in Super Bowl III. On the same side of the Baltimore defense, Lyles had been weakened by a case of tonsillitis. On the other side of the line, Bubba Smith was ailing. He had leapt to block a pass in the fourth quarter of the game against the Browns and when he turned to follow the flight of the ball he was hit hard from behind. During the two weeks before the game he wore a temporary rubber boot that extended from his groin to his foot, and his practice time had been limited.

New York's execution of "19 Straight" would prove pivotal all afternoon. On the play, Snell lined up directly behind Namath in a "Brown" formation that gave him quicker access to the corner. Boozer lined up several yards ahead of Snell and to the weak side, thus getting a good blocking angle on the outside linebacker, Shinnick. When Schmitt snapped the ball, Hill would drive into Braase, but he would also let the Colts veteran dictate the direction of the play. If Braase tried to drive his way inside, Hill would steer him in that direction, thus creating an outside running lane for Snell. If Braase took an outside rush route, Hill would ride him in that direction and Snell, reading the play, would veer inside.

On the game's first play, Snell had slanted behind Hill, and when Braase cut in, Snell took his cue and bounced the play outside. Braase took an outside charge on the Jets second play, and as Hill shoved him outside, Snell exploded through the hole for a first down.

Seeing Volk helped off the field, Snell hissed to his teammates, "These guys aren't so tough."

DeRogatis believed the same. He had seen the Jets handle Kansas City and Oakland, two of the AFL's more physical teams. For sheer size, the monstrous Chiefs were a much bigger team than the Colts. Kansas City defensive tackles Junious "Buck" Buchanan and Ernie "Big Cat" Ladd were massive. Buchanan stood 6'7" and weighed 270 pounds; Ladd was 6'9" and 290 pounds.

DeRogatis had seen the Colts play during the regular season, and while recognizing their great record and gaudy statistics, he was not awed by their physical abilities. Even Curry acknowledged that Baltimore was not as impressive physically as some teams. He had played with Vince Lombardi's NFL champions in Green Bay in 1965 and '66 and thought Lombardi's strict training regimen had molded the Packers into strong men who were unbelievable physical specimens. Fullback Jim Taylor, for instance, was such a devoted weight lifter that he had built himself up to the point where if he wanted to turn his head to talk with someone, Taylor would have to turn his whole upper body. Curry thought that Packers players looked strong enough to knock down a wall.

But when Curry joined the Colts in 1967, he looked around the locker room and wondered if he had wandered into a local YMCA. To Curry, halfback Tom Matte looked chubby; Unitas was humpbacked and bowlegged, resembling "a pair of pliers," Curry said; Morrall had ample girth around his middle, and he and Johnny U were called Rump and Hump by teammates. Shinnick had a sunken chest and sloped shoulders; tight end John Mackey was overweight; guard Dan Sullivan owned a square body with short legs. Curry described himself as both skinny and fat, a guy with thin legs and a big butt. "Maybe," he mused, "Lombardi figured I'd fit in better with these people."

Having needed just two plays to assert themselves physically and establish their running game, the Jets switched to the pass. Dropping back for the first time in the game, Namath fired a 9-yard completion to Snell. The play marked Broadway Joe's first confrontation with Baltimore's terror weapon, the blitz. As he faded to pass, Namath saw a flash of blue jersey out of the corner of his right eye. Curtis was closing fast. Spinning to his right an instant before Curtis could reach him, Namath arced the ball to Snell, who caught it in full stride for a solid gain.

Baltimore's defense steadied and stopped New York's initial drive on the Jets 38-yard line. Curley Johnson's punt carried to the Colts 18, and Timmy Brown returned it nine yards to bring the Baltimore offense on the field for the first time.

Tex Maule, who was covering the game for *Sports Illustrated*, had written in his preview that given his belief that the Colts had a superior and more coherent defense than the Jets, Baltimore could win Super Bowl III with just an average offense. "But," Maule added, "their offense is far more than that, as the Jets are likely to discover."

The Jets did discover it, as the Colts fired out on their first series and chewed up yardage in big chunks. Shula and offensive coordinator Don McCafferty, as was their custom, had scripted their first four plays. Shula had a special first-down drill; the object was to gain five or more yards on the first play of a series and put the enemy defense in a hole on second down.

On first down, Morrall flared a pass to Mackey in the left flat. Sidestepping one defender and trampling two more, the big tight end picked up 19 yards before Jets tackle John Elliott caught him from behind and drove him out of bounds. Morrall had great respect for Elliott; among the members of New York's front four, Elliott had impressed Morrall the most on film. He compared him to Green Bay's future Hall of Fame tackle Henry Jordan. Both men had great pursuit ability, Morrall thought, and Elliott's running down of Mackey from behind was another example of his hustle and desire to make a play.

Matte followed by sweeping right for 10 yards and a first down in Jets territory at the 44-yard line. Fullback Jerry Hill then hit the left side for seven more yards. On the sidelines, Pearson thought the Colts offense was moving so smoothly it appeared as if Shula was diagramming the plays on a blackboard.

Baltimore's impressive opening drive seemed to Shula to confirm what he had seen in film study of the Jets. Their defense, he thought, seemed awfully weak. It was tough showing New York's game films to his team without feeling they might get overconfident.

Morrall noticed from reviewing the Jets films that New York depended on its linebackers to aid in pass protection by getting deep in the secondary and helping out safeties Jim Hudson and Billy Baird.

Morrall would key the movements of middle linebacker Al Atkinson. If Atkinson moved left at the snap of the ball, Morrall would throw right, and vice versa. As far as their running game was concerned, the Colts would use draw plays early to bring New York's linebackers up tight so they couldn't harass the passing game. Shula believed his offensive line could control the Jets front. That being the case, Morrall, Mackey, Matte, Hill and Co. would be able to run and pass freely, Shula thought.

As the Colts moved confidently downfield, Morrall thought the first few plays had worked beautifully. Hawkins felt the Colts march matched what he had seen on film when he predicted that Baltimore might score 50 points. The Jets defense, he thought early in Super Bowl III, was posing no problems.

"Right now, Baltimore looks overpowering on offense," Gowdy said, and DeRogatis broke down the Colts power attack:

> *"Curt, let me explain what Baltimore is doing. They're going to come with real power... Three big men to the strong side and they're running at it."*

DeRogatis remarked that Morrall was great at calling a prearranged game plan. Miami Dolphins head coach George Wilson had cautioned AFL people not to underestimate the Colts quarterback. Wilson had coached Morrall in Detroit and knew he was a dedicated student of the game, a guy who spent a great deal of his own time examining game films. Morrall always made a careful study of the personnel he would be facing and prepared himself so well he could predict the types of defenses opponents would use against him. "He mixed his plays very well and would always call a good game," Wilson said.

Morrall completed a pass to tight end Tom Mitchell to put the ball at the Jets 19. Baltimore's feelings of superiority, so evident to everyone inside the Orange Bowl prior to kickoff, were increasing as the Colts moved easily against a Jets defense that was ranked No. 1 in the AFL.

The Colts were running and throwing with ease, "just ripping off yardage," Curry thought. It was too easy, and oddsmakers like Jimmy The Greek wondered if they had underestimated Baltimore by making them only 18-point favorites. Curry looked across the line at the Jets and thought they looked a little wide-eyed at the ease with which the Colts were moving. Some of the Colts felt a sense of fear in the Jets.

"It was looking bad," Sample said later. The defensive captain was in a frenzy; he screamed at his teammates in the huddle. "If we don't start doing something, we might as well walk out of here right now!"

Defensive end Gerry Philbin became just as animated. "Hit somebody, damn it! We're getting embarrassed out here!"

On the sideline, Ewbank was yelling at his players, "Keep your poise." Privately, he thought his former team looked better in person than it had on film. The Colts, he thought, looked like a powerhouse.

Morrall followed with a pair of incomplete passes. One was a drop by end Willie Richardson that would have given Baltimore a first-and-goal at the 6. Ducking under Jet pressure on third down, Morrall spun free of one sack but only got to the line of scrimmage before Atkinson hauled him down.

After giving up ground in big chunks, the Jets defense had stiffened and stopped Baltimore. On fourth down from the 19, place-kicker Lou Michaels and holder Bobby Boyd trotted onto the field. Walt Michaels saw the wind rippling the blue jersey of his younger brother; the gusts were to the Colts backs. Walt had jokingly told his players before the game that he had seen Lou and "talked him out of a field goal or two."

> Gowdy: "Boyd will hold. Michaels has hit 18-of-28 this year.
> His kick is up and... it is no good! Off to the right!"

Heading off the field, Jets linebacker Larry Grantham smiled. "Walt's pretty smart," he thought. "He actually did talk Lou out of it."

Michaels would laugh off the notion that he had conned his brother out of an early score. But he didn't laugh when he recalled that their mother and some relatives were sitting in the stands on the Jets side of the field.

"We had psychology in our favor," Michaels said, and having dodged an early score, it was starting to appear as if the underdog Jets might, indeed, have something going for them. Good vibrations, maybe? The Beach Boys had sung about them in the mid-1960s, and following the Colts missed opportunity, the Jets were suddenly experiencing good vibes, as well.

12

Jets Prepare for Takeoff

Lou Michaels' missed field goal marked a flashpoint for the New York Jets.

Sparked by the early turn of events, a current of self-confidence surged along the Jets sideline as the champions of the American Football League took control on their own 20-yard line. New York linebacker Larry Grantham said that Baltimore's botched field goal attempt "pepped us up good." Fullback Matt Snell thought he could almost feel the steam going out of the Colts. Across the field, Colts quarterback Earl Morrall felt the change in momentum, as well. The Jets had been given an emotional lift, he thought. Their confidence was bolstered.

Looking to ride the wave of emotion, the Jets offense prepared to go to work on the Colts defense. Having surprised some of the experts by running the ball on three of their first four plays from scrimmage, the Jets changed tactics on their second series of the game.

Challenging Baltimore's pass defense, Jets quarterback Joe Namath went to the air six times and completed three passes to move New York to its own 41 before giving up the ball. The most important pass of the series was not, as it turned out, a completion but an overthrown ball deep down the right sideline to streaking flanker Don Maynard. The pass was important because the Jets believed it forced the Colts into an overshifted defense that Namath would exploit the rest of the day.

Film study of New York's offense had convinced the Colts of Namath's bombs-away capabilities. "The man can throw a football into a teacup at 50 yards," Baltimore defensive tackle Billy Ray Smith said before the game. "But he hasn't seen defenses like ours in his league. Our defenses are as complex as some team's offenses."

The Colts, Smith said, had 20 variations of blitzes and five or six variations of fronts. "That lets us do a lot of things," he said.

But the Jets weren't awed. Head coach Weeb Ewbank knew Baltimore's personnel from having coached many of them just five years prior. He had installed some of the zone defenses the Colts were still running. As he and offensive coordinator Clive Rush broke down Baltimore's defense on film, Ewbank grew increasingly confident. "They're slow," he told Rush. "If we can't pass on these guys, we ought to get out of the business."

Running film of the Colts defense back and forth several times, Ewbank noticed that Baltimore's zone coverage was rotating toward veteran right cornerback Bobby Boyd.

"I think they're trying to protect him," he said. "I think he's slow."

Ewbank looked at his assistants. "We can beat these guys," he said. "We're going to win this game."

Jets tight end Pete Lammons believed the same. After days of watching film of the NFL champions, Lammons told Rush and some of his teammates, "Damn, we watch any more of these films, we're gonna get overconfident."

Baltimore's zone did indeed rotate toward Boyd as Ewbank had noticed. Colts quarterback Earl Morrall had seen it when he played against Baltimore prior to 1968. Boyd wasn't the fastest cornerback in the NFL, so he played off the receiver until the quarterback was ready to throw. Then the Colts veteran defensive captain would make his break on the ball. Baltimore's zone allowed him to play that way. If the Colts played more man-to-man defense, Boyd would have to cover a single receiver all over the field. A really fast receiver, Morrall thought, would beat him.

Maynard was one of the fastest receivers in the game. He had set a pro football record in 1968 for career receiving yards. The lithe Texan with the long sideburns and even longer stride had totaled 9,433 yards, eclipsing the previous mark set by former Colts player Raymond Berry, who had retired following the 1967 season. Maynard was never more dangerous as a playmaker than he was in 1968. He topped the 100-yard mark in receiving seven times and twice gained more than 200 yards. His best efforts came in the biggest games and against the toughest opponents. He had eight receptions for 203 yards against Kansas City in the regular season opener. Against Oakland in the Heidi Bowl, he hauled in 10 passes for a season-high 228 yards and set a team record by scoring on an 87-yard bomb against San Diego.

Fast and loose on the field, Maynard had a reputation for being tight with his money. Teammates once saw him shoving Mexican quarters into a pay phone. When his car was impounded by the New York City Police Department for parking in a no-parking zone, he let them keep it rather than pay the $50 fine. "I want to get my money's worth," he said at the time. Frugal as he was off the field, Maynard was greedy on it. He gobbled up yards with his expansive strides and his amazing 22.8 yards-per-catch average led the pass-happy AFL at a time when the league was filled with big-play receivers like Lance Alworth, Otis Taylor, and Fred Biletnikoff.

Watching film of Namath's aerial show against Oakland in the AFL Championship Game, a Baltimore defensive coach was heard to mumble in the darkened room, "He sure throws a lot of passes."

"At least fifty in this game," a Colts defensive player replied. "And a lot of them are those long ones down the sideline to Maynard."

Boyd, whose main responsibility in Super Bowl III was coverage on Maynard, had emerged from the initial session with a concerned look. Boyd told teammate Alex Hawkins the NFL champs might find themselves in a shootout.

"The Jets have a damn good offense," Boyd said. "Namath can throw the football with the best of them."

Boyd's concern startled Hawkins, who rarely saw the defensive captain worried about any NFL offense. As their film study continued, some of the Colts seemed to rationalize what they were seeing. Namath was completing a lot of long bombs, but they convinced themselves that he was only doing so because he was playing against inferior AFL defenses. Asked by reporters if Broadway Joe could burn Baltimore with his deep passing game, Boyd shook his head.

"I don't think he can," Boyd said. "Nobody in the NFL has completed a bomb on us all season. He won't get a bomb on us."

The zone coverages installed by head coach Don Shula and defensive lieutenants Bill Arnsparger and Chuck Noll were believed to have made Baltimore's defense bomb-proof. More than any other team, the Colts had pioneered the use of the zone in an era when most NFL teams still favored man-to-man. Ewbank had installed zone schemes when he took over as Colts head coach. The basic idea of the zone is simple. Of the 11 defensive players on the field, four are on the line of scrimmage rushing the quarterback on passing plays. The remaining seven defenders—three linebackers and four secondary men—drop to their zone or prearranged spot on the field. Each stays in the center of his assigned area until the ball is in the air and they converge on the intended receiver.

In 1968, Baltimore ran variations of the zone—the basic zone, strong-side roll, weak-side roll. Passing areas were divided into seven zones—four short and three deep. The three linebackers and one cornerback took the four short zones, while the second cornerback and two safeties retreated into deep zones. In the early years of the zone, there were only two variations—the strong-side and weak-side roll. The strong-side roll was the most widely used. Since most NFL teams at the time lined their tight end on the right side of the line, making that side the strong side, the Colts rolled their zone coverage in that direction. When NFL quarterbacks became adept at reading the strong-side roll and began throwing to their left, or weak side, the Colts countered by employing a weak-side roll.

Because the Colts were one of the few NFL teams using zone defenses on a regular basis, NFL quarterbacks had difficulty reading their coverages. The notable exception was Green Bay's Bart Starr, who had been tutored by head coach Vince Lombardi to attack the zone by hitting receivers in the seams, the areas between the zones.

Ewbank's response to Baltimore's complex zones was to stretch it by testing it deep, then throwing underneath the spread-out coverage. On New York's ninth offensive play of the game, the Jets offense proved the worth of Ewbank's planning. Though hampered by a painful hamstring pull, Maynard sprinted past Boyd and was yards ahead of him and safety Jerry Logan, who had rotated over to provide additional coverage. Maynard was in the clear, but Namath's deep pass sailed just beyond his receiver's outstretched fingertips at Baltimore's 20-yard line. Namath said if it wasn't for the looming specter of Bubba Smith, the Jets would have scored on that play. Colts coaches sometimes frowned upon Bubba because they thought he took plays off. But the man facing him on every down in Super Bowl III, Jets converted right tackle Dave Herman, saw a different side of Smith. "He was very aggressive, he played full speed ahead every play," Herman said.

Bubba had a reason, and Namath knew it. "The name of the game," Joe Willie said, "is kill the quarterback." Herman didn't have a problem with Broadway Joe guaranteeing victory; the entire Jets team believed from what they had seen in the films that they were better than Baltimore. After examining four Colts game films, right guard Randy Rasmussen couldn't understand what was so special about his opposite, Billy Ray Smith. After Namath guaranteed victory, Billy Ray said the rebel quarterback might keep his teeth longer if he kept his mouth shut.

Herman's only problem with the "guarantee" was that it might wake up a Baltimore team that Ewbank had been trying to lull to sleep. "I wouldn't be surprised at all if they were overconfident," Herman said of the Colts. "I could tell from what they were saying in the newspapers that they had a degree of confidence. What did the guarantee do? My concern was that it would take it to a higher intensity level. With the challenge we had up front, for Joe to say something like that was not in our best interests.

"When teams played us, they weren't just playing the New York Jets, they were playing the long-haired quarterback. That made blocking for him that much more of a challenge."

A friend of Namath's confided to *Sports Illustrated*'s AFL writer, Edwin Shrake, that Namath was talking like he was not only trying to get his team to believe like he did that they would win the game, but also to fire up the Colts. Namath had watched a lot of film of Baltimore's defense—"more hours than most people realize," Shrake was told—and knew the Colts couldn't get to him. But he wanted to get them so angry that they would practically kill themselves trying to reach him. When they found out they couldn't touch him, they would feel frustrated and let down.

The ploy seemed to be working as Bubba muscled his way toward Namath on the deep pass to Maynard. The Jets quarterback was caught in a pincer move by ends Smith and Ordell Braase, and it was Bubba who influenced Namath's overthrow by leaping high and extending his padded left arm to block the pass to Maynard.

Ewbank cursed the near-miss. "Damn. If [Maynard] legs right, that's a touchdown."

"That play was important," Namath said. "Maynard was open. He got behind their bomb-proof secondary. He put the fear of God in them the rest of the game."

Namath acknowledged that despite Maynard's injury, the Jets went to the deep sideline pattern early to show the Colts they could beat their zone. Once Baltimore knew that Maynard could beat them on a long bomb, they had to respect him. What the Colts didn't realize was how bad Maynard was hurting. It had taken tremendous effort to outrun the Colts secondary on that one play. If the Jets had needed Maynard to consistently make deep catches against the Colts, his injured leg likely wouldn't have allowed him to.

"I guess you could say we suckered the Colts," Namath said. "We showed them what they were afraid of seeing, and it changed their mentality."

"I can see what Joe is talking about," Baltimore safety Rick Volk said. "He sends Maynard deep and then starts throwing underneath. But we really didn't change our defense."

The Colts felt there was no need to. They had seen in the films that Namath had a great passing arm, and Shula emphasized that Joe had been working with the same set of outstanding and experienced receivers for years. But Arnsparger and Noll had put together a solid game plan, one in which the Colts had complete confidence.

"We called Chuck 'Knowledge Noll' because it was like being in a classroom when you were around him," Logan said. "I know he made me a smart player. He made sure you knew not only your assignment but everyone else's as well, and he'd grade you on your knowledge. He was a damn good coach, and he proved it later in Pittsburgh. He was a fiery guy, too. Not so much verbally, but he'd get his point across with little facial expressions.

"Coach Arnsparger was pretty quiet, mild-mannered. But he always put out great game plans."

Bubba Smith figured the Jets passing game would pose problems until the Colts got the timing of it and clamped down on the receivers. Then it would be open season on Broadway Joe. Maynard, however, compounded Baltimore's problem by taking extra wide splits from his flanker position, forcing the Colts to cheat on their coverage a little and giving split end George Sauer even more room to work with on the opposite side of the field. That meant that Sauer, whose 66 catches in 1968 were second in the AFL only to Alworth, would be free to work in single coverage against Lenny Lyles, who was weakened with tonsillitis. It was the same tactic Cleveland had tried unsuccessfully in the NFL Championship Game when coach Blanton Collier instructed Paul Warfield to take wider splits. New York, however, would enjoy far better results.

Few realized it, but those familiar with NFL history knew that Ewbank's strategy of going for the bomb early in Super Bowl III mirrored the tactics he had used a decade earlier in the 1958 NFL Championship Game. Against a New York Giants defense that was just as feared then as Baltimore's was in 1968, Ewbank had instructed Colts quarterback Johnny Unitas to throw deep early to Lenny Moore. Moore, like Maynard, was a speedy receiver, and the play achieved the same desired results against the Giants in 1958 as it would against the Colts in '68. New York defensive coordinator Tim Landry recognized Moore as a deep threat and assigned double coverage on him. The switch left split end Raymond Berry, like Sauer, a possession receiver, in single coverage on the weak side, and he enjoyed a great game against the Giants.

After the Jets drive stalled, Baltimore got the ball back but its offense sputtered. All-Pro tight end John Mackey was wide open at midfield when he dropped a pass from quarterback Earl Morrall. Mackey's drop surprised Morrall. He had seen the big tight end drop down to catch passes off his shoetops, then leap like a high-jumper and haul in balls thrown over his head. To Morrall, seeing Mackey drop a pass was like seeing Detroit Tigers star Al Kaline drop an easy fly ball to right field. Those things just don't happen, Morrall thought.

The incomplete pass cost the Colts, but they caught a break when David Lee's short punt hit just inside the Jets 20-yard line and took a Baltimore bounce before it was finally downed on New York's 4. Lee's 51-yard punt backed the Jets into the shadow of their goal post. Three plays later, the Colts defense forced the first turnover of Super Bowl III when Lyles jarred the ball loose from Sauer and linebacker Ron Porter recovered at the Jets 12.

The first quarter ended, surprisingly, in a tie. But Baltimore seemed certain to score when halfback Tom Matte swept left on the opening play of the second quarter and wasn't stopped until he reached the Jets 6. Eager to put points on the board after squandering an opportunity on their opening drive, the Colts went to the air. Morrall took the snap from center and retreated straight back into the pocket. He fired a quick, hard pass to tight end Tom Mitchell—Baltimore was in a two tight end alignment—on a play similar to the one the Colts had used for their initial score against Minnesota in the Western Conference playoff.

Mitchell was big—6'2", 235 pounds—and he used his size to shield defenders away from the ball. The Colts shifted into a double-wing, and Mitchell went to the left where he would be covered by cornerback Randy Beverly. Backs Tom Matte and Jerry Hill were the decoys. Matte was to slant left and get to the inside of Beverly. Morrall would throw low—his target was Mitchell's stomach area—so the tight end could catch the ball and fall into the end zone.

As he called signals, Morrall saw the Jets defense switch to the right and middle linebacker Al Atkinson take a step or two to his left. It was an AFL-style odd-front defense, and Morrall knew from film study that Atkinson would be flying to his left at the snap, thus clearing a path for the pass to Mitchell. "Beautiful," Morrall thought, "Just beautiful."

The play worked to near-perfection. Mitchell had thrown a great fake at Beverly and slipped inside him. Mitchell's arms were open and waiting. Morrall fired the ball—hard. Baltimore was about to finally get on the scoreboard.

The pass was on target. And then it wasn't. Atkinson, reaching and straining, tipped it with the fingers of his right hand. The slight deflection proved just enough to alter the trajectory of the pass. Instead of coming in low, the ball hit Mitchell high on his shoulder pads and caromed into the air. For a moment, it hung suspended, framed against the backdrop of a gray sky, until it fell into the arms of a diving Beverly in the end zone. Just a short while earlier, Beverly had taken the field hoping he wouldn't look "like a clown" against the Colts. Now he was an early hero for the Jets.

Merle Harmon called the play on Jets radio:

> *"No score, second quarter... Six yards to go for a touchdown, four yards to go for a first down... The Colts, with a slot left, Matte the lone running back... Back to pass, Morrall looks into the end zone, throws to Mitchell and... it is intercepted in the end zone off Mitchell's hands by Randy Beverly! Tom Mitchell got hit right in the breadbasket on a pass from Morrall, he was wide open, the ball bounced up into the air and Randy Beverley made a diving interception..."*

Morrall believed Beverly's interception was the turning point of the first half. If the Colts had scored at that point, he thought, they wouldn't have become so frustrated. The irony of the play, Morrall said, is that Beverly made the interception only because he had been faked out of position. "Unbelievable," Morrall said. "I was beginning to believe the stars were against us."

Colts left guard Glenn Ressler could feel the frustration mounting within the team. "We would move the ball downfield and then make a mistake," he said. "It was frustrating. We're working our butts off and then making mistakes."

The Colts had been deep in Jets territory twice, and the results had been a missed field goal and an interception. On the Baltimore sideline, Unitas watched the play unfold and shook his head in frustration as Beverly rolled over in the Jets green end zone and raised his right arm and index finger in the air. The interception had dramatically altered momentum, and Unitas knew it. Morrall knew it as well.

"The whole complexion of the game," Morrall said, "changed in those few seconds."

Across the field, Jets placekicker Jim Turner felt it, too. "That was the play," he said, "that swung the momentum in our direction." Ewbank realized it, but he also knew that the Jets had to make the most of this latest opportunity. "We had stopped the Colts again," he said. "Now it was time for Joe to get us moving."

Namath put together a drive that looked to exploit the right side of the Baltimore defense. Four straight runs by Snell, all to the Jets left side, and four passes by Namath, three of which went to his left, moved New York from its own 20 to the Colts 23. The only pass to his right was a flare to halfback Billy Mathis that beat a Baltimore blitz by outside linebacker Mike Curtis and went for six yards before Bubba Smith ran down Mathis from behind. Smith's hustle startled Namath. He looked at Bubba as the consummate pass rusher, but the fact that Smith had the speed to get out into the flat and make the sideline tackle on Mathis was surprising. Just awesome, Namath thought.

Namath narrowly missed turning the ball over when Don Shinnick, the NFL's all-time interception leader among linebackers, dropped into zone coverage and had both hands on a pass intended for Sauer near midfield but couldn't hold the ball. Given a reprieve, Broadway Joe resumed his attack on the Colts left side and hit Sauer on passes of 14 and 11 yards. But the real key to the drive was New York's success running Snell on the weak-side slant. The Jets were winning the line battles on their left side—tackle Winston Hill opposite end Ordell Braase; guard Bob Talamini against tackle Fred Miller—in part because of each team's personality.

Baltimore's defensive linemen had been taught to play the run by reading their keys, controlling their blocks, and holding their positions. Braase called it a "battle of balance," and because he had more than 10 years of NFL experience, he knew from the formation the Jets were using—a "Brown" formation in which Snell is directly behind Namath and halfback Emerson Boozer is set to Snell's left—which type of running play New York would run.

Yet even though the Colts defense knew what was coming, their personality of reading and holding set them up for the hard charge of Hill and Talamini. The massive Hill, who at 280 pounds outweighed Braase by 35 pounds, was the Jets best run blocker. Talamini, a thickly built weightlifter who had been an All-AFL guard with Houston during the Oilers championship years in the early 1960s, wasn't far behind Hill as a drive blocker. Both men were agile, since they both played tennis in the offseason. Hill and Talamini used their size, strength, and agility to ride Braase and Miller out of the way. The weakside slant was a no-frills power play perfectly suited to the skills and temperament of both Talamini and Hill. "You hit someone," Talamini said, "and knock him a country mile."

"I did what I did all season," Hill said. "When we played Baltimore in the Super Bowl, I didn't believe in trying to play above my head. I played to my potential. I don't think Matt Snell, Emerson Boozer, or Dave Herman has ever received enough credit for what they did that day. Dave Herman was giving away 30, 40 pounds to Bubba Smith, and he was playing a new position against a superstar. I was playing against a guy [Braase] who was 36 years old."

In boxing, the credo is that styles make fights. The same can be said for football, as well. The areas where the Baltimore defense was suspect were the same areas where the New York offense was strongest.

On the NBC-TV broadcast, analyst Kyle Rote grasped what the Jets were doing and explained it to a startled viewing audience:

> "You see the straight type of running game, and this is what the Jets have to do to penetrate that Baltimore line. As Al [DeRogatis] pointed out earlier, they're not a penetrating line where you can trap them in and create big holes. They hit, they slide, they have tremendous lateral movement... You really have to drive a team like that straight back."

On the Colts sideline, Hawkins was surprised but impressed. It's a beautifully executed drive, he thought. Namath had predicted he would pick the Colts apart, but Baltimore had believed he was going to try to do that through the air. Instead, the AFL champs were pushing the Colts back by running, of all things, an NFL-style play. From his spot on the sideline, Hawkins studied Namath. The undisciplined one, he thought, is calling a disciplined game.

Namath was also beating Baltimore's feared blitz. But he came within a half-step of disaster for the second time on the drive when he threw an 11-yard square-out to Sauer that Lyles gambled on and almost intercepted. Had Lyles reacted a split-second sooner, he might have picked off Namath and gone all the way for a score.

"I was lucky on that one," Namath admitted. Some of his teammates, however, felt that Lyles mistimed his break on the ball because no NFL quarterback threw passes as fast as Namath.

In the NBC-TV booth, Curt Gowdy said during his play-by-play broadcast that the Jets were driving due in part to Namath's handling of the blitz. DeRogatis agreed and pointed out the great job Boozer was doing in picking up the Colts linebackers:

> "Curt, you've talked about the great protection, and Emerson Boozer did another great job. He sees Number 66, Don Shinnick, the weak-side linebacker, blitzing. Boozer steps up and gives him a good pop. And Joe Namath is still standing erect."

The Jets huddle was gaining in noise and confidence. "We felt we could handle their defense after the first couple of series," Talamini said. "They had used up their repertoire, and we were blowing them out."

Boozer turned to Snell and said, "Follow me. I'm splitting [Shinnick] down the middle." Before the game, Snell and Boozer had made a pact. Whichever one was called on to run, the other would do whatever was necessary to make the play work. Boozer was blocking exceptionally well and Snell, who ran better to his left even though he was right-handed, was running "19-Straight" and its variants "19-Option" and "19-Cutback" to near perfection.

Rote called attention to the ongoing strategic duel between Namath and middle linebacker Dennis Gaubatz:

*"You watch Gaubatz calling the defensive signals and
Namath calling the offensive signals and what a battle of
wits is going on. Gaubatz, of course, trying to conceal the
Red Dog [blitz]... Namath trying to automatic [audible]."*

Boyd could see what was happening: Namath was reading the Colts
defense and dissecting it with the skill of a surgeon. Boyd was startled
early on when he heard Namath calling check-offs at the line of scrimmage and they were the same ones used by Baltimore. Namath looked
toward the Colts sideline during one audible and saw Unitas mouthing
the words along with him.

"Weeb had coached in Baltimore, so they had the same exact system we had," Boyd said. "Their check-offs were the same as ours."

It could have been a big break for Baltimore to know what plays
Namath was calling, but when Boyd told Noll of his discovery at the
close of the first quarter, he said Noll bushed it off. "He said, 'Oh no,
you can't trust that.'"

Namath beat a blitz by flaring a pass to Snell that carried for 12
yards. Gaubatz forced a fumble at the end of the play, but the ball
bounced right back into Snell's arms, another good omen for New
York.

Gowdy: *"You're seeing Baltimore put the heavy blitz on
Namath, and as soon as he reads that, he dumps the ball off
to his backs flaring out to the side."*
DeRogatis: *"Exactly right, Curt. And he's not only reading the blitz so well, he's playing that zone perfectly."*

Los Angeles Rams coach George Allen watched the game and saw
something familiar in the Jets strategy. A year earlier, Allen had put
together a game plan to beat a Colts team that entered the final game
of the season 11–0–2. Allen's plan was built around protecting quarterback Roman Gabriel from the Colts pass rush. "Their front four and
three linebackers could kill you," Allen said. "We had to be ready to
pick up the [blitz]."

Allen instructed Gabriel to read the defense and audible plays
at the line. To beat the Colts zone, Gabriel would have to find his

receivers between the defenders—in the seams of the zone—or in front of them. The strategy worked, and the Rams won 34–10 to clinch a playoff spot and end the Colts season.

A similar plan was now working for the Jets. With the ball at the Baltimore 9-yard line, Snell veered right for five yards. The Colts sent in their goal-line defense, and DeRogatis mentioned that the Jets should adjust, as well:

> *"It's going to be a tough defense to hit straight on. The slants probably will be more effective."*

Namath saw Lou Michaels, his barroom antagonist, heading into the Colts huddle and knew from studying films that Baltimore was going to shift into a tight, five-man front. Bending into the Jets huddle, Namath called 19-Straight. "We'll go on the first sound," he said.

Realizing that a wide-sweep would work against Baltimore's tightly bunched line, Namath also realized that going on the first sound for the first time in the game might catch the Colts unaware. Striding to the line in his white leather shoes and white-and-green trimmed uniform, Namath paused behind center John Schmitt, then got into his stance. "Now!" he shouted.

> Gowdy: *"Here's a handoff to Snell... He may go..."*

Taking Namath's handoff, Snell veered to his left and bounced outside Baltimore's flank. Because the ball had been placed on the right hashmark, Snell had a long run to reach the wide side of the field. As he ran, Snell felt as if he was moving in slow motion. He read the blocks of Hill and Talamini and escaped a tackle attempt by Volk, who was charging in from his safety position. Snell wondered for a moment if he was ever going to reach the goal line. When he did, he lowered his helmet, burst past Gaubatz and into the Colts blue end zone, where he rolled under Lyles.

Harmon called the historic play that gave the AFL the lead for the first time in a Super Bowl:

> *"Namath, on a handoff to Matt Snell... Snell at the 5, Snell at the 3, Snell... Touchdown! Matt Snell in the end zone on*

a wide sweep to the left... He shook Rick Volk at the 5-yard line and banged into the end zone where Lenny Lyles hit him, and this crowd is up and standing and yelling as the Jets have drawn first blood. Bob Talamini made an outstanding block to help Snell get into the end zone..."

Few knew it, but in striving to get outside of the pursuit of Gaubatz, Snell had aggravated an old injury in his scarred right knee. Sitting on the bench after the score, he was thankful for the warm weather of Miami. Jets team trainer Jeff Snedeker taped the outside of Snell's pant leg to take pressure off his knee.

Turner, whose extra point gave New York a 7–0 lead with 9:03 left in the first half, marveled at Snell's long run to the end zone. "Was that ever pretty," he said.

Gowdy: *"The Jets score first. They're anywhere from 18- to 20-point underdogs, more than the College All-Stars were against the Packers last August."*

New York's scoring drive covered 80 yards and 12 plays and drained more than five minutes off the scoreboard clock. More importantly for the Jets, it also drained some of the confidence from the Colts. Almost to a man, Baltimore seemed unable or unwilling to believe that a loose cannon like Namath, who had thrown 49 passes in the AFL Championship Game, would continue to call this most basic of game plans.

The Jets had appeared at times during the league season to be using five footballs at once, but they were beating the Colts with an NFL-style game plan based on power running and conservative, albeit precision, passing. Frustration enveloped the heavily favored Colts. Snell saw desperation in the face of Braase, who was being handled by Hill. Billy Ray Smith felt like the Jets were taking away the Colts pride. Schmitt could hear the NFL champs cursing themselves. "They were mad as hell that we were moving," Schmitt said. Bubba Smith was shocked the Jets were leading. "We walked out of the hotel that morning like the Jets were going to be too scared to show up," Smith said. "I think we even got to believe what the papers said—that we were going to win by 17, 18 points."

Trailing in a game for the first time since November, the Colts looked to counter quickly. Matte gathered in Morrall's short toss along the sideline in front of the Baltimore bench and ripped off a 30-yard gain. Three plays later from the New York 38, Morrall spotted Mackey running free through the secondary. This is where we get even, Morrall thought. But he hurried his throw, and it was off to the right. Mackey turned to try to get his hands on it. Sample, who had read the play and left his coverage on Willie Richardson, arrived at the same time as the ball and crashed into Mackey from the blind side. The ball fell to the turf. Another big play, thought Morrall. Another missed opportunity.

Sample stood over Mackey, chiding him. "Big boy, you're going to have a tough time out here today," he said. "You may run over rinky-dinky backs in the NFL, but you don't do it over here."

Mackey snorted in disdain. "I'll be back."

Moments later, Baltimore missed on its third scoring chance of the opening half when Michaels misfired on his second field goal attempt, this time from 46 yards out. New York's underrated defense was riled up. When Matte congratulated Larry Grantham after a hard tackle, the Jets outside linebacker sneered. "Screw you," Grantham said. Walt Michaels and Buddy Ryan had devised New York's defensive game plan, and it was left to Grantham to call the signals on the field, just as Namath was doing for the offense. Defensive tackle Paul Rochester said Grantham knew what everyone on the defense was supposed to be doing on every play. Grantham deciphered the Colts offensive game plan and could see that Baltimore was running behind Mackey and at Rochester and defensive end Gerry Philbin on the Jets left side. Grantham kept calling the same defense. "They're coming your way," he'd yell at Rochester and Philbin. "Just keep stopping 'em."

Herman thought the Jets defense, and the team as a whole, got its fiery emotion from Ryan. "Buddy was one of the keys to that team, and not just the defense," Herman said. "He would lend you the intensity he had and also lend you the confidence he had. Walt had a quiet intensity. Buddy was more vocal."

Turner followed by missing a 41-yard attempt on New York's next series. Gaubatz finally got back at his tormentor on the drive when he broke through and sacked Namath. The Colts offense came back with another drive, and Matte was again the catalyst. Sweeping right, he followed the blocking of Ressler and ran through an attempted tackle by safety Jim Hudson on a 58-yard run.

> *Gowdy: Second down and 4, Baltimore on their 26. Tom Matte, cutting back, breaks away! He may be caught from behind... Billy Baird finally wrestles him down and, some unhappiness now. Matte and Johnny Sample."*

Baird had given chase from his safety position and pulled Matte down from behind at the Jets 16-yard line. Sample arrived late and fell on the pileup. A brief scuffle ensued when Matte charged Sample and accused the Jets cornerback of piling on, knees first.

"You're a dirty player," Matte screamed into Sample's face.

Sample grabbed the Colts halfback by the front of his jersey. "You ain't nothin'!" he shouted. "You oughta be ashamed of yourself. Anybody who can't score when he's this far out in front shouldn't even be wearing a uniform."

Super Bowl III was the most productive game of Matte's career. The 58-yard run was his longest of the season and he would go on to lead the Colts with 116 yards on just 11 carries. He averaged a game-high 10.6 yards per run. Had Baltimore not been forced to abandon the running game in the second half in favor of a passing attack, Matte would have certainly surpassed Snell as the game's leading rusher and would have set a new Super Bowl rushing record. Forced to make a comeback, the Colts went away from their productive ground game and Matte finished five yards short of Snell's then Super Bowl-record 121 yards rushing.

For much of the second quarter, Super Bowl III was a showdown between Matte and Snell. The two men shared similarities beyond their almost identical height and weight. Both hailed from Ohio State, and for one season had shared the same backfield as Buckeyes. Matte at the time was a senior quarterback, and Snell a freshman fullback. Blocking for Matte and Snell on that Ohio State squad was tackle Bob

Vogel, a starter for the Colts in Super Bowl III. Both Matte and Snell were first-round draft picks, and as pros, both wore No. 41. They were versatile backs who could run, catch, block, and throw the option pass. Each would play for a world champion whose Super Bowl victory would come in the Miami Orange Bowl, and both would suffer knee injuries before eventually retiring in 1972.

Two plays after Matte's long gain, Morrall dropped back and saw Richardson a step ahead of Sample at the Jets goal line. A good pass would have resulted in a game-tying touchdown, but Morrall threw low and behind his receiver. Though trailing on the play, the poor pass put Sample in perfect position to make the interception at the 2-yard line.

"I blew it," Morrall said of his pass to Richardson. "I threw behind him."

Fueled by his private grudge with the Colts and the NFL, Sample was in a frenzy when the game started. He remained in a froth for much of the afternoon. He screamed at teammates, almost brawled with Matte, and taunted Richardson. During the week, he read comments attributed to Richardson that the difference between Baltimore's receivers and the receivers on the Jets was that the Colts were used to working against NFL defenses. To Sample, the implication was clear. The Jets were inferior because they played in a weaker league.

To the Jets, it was another case of the NFL lording it over the AFL. Only this time, Snell said, the NFL didn't have the Lombardi Packers going into battle for them. Sample was determined to stick the notion of NFL superiority—and AFL inferiority—in the face of the Colts, literally, as well as figuratively. Rising from the ground, the snarling Sample tapped Richardson on the helmet with the ball. "Is this what you're looking for?" he mockingly asked.

As he prepared to take the field to play defense, Curtis knew the Colts were in trouble. "Instead of two touchdowns for the Colts," he said, "it became two interceptions for the Jets."

Baltimore had outscored NFL opponents by an average of 29–10 during the regular season, so their inability to convert numerous scoring opportunities against the Jets was inexplicable to them. Curtis could feel the Colts starting to press, and some members of the Jets could sense as well that the NFL champs were starting to panic. All season long, Baltimore's defense had fueled its offense. And the defense was still doing its job. The high-powered Jets offense had only managed a single touchdown thus far. It was the Baltimore offense that was sputtering, and some members of the Colts were already looking anxiously toward John Unitas.

"Unitas was ready to play," Gaubatz said. "But they didn't let him. I liked Earl, but when I found out they wouldn't let John start, I thought, 'Oh, man.'"

Shula would say later that Unitas had approached him before the game and told him he felt well enough to start. Shula countered that he was going to stick with Morrall. The decision made sense. Morrall had started every game that season, had helped lead the Colts to the Western Conference championship, the NFL title, and the most wins by a team in NFL history. He was the league's MVP. Unitas had limited playing time during the season, and his arm strength was still suspect. The fact that the Jets defense didn't look like it was going to pose many problems also likely played a part in Shula's decision.

Yet when it became clear in the first half that Morrall was not having a good game, some of the Colts said they approached Shula and begged him to put in Unitas. But Johnny U remained on the sideline.

The enormous Orange Bowl crowd, which had been pro-Baltimore in the beginning, could sense a historic upset in the making and began switching its allegiance to the underdogs from the AFL. Jets guard Randy Rasmussen felt the change in the sellout crowd and thought it might be that while the Jets had their share of fans at the game, they had kept quiet in the early going because they were afraid to say anything. They had stayed subdued while Colts fans had not. Tight end Pete Lammons thought the mood of the crowd during the pregame had been hostile to the Jets. One Baltimore fan sitting behind the wives of the Jets players referred to the Colts as "Big Boys" and the Jets as "Little Boys." At the kickoff, the fan jeered the Jets wives. "The Big Boys," he said, "are going to show the Little Boys."

As the game progressed, fans of the Jets and the AFL became more vocal, and Rasmussen thought the entire Orange Bowl crowd had erupted when Snell scored to give New York the lead.

Morrall sensed a change in the mood of both the Jets and the crowd. "The Jets were fired up," he said, "and I could see the crowd shifting its allegiance to them. Namath was becoming the dragon-slayer just as he said he would, and I just couldn't believe that."

The Jets were controlling the game and the clock; they owned possession of the ball for 18 of the game's first 30 minutes. Still, the Colts were trailing by only a touchdown. As the first half wound down, Baltimore knew a late score would give them momentum going into the break. The football gods granted them two scoring opportunities. With just less than a minute left and the Jets offense backed up in its own end of the field, punter Curley Johnson kicked from deep in his end zone. The Colts had two choices. They could crowd the line of scrimmage, overload the Jets at the point of attack and try to block the punt, or they could drop back into a blocking wedge and set up a return.

Baltimore chose the former. The Colts set up in a 10-man front; they were going for the block rather than the return. From his left end position, Alex Hawkins prepared himself. He knew any big play that happens before halftime is magnified, and he knew that a blocked punt could turn momentum in the Colts favor.

Gowdy: "*Look at that, a 10-man front for Baltimore. They're going after [Johnson]."*

At the snap, Hawkins sprinted toward the Jets punter. He had timed his move perfectly and had burst into the backfield untouched. For a split second, Hawkins thought he might reach Johnson before he punted. Should he tackle the punter in the end zone for a safety or try to block the punt and possibly set up a touchdown? A moment's hesitation in his thinking destroyed Hawkins' timing. "I froze for just a tick," he said. Raising his arms to block the kick, Hawkins was startled when Johnson's punt actually sailed beneath his outstretched arms.

Johnson got his punt away, and the Colts had missed yet another scoring opportunity. They would have one more chance before the end of the half. On second down at New York's 41, Shula called for a timeout and Morrall trotted to the sideline. There were 25 seconds remaining in the half. Shula had several options. Give the ball to Matte, who had already broken loose on two long gains? Set up a pass play that would put the Colts closer to a field goal attempt that could cut the Jets lead to just 7-3?

Earlier in the season, when the Colts were struggling to subdue the upstart Atlanta Falcons, Shula had used some razzle-dazzle, a flea-flicker play, to give Baltimore some life. Ewbank knew about it, and the Jets defense had worked on it during the two weeks leading up to the game. They never did defend it successfully in practice. The gadget play—"38 Flow Special" in the Baltimore playbook—called for Morrall to hand off to Matte, who would simulate a running play by sweeping right. When he got wide of the tight end, Matte would stop, turn, and throw a lateral pass back to Morrall. The Colts quarterback would then look downfield for Jimmy Orr, the primary receiver on the play.

The call worked against Atlanta and helped give Baltimore a 28-20 win. The irony of the Colts having to call it against the Jets was that most experts felt it would be New York, not Baltimore, who would have to resort to desperation tactics to score in Super Bowl III.

Walt Michaels' plan was to have the cornerback covering Orr, Randy Beverly, play the run and let the onside safety—Baird—cover Orr deep. Yet every time the Jets practiced against the flea flicker, it resulted in a touchdown. As Matte took Morrall's handoff and the play unfolded, the Jets blew coverage again. Beverly and Baird both moved up to stop the run.

As Orr raced toward the end zone, he also ran toward the Baltimore Colts Marching Band, which had taken up seats on metal folding chairs in the east end of the Orange Bowl and were dressed in blue-and-white uniforms that matched the color of the Colts jerseys.

Conservative estimates put Orr 20 yards behind the Jets defense. "I was open from here to Tampa," he said. "I was waving my arms in the end zone, 37 yards away from the nearest guy. It was the perfect play."

"It was a certain touchdown," Shula said. Curry believed the same. His job on the flea flicker was to block the defensive tackle opposite him—John Elliott—then slide back and protect Morrall. As he looked downfield, Curry saw Orr so alone he was "standing in the end zone as if he were waiting for a bus."

This, Curry thought, is going to get us back in the game. It's a sure touchdown.

Except that it wasn't. Morrall never saw Orr open downfield. As he turned to catch the lateral pass, the Colts quarterback looked downfield. "There was Jerry Hill racing down the middle," he said. "He had plenty of room so I just sort of arched the ball instead of throwing hard. It floated..."

Baltimore Sun sportswriter John Steadman theorized that Morrall failed to see Orr because the Colts receiver was in direct line with the marching band and his uniform blended with theirs.

Orr waved his arms frantically, trying to get Morrall's attention. "Everyone in the stadium saw Orr," Hawkins said. "Everyone except Morrall."

Gowdy saw Orr from the broadcast booth:

> "All alone is Jimmy Orr! But they hit down the middle... Intercepted by Jim Hudson, the third interception for New York! Baltimore trying a trick play... They had Jimmy Orr all alone and they didn't see him."
>
> DeRogatis: "A very smart play. Earl is in a great spot and he completely loses Jimmy Orr. That was a tremendous play, Curt."
>
> Gowdy: "Orr could have walked in. He was wide open on the 10-yard line. Nobody within 15 yards of him, Kyle."
>
> Rote: "There really wasn't. He was just so wide open."

The Colts failed flea flicker remains one of the most controversial and discussed plays in Super Bowl history. The game film shows Morrall doing a half turn as he looked downfield. He then looked toward the middle of the field to find his secondary receiver, Hill. Hill was open as well, but Morrall floated a pass that had just enough air beneath it to allow Hudson to cut in front of Hill and make the interception at the Jets 12-yard line. Sample had played against Morrall in the NFL, and he told teammates before the Super Bowl that Morrall threw a soft pass 90 percent of the time. That Morrall tended to lob some of his passes, Sample said, would give Jets defensive backs recovery time to either knock the ball down or intercept it. Hudson's interception, Sample thought, had proved a prime example.

Hudson's return ran out the clock, and the Jets headed into half-time still leading 7–0. Baltimore had wasted numerous scoring opportunities, had left as many as 27 points on the field, and turned over the ball three times. It was the first time all season the Colts were shut out in the first half, and their frustrations were summed up by their failure on the flea flicker.

There are two explanations for this seemingly unexplainable play. First, there's the belief put forth by Steadman that Orr's uniform blended in with those of the Colts Marching Band behind him and thus Morrall couldn't see him. Another reason, and an often overlooked one, is that Morrall had been hurried by John Elliott. Curry saw Elliott charging Morrall and reached him just as Morrall was releasing the ball. Yet Elliott has never received enough credit for forcing Morrall to throw a fraction of a second before he was ready to.

The blame for the failure of this critical play has fallen on Morrall, but Grantham exonerates the Colts quarterback.

"My game film shows Beverly within 10 yards of Orr," he said. "And [Elliott] was right in Morrall's face when he threw the ball."

Walt Michaels and Buddy Ryan were angry. At halftime, they approached several members of their defense. "What happened?" they asked. "I guess they outsmarted us on that play," Sample said. "Orr was wide open."

The Colts seemed to be emotionally crushed as they trudged toward their locker room. Matte looked toward the heavens and shook his head, as if questioning his team's fate. Orr ran toward Morrall and began shouting.

"Didn't you see me, Earl? Didn't you see me?"

"No, Jimmy, I didn't."

Shula turned to one of his assistants. "Damn it, the flea flicker is designed especially for Orr," he said angrily. "Morrall's supposed to look for him. What in hell is happening?"

Curtis came unglued. He began screaming obscenities. Mad Dog's frustration was two-fold. He was angered by the offense's inability to score and because the Jets had spent almost the entire first half running their plays away from his side of the field. Curtis became so anxious to make a play that when the Jets did attack in his direction, he forgot his responsibilities. He was so anxious to get to Namath—Hollywood, as he called him—that Curtis vacated his coverage area on one play and left Snell wide open in the flat. Namath found Snell for a short gain.

The Colts confidence was depleted. As he trudged toward the locker room, Morrall made a mental list of Baltimore's missed opportunities in the first half:

The failed pass to Richardson; Mackey's drop; Beverley's "fluke" interception; the pass by Namath that slipped through Lyles' hands; Lou Michaels' missed field goals; the failed flea flicker.

God, Morrall thought, it was a long list.

13

Cowboy at the Mike

As the Jets and Colts headed off the field at halftime, NBC cut away from its live broadcast to commercials.

To the background of *"You can take Salem out of the country but... You can't take the country out of Salem,"* Curt Gowdy turned to broadcast partner Al DeRogatis.

"We may be sitting in on one of the biggest upsets of all time," Gowdy said.

Down on the field, some of the Colts began to realize the same. Several players said they had approached the coaching staff during the first half and pleaded for changes, only to be rebuffed. Defensive backfield coach Chuck Noll had waved off defensive captain Bobby Boyd's information about Joe Namath's check-offs at the line, and head coach Don Shula had resisted the notion of bringing in John Unitas to replace Earl Morrall at quarterback. Some of the things that happened in the first half, Shula said, were not Morrall's fault.

Some Colts, like middle linebacker Dennis Gaubatz, thought Unitas should have started the game. Others, like safety Jerry Logan, were looking for Johnny U not long after. "John should have come on in the first quarter," Logan said. "Earl had a great season, but he was having a bad day."

Gaubatz also thought that the Colts coaches should have replaced aging right linebacker Don Shinnick with younger Ron Porter. Shinnick was 33, Porter 23 and, according to Gaubatz, better against the run.

"Shinnick was great against the pass, but he couldn't stop the run," Gaubatz said. "Porter could."

The white-on-green lights of the scoreboard in the Miami Orange Bowl told the stunning story: Jets 7, Colts 0. The audience inside the stadium and millions watching on television or listening to the radio broadcast buzzed with excitement at the possibility of a historic upset.

Shula's question to an assistant at halftime—"What in hell is happening?"—hung suspended and unanswered in the south Florida air. His opposite, Jets coach Weeb Ewbank, wasn't surprised by what had taken place during the first two quarters of Super Bowl III. Ewbank knew the Colts weren't the invincible machine portrayed by the media—"self-designated experts" is what Ewbank mockingly called the hundreds of writers and TV and radio personnel who had descended on Miami to report on the game.

Yet many of those same experts were shocked by what they had witnessed on the field. The vaunted Colts, a team that had lost just once in a record-shattering season, a team considered one of the greatest if not the greatest in NFL history, had three turnovers and zero points in the first half. *Detroit News* columnist Jerry Green had called the Colts the "team supreme of the NFL," but it dawned on him as he followed the action on the field below that strange things were happening in this game.

Baltimore had wasted several scoring opportunities; had missed out on as many as 27 first-half points. Quarterback Earl Morrall, who had been intercepted just twice in the previous five games against NFL opponents, had been picked off three times in the first half alone by the AFL upstarts. Lou Michaels had misfired on two field goal attempts; Alex Hawkins had mistimed his jump on a punt block attempt.

The ferocious Colts charge, headed by big Bubba Smith and Mike "The Animal" Curtis, had barely touched Broadway Joe Namath. Unsung fullback Matt Snell was succeeding where NFL rushing leader Leroy Kelly and the explosive Gale Sayers, future Hall of Famers both, had failed.

A year earlier, NFL writers had sat in the same Orange Bowl press box and watched the Green Bay Packers pound the Oakland Raiders 33-14. The NFL media gloated long into the night at the expense of their AFL counterparts. Noting that Oakland's 19-point loss to Vince Lomabrdi's all-conquerors was six less than Kansas City had suffered in its 35-10 loss to the Pack in Super Bowl I, an NFL writer chided his AFL counterparts. "Hey, they're getting closer. Three years from now, they'll only lose by one."

Jerry Izenberg of the *Newark (N.J.) Star-Ledger* wrote in his column the day after Super Bowl II that at the AFL's current rate of success against the NFL, the younger league should be able to manage a tie in 1971.

Members of the NFL and AFL media felt they had personal stakes in the outcome of each Super Bowl. When the Colts began losing, some NFL writers felt as if they were losing, too. When Jimmy Orr ran free through the Jets defense on the flea-flicker play, a few NFL writers jumped from their seats, pointed downfield, and yelled at Morrall. "Look at Orr!"

Don Weiss, the NFL's public relations director, felt the afternoon was growing more ominous by the moment. For years, he and his staff had tried to make the AFL look as bad as possible. They were NFL fans, and by halftime of Super Bow III, their emotions were consuming them. At the moment, they didn't care what a Jets victory would mean to the Super Bowl as a sporting event or to the future of pro football. They worked for the NFL, and what they were watching, Weiss thought, was an outrage.

AFL writer Larry Felser of the *Buffalo Evening-News* thought there was a "stupendous smell of upset" inside the Orange Bowl. The Colts, he believed, were a psychological mess. They had started the game so strongly it appeared as if the massive betting line was an underlay. But Felser thought that Namath had scared the Colts defense with the "most famous incomplete pass in Super Bowl history"—the early bomb to Don Maynard. The Jets then stepped out of character, playing methodical, ball-control football that was more suited to the NFL than the AFL and were taking it to the Colts physically.

Not far away from Felser in the press box, NFL writer Jerry Green of the *Detroit News* was experiencing the same realization. The Colts, Green thought, are not annihilating the Jets as expected. Baltimore had three opportunities to score touchdowns and had failed. Lou Michaels had missed a chipshot field goal. Namath was riding herd on a controlled offense, and Bubba Smith wasn't killing him. Story leads began flipping through Green's mind:

"It happened. Space has been conquered and the New York Jets are the professional champions of the universe...

"Joe Namath, the Broadway loudmouth, is the king of quarterbacks and the American Football League is equal..."

While NFL writers struggled to explain the Colts sudden difficulties scoring, AFL writers could barely conceal their glee. Some took particular delight in the pained and puzzled expression of their NFL counterparts, most notably Tex Maule of *Sports Illustrated*.

Maule was a proponent of the established NFL and considered the AFL a vastly inferior product. He had said before the game that the Colts would "whip the Jets about as they pleased." He acknowledged that Namath was a better passer than Morrall, though their respective statistics from the 1968 season did not bear out that fact. But he believed that the Jets just did not have the overall team strength to match the Colts.

Maule's AFL counterpart at *Sports Illustrated*, Edwin Shrake, disagreed. A month earlier, Shrake had written a cover story for *Sports Illustrated* titled "A Champagne Party For Joe and Weeb." In it, Shrake predicted a Jets victory over Baltimore. The story would prove amazingly prescient since the AFL and NFL playoffs had not yet even begun, yet Shrake was not only forecasting the Jets and Colts as league champions but also stating that New York would beat Baltimore with Namath's strategic passing, a ball-control attack, and big-play defense. Shrake wrote that Unitas would replace Morrall at quarterback—due to injury, not incompetence—but that Namath would still guide the Jets to a stunning upset victory.

Maule, having accurately forecast Green Bay's one-sided wins in Super Bowls I and II, still felt comfortable predicting that Baltimore would win Super Bowl III. "By a rather comfortable margin," he said.

At halftime, he had become impressed by Namath's remarkable ability to beat the Baltimore blitz, by fullback Matt Snell's power running, and by split end George Sauer's soft hands. But Maule felt New York had been lucky, as well. Given a little more good fortune, he thought the Colts could have already put the game away.

Maule was not the only member of the media groping to cope with the possibility of a Jets victory. ABC sportscaster Howard Cosell was pacing the press box in a somewhat confused state. Prior to the game, Cosell had told Gowdy, "Cowboy, the Colts will break both of Joe Namath's legs."

As the game unfolded, Cosell couldn't grasp the fact that the Jets were outplaying the Colts. During stoppages in play, he would rise from his seat next to WABC radio broadcasters Merle Harmon and Sam DeLuca, the voices of the Jets, and ask them, "What the hell is going on? Why are they winning?"

Cosell was looking for answers, and DeLuca said he didn't have any, other than the Jets were playing solid football and the Colts were making mistakes. And that, the former AFL lineman told Cosell, is how most games are won and lost.

In the NBC-TV booth, the broadcast team of play-by-plan man Gowdy and color men Al DeRogatis and Kyle Rote was providing viewers with the same calm, unruffled analysis. NBC's understated approach was quintessential Gowdy. Despite the importance of the events he covered, he never lost sight of the fact that these were still *games*.

Gowdy would sit in production meetings held before each event and listen quietly as NBC producers droned on about the opening and close of each game. To Gowdy, the producers sounded as if each one was Cecil B. DeMille. Finally, he would put his hand up.

"Yes, Gowdy?"

"What about the game?"

"Oh, hell with the game. We've got to have the opening and close."

"Yeah, but fellas, we're here because of the *game*."

Just as Ray Scott's clipped, concise tones ("Starr... Dowler... Touchdown!") symbolized the NFL on CBS in the 1960s, Gowdy's resonant voice was the sound of the AFL on first ABC and then NBC. Gowdy, however, had to survive attempts to fire him and broadcast partner Paul Christman when the two were doing games on ABC in the early part of the decade. Unhappy that Gowdy and Christman were not doing more to build up the young league during their broadcasts, some AFL owners contacted league president Joe Foss and asked him to pressure the network to fire Gowdy and Christman.

When Gowdy learned of the attempted coup, he went to his bosses at ABC. "Look," he said, "we're not going to say things we don't believe. Are we going to be harassed by these owners?"

ABC brass told Foss that Gowdy and Christman worked for the network, not for the AFL.

Gowdy was one of the better and more versatile sportscasters in the business. He was also a man who was good to his working partners, as well. Tony Kubek worked with Gowdy covering baseball games on NBC and called him the best broadcast partner he's ever had.

A year after Super Bowl III, Gowdy became the first sportscaster to receive the George Foster Peabody Award for highest achievement in radio and television. Five times he was named top sportscaster in the country by his peers.

Remembered today as the voice behind NBC's coverage of the Super Bowl, Rose Bowl, and World Series, Gowdy was, at heart, a basketball man. Born in Green River, Wyoming, and raised in nearby Cheyenne, Gowdy was the son of a railroad man who became chief dispatcher for the Union Pacific Railroad. Young Curt's lifelong love affair with the outdoors began during a childhood spent hunting and fishing. Despite his small size and slight build, he played basketball at the University of Wyoming. He was a set-shot specialist until a back condition shortened his athletic career. It also ended his Army career during World War II, and he returned to Cheyenne.

Gowdy began his career in the media in the 1940s as a part-time reporter covering high school sports for the *Wyoming Eagle*. He spent his spare time broadcasting make-believe games in his room. His mother encouraged him to apply for a job at a local radio station and drove him to his first broadcast. It was a six-man football game between Pine Bluff and St. Mary's four blocks from his house.

The temperature in Cheyenne that afternoon was in the sub-zero range, and Gowdy later estimated the crowd at some 15 people.

Fourteen of those, he said, were relatives. The field was bare of sidelines and goal posts. When the players took the field, Gowdy realized they didn't have numerals on their jerseys.

He laughed at the memory years later. "I made up the whole game," he said. "Still the best broadcast I ever did."

He spent a year doing local broadcasts in Cheyenne, then was hired to do University of Oklahoma football games for station KOMA in Oklahoma City. Gowdy was doing Sooner football when a phone call to his home changed his life.

"Curt, this is Red Barber in New York."

Barber was sports director at CBS and wanted Gowdy to do the network's nationally televised Oklahoma-Texas Christian football game the following Saturday. The game gave Gowdy national exposure and paved the way for his next opportunity—the No. 2 man behind Mel Allen on New York Yankees radio broadcasts. Russ Hodges had left the Yankees broadcasting booth to become the top announcer for the New York Giants baseball team. Needing a new No. 2 man, Yankees general manager George Weiss hired Gowdy. The Wyoming Cowboy stayed in New York for a year and supplemented his coverage of Yankees baseball by broadcasting college basketball games and boxing from Madison Square Garden. One year later, Gowdy was hired to be the lead announcer for the Boston Red Sox.

He began covering the AFL for ABC in 1960. After NBC purchased the rights to broadcast AFL games in 1964, Gowdy switched networks in 1965 and became the lead announcer. His career with the Peacock Network would span two decades and include 16 baseball All-Star Games, 13 World Series, and nine Super Bowls. Yet he always considered Super Bowl III to be the most memorable sports event he covered.

"The Jets were a good team, very quick, and I thought they would give Baltimore a good game," Gowdy said. "I thought Baltimore would win, but I thought the Jets would be more formidable [than the AFL's first two Super Bowl representatives, Kansas City and Oakland]. But if you were with the AFL at that time, you were caught in a trap, laughed at. I remember Cosell telling me, 'Cowboy, you're an idiot. The Colts will break both of Joe Namath's legs.'"

Throughout the afternoon, DeRogatis and Rote complemented Gowdy's crisp play-by-play broadcast with insightful analysis. DeRogatis told viewers in the pregame that one of the keys for the Jets was to establish the running game. It was a startling comment, since most experts believed that the only hope New York had for an upset was if Namath could have a huge game passing.

> DeRogatis: "If the New York Jets get 120, 130 yards on the ground, and nine to 13 first downs (rushing)... they have a whale of a chance to win the game."

To NFL fans, the idea must have sounded ridiculous. Only one man had run with any success on Baltimore's defense all season, and that was Cleveland's Leroy Kelly. His 130 yards rushing back in October would be more than any two backs had combined to gain against the Colts in a game all season. Bubba Smith, Mike Curtis, and Co. had evened the score with Kelly in the NFL Championship Game, holding the NFL's rushing leader to a mere 28 yards.

But DeRogatis, an All-America player at Duke and a former All-Pro with the New York Giants, knew football. Marty Glickman worked with DeRo on Giants radio broadcasts and was amazed how many times his analyst would correctly predict what was about to happen.

Gowdy later called DeRo's prediction regarding the Jets running game in Super Bowl III one of the great calls of all time. "But," Gowdy added, "he never got credit for it."

DeRogatis smiled. "Curt, I told you."

Amid commercials for the Chrysler Corporation, Winston cigarettes, Phillips 66, RCA ("The first name in home entertainment"), and TWA ("Up, up, and away, TWA"), NBC's halftime show featured a Four Freedoms theme, complete with patriotic costumes, colorful parade floats, and the "Battle Hymn of the Republic." Compared to the halftime extravaganzas at future Super Bowls, where pop stars and mega-personalities would dominate the stage, the proceedings at Super Bowl III seemed quaint by comparison.

The solid reporting done on NBC television was matched in the network's radio booth by play-by-play announcer Charlie Jones and analysts Pat Summerall and George Ratterman. Speaking above a wave of almost continuous crowd noise, the trio dovetailed their comments and provided inside information on the two teams and the game.

Summerall realized early on that the strategy of Ewbank and offensive coordinator Clive Rush was to work on the three aging veterans—end Ordell Braase, outside linebacker Don Shinnick, and cornerback Lenny Lyles—on the right side of the Colts defense. He also noted that New York was tipping its plays. When Emerson Boozer was in the backfield, the Jets were likely going to run the ball. When Bill Mathis came in, it usually signified a pass play.

Ratterman remarked that the Jets appeared more nervous than the Colts in the opening minutes of the game, and cited that as the reason New York's linebackers and secondary were taking deeper drops in coverage than usual to keep Baltimore's playmakers in front of them and prevent the big play. After the Jets took the lead in the second quarter, Ratterman thought the AFL champions had settled down. New York's defense, he said, so tentative in the early going, was now challenging the Colts with aggressive play.

Jones told his listening audience in the second quarter that Morrall had fallen into a predictable pattern of play-calling and was consistently throwing deep on first down. On the field, NBC sideline reporter Jim Simpson stood with comedian Bob Hope. Seconds before the start of their interview, Hope removed his sporty checkered hat and told Simpson, "You know, there has been some betting on this game. If this keeps up, a few of my friends will have to start new careers."

Simpson laughed. He knew Hope was an NFL fan who was rooting for the Colts. Simpson thought of the millions who, along with Bob Hope, were trying to figure out how and why the Colts were losing. When the signal came from the booth, Simpson and Hope went on the air.

> Simpson: *"Our special guest is the nation's number one comedian and turning out to be the number one sports fan. We see you at the World Series and now at the Super Bowl."*
>
> Hope: *Well, I'll tell ya, I'm really shocked by this game today. These Jets are doing something, aren't they?"*

> Simpson: "*What about the New York Jets? I understand*
> *you came in here as a Baltimore supporter. Are you changing*
> *your mind?*"
>
> Hope: "*Actually, I think the Jets forgot to read the*
> *papers. This is a thrilling game, I'll tell ya that.*"

As Simpson signed off, he thought of the first two Super Bowls, and how Kansas City and Oakland had fallen apart following halftime after playing competitively in the first two quarters. But he also recalled that those two teams had been beaten by Green Bay, and the Colts weren't looking like those champion Packers this day.

Simpson was anxious to see which pattern would dominate the second half. The pattern of NFL superiority set forth by Vince Lombardi or that of the AFL rebels being established by the Jets.

Jets linebacker Larry Grantham wasn't concerned. Grantham had seen the Packers play in the first two Super Bowls. The Colts, he thought, weren't as good.

"Green Bay was head and shoulders above everybody in the National Football League," Grantham said. "They were a dominant team. They lined up and executed. When we sat down and analyzed Baltimore, Tom Matte was a great back but he wasn't going to beat you. Jerry Hill was a tough runner, but he wasn't going to beat you. Jimmy Orr was a good receiver with good hands, but he wasn't going to beat you. Willie Richardson was a great receiver on 'Out' patterns, but he didn't go over the middle.

"And then you look at John Mackey. He's the one guy who can beat you. So we kept double-teaming Mackey the entire game.

"The Colts won because they caused a lot of breaks on defense. That's how they beat people. But I knew we could get points against them. I thought Joe could get 20, 30 points against their defense. That's how confident I was."

Don Maynard felt the same sense of confidence from his teammates "All week long, Pete Lammons said, among the players, 'We're going to win.' The defensive guys were saying they were going to intercept five passes."

As the second half approached, Rush approached Namath. Because Broadway Joe's play-calling and audibles at the line had been nearly perfect, Rush hadn't suggested a single play during the first two quarters.

"Just stay with it," he told Namath at halftime. "Do things the way we did in the first half."

Namath nodded.

But he was thinking. Morrall had such a frustrating first half. It was only a matter of time, Namath believed, before the Great One got into the game for Baltimore.

14

No Ordinary Joe

Earl Morrall sat in the Baltimore Colts locker room at halftime, unable and unwilling to believe how badly things were going for the NFL champions. Over and over, the NFL's MVP kept asking himself, "What do we have to do?"

"Everything that could go wrong did go wrong," halfback Tom Matte said. "Jimmy Orr is wide open, but Earl throws underneath to Jerry Hill and it's intercepted. We're 18-point favorites. We're supposed to kick their ass."

The Colts were only trailing the New York Jets by a touchdown, but they acted as if they were down by four or five scores. They had started to panic in the second quarter, and had started to abandon their game plan. Matte was having his greatest game as a pro, but Baltimore was looking to pass rather than run. Rather than stick with their ground game, the Colts began looking for the quick score. Morrall, who did not own a strong arm, had fallen into a pattern of firing deep passes. It was clear that a team ranked as an overwhelming favorite felt not only a need to win, but to win in convincing fashion.

Morrall gave voice before the game to the pressure the Colts were feeling. "What are we, 18-point favorites?" he asked a reporter. "That puts the pressure on us to win big. A close victory by us would be a moral victory for them."

Jets defensive tackle Paul Rochester could relate. During the AFL's regular season, New York had lost the two games in which it had been most heavily favored to win. "I'd rather be 17-point underdogs," he said, "than 19-point favorites."

In terms of total yards, the Colts had only been outgained by the Jets 175–162, and New York's lead was just seven points. But Baltimore's costly mistakes—they turned the ball over 34 times during the regular season, six more than the Jets—was haunting them. Morrall had thrown three interceptions in the first half and was just 5-of-15 passing.

Baltimore's plight in Super Bowl III was not unlike that which had faced Green Bay two years before in the first AFL-NFL World Championship Game. The heavily favored Packers had gone into halftime leading the Kansas City Chiefs by just 14–10. Since it was the first meeting between teams from the NFL and AFL, the Packers were pressured to win big and establish the older league's dominance over their young rivals. Green Bay at the time was a tough, seasoned team that had played in five NFL Championship Games during the decade and won four of them. Bullied and bossed by Vince Lombardi, the Packers seemed immune to pressure. But carrying the NFL colors into the first Super Bowl proved enough to rattle even the two-time defending league champs. Lombardi shook from nerves prior to the game-opening kickoff, and defensive captain Willie Davis acknowledged his teammates were uncharacteristically wound tight throughout the first half.

Baltimore had played the first half of Super Bowl III in similar fashion. By halftime, it was obvious that the Colts were a frustrated team, a team that felt it not only had to beat the Jets, but beat the AFL upstarts by the 18-point spread. The Packers had felt similar pressure in Super Bowl I. They took a surprisingly small lead into the locker room at halftime, assessed the situation, and outscored the Chiefs, 21–0, in the second half.

Reactions to the first half were varied inside Baltimore's locker room. Preston Pearson felt that outside of the Jets lone touchdown drive, New York's heralded offense hadn't shown much. By his calculations, Pearson figured the Colts should have scored at least 24 points in the first half. That meant Baltimore should have been on pace to a 48-point outing, a total that many experts had predicted in the pregame. Since he didn't believe the Jets could score 48 points against Baltimore's defense in a season's worth of games, Pearson thought that the Colts should have been well on their way to achieving the expected rout.

Missed opportunities gnawed at the NFL champions. "We had a chance to have 27 points in the first half," Matte said. "It was right there. We didn't get any."

Still, with two quarters to be played, most of the Colts refused to believe they could be beaten. They were certain they would come back and win. Some, however, seemed less certain. "I remember sitting around at halftime of that game and thinking how bad it was, how unprepared we were," tight end John Mackey said. The Colts had assumed it was an automatic win. "We cut up the shares at the pregame meal," Mackey said.

Several Colts thought back to the relaxed preparation they had during the week. "Some of the guys brought their wives and families with them," linebacker Mike Curtis said. "The kids were running around, raising hell." No one knew the despair, the abject humiliation the Colts were feeling, Curtis said. The 1968 Baltimore Colts were a perfect football machine. They had crushed every opponent but one on a tough schedule. The 1968 Baltimore Colts...would they be the first National Football League team to lose the Super Bowl? Cutis felt great anger inside of him. "Those damn Jets," he said, "were holding as if they were never going to hold again."

Offensive guard Glenn Ressler though the Colts had seriously underestimated the Jets. "We had a very good team," he said. "But when you look at the talent the Jets had on that team, it was tremendous. They were a very talented team. We took them too lightly."

Defensive end Bubba Smith approached coordinator Bill Arnsparger. "What's happening to us?" Smith asked.

Bubba had spent a frustrating first half hand-fighting tackle Dave Herman in an attempt to sack Jets quarterback Joe Namath or run down backs Matt Snell, Emerson Boozer, and Bill Mathis. It was evident that New York's offensive game plan called for the Jets to direct their attack away from Baltimore's left side, where Smith and Curtis were waiting for them. Smith thought he had a solution to the problem and brought it to head coach Don Shula.

"Place me in the middle of the defense," Smith said, "so I can get into the flow of the game."

Shula's response was brief. "Just play your position."

The rebuke caused big Bubba to roll his shoulders in a shrug. "Hey man, it's your team."

Smith thought that by playing the middle of the line as he did on special teams, he could disrupt the Jets blocking schemes. It was an intriguing idea, but most of the Colts believed a change in strategy wasn't what the team needed. Alex Hawkins felt there were very few adjustments that had to be made. The right side of the Colts defense had surrendered yardage in the first half, but the Jets still had only seven points on the scoreboard. It was a total on par with what the Packers had allowed in the first half in the first two Super Bowls. The frustration for Baltimore lay in the fact that its offense wasn't nearly as productive as Green Bay's had been. Colts miscues and big plays by the Jets defense had combined to turn Baltimore's opportunities to ashes.

Gathering his team around him, Shula blistered the locker room. "We're making stupid mistakes, we're stopping ourselves!" he shouted. "You've got them believing in themselves. You've got them believing they're better than we are."

Shula's outrage left his team transfixed. "He was hot," Morrall said. The Colts had seen him react so strongly just twice that season—against Atlanta in a game Baltimore rallied to win, and against Cleveland in the Colts lone loss. Shula's fiery speech lasted three or four minutes and had a dramatic impact on his players. Morrall looked around the locker room and saw the faces of his teammates reddening in anger. Bubba Smith sat in front of his locker nervously chain-smoking cigarettes.

"Let's go out there," Shula said, "and take charge of the game the way we know we can."

The Colts stormed out for the second half, then immediately turned the ball over on their opening drive. Matte followed Ressler for a gain of eight yards but fumbled the ball when he was bear-hugged from behind by 6'4", 270-pound defensive end Verlon Biggs. Linebacker

Ralph Baker covered the loose ball at the Baltimore 33-yard line. It was the Colts fourth turnover of the game.

NBC's Curt Gowdy made the call on a play some of the Jets thought was the turning point of Super Bowl III:

> Gowdy: "Now let's see what Baltimore does. Morrall gives the ball to Matte and... Matte fumbles and it's a New York recovery! Verlon Biggs hit him and jarred it loose and there on the ball is Ralph Baker. Biggs came over from right end, great pursuit by Verlon Biggs."

In the Jets halftime locker room, Weeb Ewbank had given his team a short talk warning against overconfidence. "We've only got one more half to go," he said. "But I want you to think of the score as 0-0. I want us to go out there and play like we have to win the game in the second half, not just hold the lead."

Namath stayed with the offensive game plan that had worked so well in the first half. He told defensive captain Johnny Sample at halftime that he wasn't going to take any unnecessary risks. "The defense is holding up good, there's no sense taking a chance on something happening," he said. "Keep it up."

Boozer and Snell combined to pick up 14 yards on three carries, and Namath followed with a 5-yard flare pass to Snell. The big fullback churned for three more yards to put the ball at the Baltimore 11. NBC-TV analyst Al DeRogatis told viewers that this series could be the biggest of the game for the Colts defense. "This," he said, "is where their defense is going to be tested."

Baltimore responded and showed why its defense was considered one of the best in NFL history. On first down, Boozer was pinned for a 5-yard loss on a sweep left when safety Rick Volk charged in and forced the play wide. Smith followed on the next play by finally breaking free of Herman's block. A sellout crowd and national television audience held its collective breath as the 295-pound end closed on the star quarterback. If the game had been in Baltimore, "Kill, Bubba, Kill" would have been the crowd's chant.

"I was dead on toward Joe Willie," Smith said. The massive end realized he had two choices—fire in low and possibly put an end to Broadway Joe's career by crushing his crippled knees, or hit him high.

"I chose to let Namath live," he said. "Even though Namath was turning into a quarterback machine, I couldn't cripple him."

Perhaps shaken by the Colts second sack of the game, Namath threw one of his few poor passes of the afternoon. Trying to find tight end Pete Lammons, Namath forced the pass. Safety Jerry Logan read the play and got his hands on the ball. There were 75 yards of open field in front of him, but Logan dropped the ball.

"I still don't know why I threw the ball," Namath said. "I should have eaten it."

Having dodged Logan's potential interception and return for a game-tying score, the Jets gladly took a 32-yard field goal from Turner. With 10:08 left in the third quarter, New York led 10-0. Ewbank breathed a sigh of relief. "Ten points," he said, "is a hell of a lot better than seven."

On Baltimore's next series, Morrall had Mackey open downfield but overthrew him. Two plays later, Morrall was dropped by Carl McAdams for a 2-yard loss and the Colts were forced to punt. The rest of the third quarter belonged to Broadway Joe.

With his white uniform, bulky knee braces, and white leather shoes, Namath played his position that day with a flair and style that were uniquely his own. Green Bay's Bart Starr had won the MVP award in each of the first two Super Bowls with a classic passing form—the solid plant of the right foot, the deliberate step toward the receiver, the precise overhand delivery. Each of the top quarterbacks of the era had his own recognizable style. Baltimore's Johnny Unitas flipped his passes with an exaggerated overhand motion; Washington's Sonny Jurgensen had a roundhouse delivery that gave an arc to his passes.

Namath's style was different than what the Colts had seen in the NFL. Chants of "Joe! Joe!" rang out in a loud chorus from the Orange Bowl crowd. Morrall listened to the chants and thought that the fans who had cheered the Colts at the start of the game had been won over by Namath. "You could sense the crowd shifting its allegiance to him," he said.

Oakland Raiders star George Blanda thought Namath had succeeded in psyching not only the crowd, but both teams. "He psyched the Colts into thinking they could lose," he said, "and psyched the Jets into thinking they could win."

Namath's individuality and self-expression coincided perfectly with the cultural revolution the country was experiencing. In an era of long hair and free speech, Namath's shaggy mane and swinging lifestyle brought him more notoriety than most athletes. The pop generation loved Joe Willie White Shoes. But he was more than just Broadway Joe, as the Colts were finding out. Namath was also proving himself to be an astute field general.

Because the Baltimore defense shifted as much as it did, Namath was calling more audibles than usual. "Play at the line," he told teammates in the huddle. "Check with me." What was unknown to the Colts was that many of Namath's line calls were fake. The Jets went into Super Bowl III with three "live" colors—red, white, and blue. The color preceded each play call. When Namath called "green," the Colts would shift their defense prematurely. Namath would read the movements of the defense and then call out the "live" color and the actual play that New York was going to run.

The Colts knew Namath was a good passer. But as they lined up against him, they found themselves increasingly frustrated by Namath's ability to speed-read their defense. What they failed to grasp, center John Schmitt said, was that unlike many NFL teams, which went with just one "live" color, the AFL champs were using three.

Namath also confused the Colts with his snap counts. Varying his count each time, he would call for the center snap on a quick count on one down, and then hold for a long count on the next. On passing plays, he burned the Baltimore blitz with a variety of short and deep drops, quick releases, and precision passes. Throughout the game, he continued to take advantage of the Colts rotating zones. Because Baltimore's zone was rotating to the Jets right, where Don Maynard lined up on most downs, Namath felt that he could work the ball to George Sauer.

Nobody could read defenses like Namath, Maynard said. "We'd get in the huddle, and he'd call 'Play at the line.' That meant that we didn't have a set play, that he'd call it when we got up to the line. I'd say he did that almost half the time."

The way the Jets read the blitz was key, Namath said. After a couple of years of playing together, he and Sauer had an automatic play. Any time the safety would come up and blitz, Sauer would break off his pattern and slant inside.

The Jets read the blitz expertly. When Namath dropped back to pass, the first Colts defender he looked for was Logan. At the snap of the ball, Logan was usually positioned just more than 10 yards away from Namath. What Logan did after Schmitt's snap gave Namath a clue which defense Baltimore would be in. If Logan moved up to play tight end Pete Lammons, Namath knew the Colts were in man-to-man coverage. If Logan headed to the weak side of the formation, Baltimore was in a weak-side zone rotation. If Logan went to the strong side of the formation, they were in a strong-side zone. If he ran toward left cornerback Bobby Boyd, the Colts were in a safety zone.

After checking Logan's initial movements, Namath would next look to the other safety, Rick Volk, and then to middle linebacker Dennis Gaubatz. It would take Namath just one step back, sometimes two, to read the movements of the three key players in the middle of the Baltimore defense. The Colts had a tendency, Namath said, to telegraph their coverages. Film of the game shows him stepping to the line of scrimmage, pausing, reading the defensive alignment, then getting in his familiar hunched stance behind Schmitt. He would call the appropriate play based on the strength of the defense, then attack the Colts at their weakest point. When he wasn't picking the Colts apart with the pass, he was pounding them with bruising runs by fullback Matt Snell.

"Namath was a good quarterback," Gaubatz said. "The plays the Jets were running forced Lenny Lyles to come up [from his cornerback position]. I told our guys in the huddle, 'Let's stop that damn run.'"

With Maynard acting as a decoy, Namath continued to hit Sauer, who was working one-on-one against Lyles, in the seams of the zone. *Sports Illustrated* writer and pro football expert Paul Zimmerman covered the 1968 Jets for the *New York Post*. In his book *A Thinking Man's Guide to Pro Football*, Zimmerman wrote that people who knew Namath only for his long hair, mink coat, and great passing arm saw a scientist at work in Super Bowl III. What Namath was doing to the NFL's best defense, Zimmerman thought, was a clinical study on how to beat a rotating zone.

Namath would complete 17-of-28 passes for 206 yards in the game. His passing chart shows that almost half (12) of his attempted passes went to Sauer. Juking his way through the defense, dropping to his knees to make one catch, hauling in a pass over his shoulder on another, Sauer would eventually finish with a then-Super Bowl record eight catches for 133 yards. Sauer benefited from pregame advice he received from Johnny Sample. Years earlier, Sample played alongside Lyles in the Baltimore secondary. He told Sauer that if he made his first fake very hard—"really cut sharp," Sample told him—Lyles would probably bite on the fake. With Lyles out of position, Sauer would then be free to beat him to the ball. At one point in the NBC-TV broadcast, color analyst Kyle Rote remarked that Sauer was making moves on Lyles all the way downfield.

Sauer was also, as Namath pointed out, "making some great catches." Yet it wasn't just Sauer who was dissecting the Colts intricate coverages. New York's trio of Texans—Sauer, Maynard, and Lammons—were reading Baltimore's zones and finding the open seams. Jets coach Weeb Ewbank had spoken before the game about finding the soft spots in the defense. He told Sauer, "Find the dead spots in the zone, hook up, and Joe will hit you." During the game, Namath would throw to the vulnerable area 15 times and complete 11 passes.

"They were picking on our left side, running Snell on '19-Straight' and hitting Sauer on short patterns," Volk said. "They controlled the ball and controlled the clock. They were making the plays on offense."

After completing just one pass on New York's opening series of the second half, Namath came out firing when New York got the ball back. Taking over on the Jets 32-yard line following Baltimore's three-and-out, Namath hit Mathis for a 1-yard gain and then Sauer for 14. Two plays later, Namath connected with Lammons for 11 yards.

Merle Harmon described Namath's masterful performance on Jets radio:

"Namath, back to pass, Joe looking, throwing... It is complete on the 47-yard line to Sauer, he is brought down immediately by Rick Volk... Winston Hill doing a great job of pass blocking. He has given Ordell Braase fits today...

"Big third down play for New York... Over the ball is John Schmitt, Namath calling signals... Namath goes back to pass, he throws over the middle to Lammons, slant-in, he's got the ball at the 40-yard line of Baltimore, and he bounces off a tackler, Logan, and goes down to the 38-yard line..."

To keep the Colts honest, Namath went deep to Maynard, and again the speedy flanker got behind the Baltimore defense. The huge Orange Bowl crowd rose to its feet at the sight of Maynard sprinting through the end zone. But the pass was overthrown. Maynard caught it but was correctly ruled out of bounds in the back of the end zone.

Namath followed with a 14-yard completion to Snell, then threw incomplete to Maynard. Suddenly, Namath turned and trotted toward the Jets sideline. He was shaking his right hand, the same hand that had been injured in the AFL Championship Game against Oakland.

Gowdy: "Namath is injured... What a turning point that could be in this game..."

Namath had dislocated his right thumb after his passing hand hit the helmet of Colts tackle Fred Miller on the follow-through of his incomplete pass to Maynard. Jets team doctor James Nicholas was waiting for Namath on the sideline. He advised an injection of pain killer but Namath shook his head.

"No," he said. "I won't be able to feel the ball."

Gowdy: "The big question now is Joe Namath. He has played a spectacular game here. He has run his offense beautifully, he's read the blitzes."

Backup Vito "Babe" Parilli replaced Namath, who had completed four passes for 40 yards on the drive. Turner capped the march with his third field goal of the game, this from 30 yards out, and the Jets were in front by the shocking score of 13–0.

Namath was succeeding where NFL quarterbacks had failed in part because AFL defenses had been using zone coverages with more frequency than their NFL counterparts. Hank Stram, who coached the AFL's Kansas City Chiefs in Super Bowls I and IV, recalled a meeting he had with NFL coaches in 1960. It was the AFL's first year of operations and Stram, a former college coach, asked about the frequency of zone coverage in pro football. NFL coaches grinned at his question. Zone coverage would never work in the pros, they said, because an experienced quarterback would pick it apart.

The NFL viewed the zone as a college-style defense. But AFL coaches like Stram, who had coached in the college ranks, adapted it to the pro game. Stram first used the zone in a 1960 game against the Houston Oilers. The Oilers featured a pass-oriented offense led by bombs-away quarterback George Blanda and a pair of fleet receivers in Charley Hennigan and Bill Groman. Both could run the 100-yard dash in 9.5 seconds. Stram's cornerbacks at the time were David Grayson and Carroll Zaruba, each of whom ran a 10-flat in the 100. Fearing a series of big plays, Stram installed a double-zone. The strategy worked. Stram's team picked off three passes in a 24–0 win. Other AFL coaches took note and began using zones with more frequency and proficiency.

By 1968, Namath had so much experience deciphering the exotic zone coverages used by AFL defenses that the Colts zone looked simple in comparison. He was reading coverages with ease and puncturing it with precision passes.

> Gowdy: *"Namath has the time, shoots the ball, and completes it. George Sauer has a first down. How that Namath can rifle that ball."*
>
> Rote: *"That was a 25-yard pass, just like a bullet."*

As Namath's rocket right arm riddled the Colts pass coverage, and as his white cleats carried him away from the blitz, Baltimore's defense grew increasingly flustered. Snell could see that the Colts were pressing and could see the frustration and worry on their faces. One of the distinctive memories he has from that game is the look of bewilderment on the faces of the Colts defense. Members of the Jets offense could also hear the Colts cursing themselves and questioning each other:

"How come you didn't get through?"

"I had a man on me."

"So did I."

"Well, one of us was supposed to be free."

New York was handling the heralded Colts blitz three ways. Ewbank had helped Paul Brown develop the concept of "pocket protection" in Cleveland a decade earlier, and to blunt the blitz, the Jets would pull their free lineman, the one unoccupied, and slide him to the side where the blitz was coming from. DeRogatis, a former NFL lineman, saw what was happening and praised New York's offensive linemen:

> "Curt, let me just talk about some people that kind of go unsung. This offensive line of New York has been superb. John Schmitt at center, outstanding blocking. Randy Rasmussen, who moved from left guard to right guard, is doing a great job on Billy Ray Smith. Dave Herman, outweighed substantially, is doing a terrific job, as is [Bob] Talamini on the left side and Winston Hill."

Hill was doing such a great job on his former tormentor in Colts training camp, Ordell Braase, it would cause Snell to say later that "Braase pretty much faded out."

Brown, who was intently watching the game that matched former pupils Ewbank and Shula and former players Walt Michaels and Chuck Noll, found himself admiring Namath's abilities. "He can really wing that ball in there," he said later. "He had strength and accuracy, and you'd better get to him or he'll pass you out of the park."

The swaggering Namath was calling a precise, patient game. "Standing in that press box and watching Namath unravel the NFL myth," Howard Cosell said later, "was a thing to behold."

Shula watched Broadway Joe pick apart his defense and thought, "Not many quarterbacks can do that to us." He was also impressed with the skill that Snell, Boozer, and Mathis showed in picking up blitzing linebackers and safeties. Shula knew the Jets backs could block; he didn't know they could block *that* well.

New York also used what Ewbank called "blitz control," a concept similar to safety-valve passing and hot reads. Whichever Jets running back was not kept in to block would release into the open flat and thus give Namath an extra receiver to go to if he was pressured or if his downfield receivers were covered. AFL teams had learned it wasn't such a good idea to blitz the Jets, Ewbank said. "Joe has such quick wrists—bing! It's there. We like the blitz."

Stunting and looping, shifting their fronts, blitzing their linebackers and safeties, sending eight, sometimes nine men after Namath, the veteran Colts threw their whole defensive package at the young quarterback.

> Gowdy: *"Baltimore has gone to the blitz heavy. They're behind, and they're trying to get in there on Namath. And Namath has been reading those blitzes."*

From his cornerback position, Boyd saw what New York was doing and thought it was a smart plan. "Every time they read a weak safety blitz, Sauer ran an I-cut [inside slant] automatically," he said. "He just took off, and Namath hit him with those quick passes."

> Gowdy: *"Baltimore stunting around... Namath, nice protection, completes it to Snell... It's a first down and Namath is picking the vaunted Baltimore secondary to pieces."*
>
> Rote: *"Again, you see where Namath throws that ball without hardly setting up at all. He's still leaning backwards, and he fires that ball on a line."*

On running plays, Namath continued to hand off to Snell, who hammered away at the sagging right side of the defense. Running "19-Straight" or "19-Cutback," Snell followed Hill, Talamini, Boozer, and sometimes Mathis for steady gains. "Joe was content to play a cautious game," Sample said. As the game wore on, the Colts aging veterans on the right side—the 36-year-old Braase, the 33-year-old Lyles and Shinnick—wore down under the hammering blows on New York's weak-side slant.

"We knew Namath could throw the football," Logan said. "But it really wasn't Namath's passing, it was Snell's running that made the difference."

The Colts could feel the Jets adrenaline pumping a little more with each play. Gone was the wide-eyed fear Baltimore center Bill Curry thought he had seen in the Jets eyes at the start of the game. It had been replaced by what Curry described as a "brightness." The Colts not only saw a transformation in the Jets, they felt it as well. The tempo of New York's hitting increased as the game turned in their favor.

The Jets felt the change, as well. New York's linemen noticed that the Colts were beginning to hang their heads. Defensive end Gerry Philbin, who spent the afternoon battling tackle Sam Ball, thought old age, heat, and frustration were combining to wear down Baltimore.

While the starting lineups were nearly identical in physical size, the Jets averaged five years of pro football experience, the Colts seven. Ewbank thought the two-year difference was significant in terms of physical and emotional resiliency. He believed that pro players reached their peak in their fourth and fifth seasons. Once beyond that, he thought they had a harder time sustaining a big effort for a prolonged time.

Braase had alluded to that fact before the game. "I'll tell you one thing about the game of football," he said. "The older you get, the more of a strain it becomes."

The third quarter was draining away, and so was the Colts confidence. Baltimore's ferocious defense was battered. Braase had been driven from the game with a bad back; the aging Shinnick had been replaced at left linebacker; Volk, still suffering from a concussion, was vomiting on the sideline. Sideline cameras showed several of the Colts taped up and limping; others were receiving smelling salts to clear their heads. The Jets were hurting, as well. Middle linebacker Al Atkinson had injured his shoulder just before halftime and had been replaced for a few plays by Grantham, who moved from outside linebacker to the middle. Team doctor James Nicholas told Atkinson he had suffered a badly bruised shoulder, but he returned to the field. "I'm gonna play if that arm falls off," Atkinson said. Snell had re-injured his knee on his touchdown run, and Namath had re-injured his passing hand.

The intense hitting in Super Bowl III was taking a toll on both sides. On the Jets sideline, the team's artist-in-residence, LeRoy Neiman, was capturing the drama in his signature splashy sketches. The game had such an impact on him that more than 40 years later, Neiman could still recall all the elements of the battle—the breathing, the profanity, the sweat, the clashing of pads.

Running a cautious, conservative offense, New York had controlled the ball for all but two minutes of the third quarter. To Preston Pearson, this was ball-control football at its best. Baltimore's offense, meanwhile, had been on the field for just seven plays.

Dusk was descending on the Orange Bowl. For the proud Colts, a day that had dawned with such great expectations was becoming a day of defeat. Pacing the sideline, Shula turned to the one man who had proved himself the champion of such seemingly lost causes.

With 3:51 showing in the third quarter, John Unitas was called upon to recapture the magic that had made him a legend. In his weakened arm and champion's heart lay the last hope for Baltimore and the NFL.

15

Two Champions
on a Sunday Afternoon

As John Unitas pulled on his Colts helmet and prepared to rescue the NFL champions from a distastrous defeat late in the third quarter, he felt a tap on his shoulder. The old master turned around.

"Good luck, John," Earl Morrall said.

The sight of No. 19 taking the field sent shivers of excitement through both teams and throughout the Orange Bowl. The sellout crowd greeted him with a rousing ovation. Preston Pearson listened to the roar and thought it a mix of surprise and joy. The cheers grew louder, so loud that Pearson later described it as a sound that one could touch and feel.

Jets cornerback Johnny Sample heard the commotion, then turned and saw a familiar figure entering the game. "Damn," Sample said. "Here comes Unitas."

As NBC-TV cameras showed Johnny U jogging onto the field, Curt Gowdy made the dramatic announcement above the cascade of noise:

> "Unitas is going into the game now and Unitas gets, well, almost a standing ovation, as he should... One of the greatest players in the history of pro football."

Al DeRogatis watched Unitas take his familiar place in the Baltimore huddle. The dramatic entrance of the NFL's greatest quarterback, he said, made this the point in the game where the champions of the AFL had to make their stand.

> DeRogatis: *"This is really the series where the Jets have to come on, because of the inspirational leadership of John Unitas. He was brilliant in the past, still has it, and this man can really move a football team."*

Johnny U's presence stirred the Colts hopes. Pearson was so excited he wanted to join the more than 75,000 fans inside the Orange Bowl and cheer. Alex Hawkins looked at Unitas as the Miracle Man. Johnny U had conquered similar odds in the past. Now he was the Colts only hope, Hawkins thought. Guard Glenn Ressler felt the same surge of confidence.

"We were really frustrated," he said. "But when Unitas came in, we felt like we were going to move the ball."

Halfback Tom Matte looked at Unitas and thought, "There's still time. When John came into the huddle, everyone came to attention," he said. "Unitas was the guy, he was the leader. He stepped up."

On the Colts sideline, the defense perked up, as well. Heads that had been bowed in despair were now being lifted in hope. "When John went in the game," safety Jerry Logan said, "our attitude changed."

Offensive coach Don McCafferty thought that if he had to play catch-up football, he'd rather go with Johnny U than anyone.

Across the field, Weeb Ewbank saw Unitas head into the Colts huddle and instantly became nervous. With Unitas, even an ailing Unitas, he thought, anything could happen. "When I saw Unitas, I was scared," he said. "I'd seen John do so many great things before."

Unitas' dramatic entry threatened to change the complexion of the game. His teammates thought Johnny U had the look of a legend about him. In fact, they called him Legend. When he took his place in the huddle, they would ask, "What'd ya say, Legend?" But it was never said with irreverence; to them, and others, Johnny U really was a legend. Tight end John Mackey felt there was something special about being in the huddle with Unitas in big games. It was, Mackey said, "like being in the huddle with God."

Teammates would stare into his eyes, see the scar on his crooked nose, and believe that everything was going to be fine. That Johnny U would win the game for them almost seemed matter-of-fact. Inside the huddle, Unitas rarely gave pep talks. He approached each situation in a straight-forward manner. He would ask his receivers, "What ya got?" and tell his linemen, "Let's go, keep them out."

As Unitas prepared to call his first play in Super Bowl III, teammates wondered if Johnny U might flip the script, might say something dramatic. Something along the lines of "All right, men. We are the Baltimore Colts from the NFL. Let's handle ourselves accordingly and win this game."

Instead, Unitas stayed with his business-like approach. "Okay, we gotta get two touchdowns," he said. "Let's do it."

Ressler felt a surge of confidence. "John could make something happen," he said. "Everything you expected a sports hero to be, he was it."

Showing a spark that had been missing, the Colts spun from the huddle and charged to the line in a suppressed dog-trot. Members of the Jets defense saw Unitas striding to the line of scrimmage and tightened up. Sample, a teammate of Johnny U's on Baltimore's title teams a decade earlier, tried to break the tension.

"Man, you know you don't want to play today," he shouted at Unitas.

The old master grinned. Sample sweated. He considered Unitas the greatest quarterback ever, a man who was as much a leader as he was a player. Unitas was hurting physically and his arm may not be what it once was, but Sample knew Johnny U would remain calm and cool and that he would inspire the rest of the Colts. He understood the psychological boost Baltimore would get by having their old champion in the game. Unitas had pulled the Colts out of seemingly hopeless situations before, and Sample found himself wondering, could Johnny U do it again?

Jets linebacker Larry Grantham wondered, as well. Grantham had heard the stories emanating from the NFL through the years about the Unitas magic; he had seen it for himself on occasion in televised games. Like most of the Jets, Grantham had never been on the same field with Johnny U, until now. The AFL veteran and his teammates feared Unitas' history as a clutch quarterback.

"Unitas had a big mental impact on us," Grantham said.

Jets safety Bill Baird believed it. He remembered his rookie camp with the Colts in 1963 and thought of the Unitas he knew then the passing master with the golden arm. Baird grew nervous. On New York's sideline, guard Dave Herman looked on with worry. Just a few moments earlier, Herman had been part of an offensive huddle that was so loose it was fun. Namath was smiling and asking teammates, "How's everything goin' guys?" and the linemen would respond by talking confidently about what they were going to do to their Colts counterparts on the next play. But Herman looked at Unitas calling signals and thought he saw a legend in Baltimore blue-and-white. Who knew whether he had one more great comeback in him?

"We had set the tone for the game and were thinking, 'This is great. We're gonna win,'" Herman said. "Then I saw Unitas. And I thought 'Oh my God. Here he comes. It's over with.'"

Namath's mood turned serious, as well. If there was an NFL mystique, he thought, no one defined it more than Johnny U, his boyhood idol. Team physician Dr. James Nicholas noticed that Namath was suddenly pacing the sidelines, urging his teammates not to let down. "When we get the ball, we gotta score!" Namath shouted. "We gotta score!" Namath would say later that at that point in Super Bowl III, the only thing standing between the Jets and a world championship was a three syllable word—"Unitas."

Ewbank, for a brief moment, lapsed into the misty past, when he coached Johnny U in Baltimore. "No interceptions now, John," he said.

On his first play, Unitas turned and handed off to Matte, who swept right for five yards. On second down, Unitas decided to test his sore arm. As he took the center snap and backpedaled in classic fashion, the Orange Bowl audience and millions of fans across the nation leaned forward in their seats. If Johnny U could throw without overwhelming pain, there was still time for a Colts rally. Unitas pivoted to his right and completed a short pass to Matte, but Grantham stopped him for no gain. He followed with another short throw, this time to Jimmy Orr, but the pass was dropped.

> *Gowdy: "The ball wobbled out there. It wasn't a typical Unitas pass."*

As day turned to night and a bright moon appeared over Miami, Namath resumed his attack on the Colts right flank. Snell, his white uniform bearing streaks of grass stains from his collisions with the soggy Orange Bowl turf, continued to provide the thunder to Namath's lightning. Joe Willie, his white shoes flashing beneath the stadium lights, continued to pick apart Baltimore's zone. He found split end George Sauer for 11 yards and then for 39.

> *Gowdy: "The Jets on the 50 with a first down. They have 16 first downs to six for Baltimore... [Namath] deep, retreats, a long shot to Sauer... He's got it! He had the inside step on Lenny Lyles again... And what a job this interior line is doing for Namath..."*

By this time in the game, even the Colts were impressed by Namath. Center Bill Curry had joined the NFL as a member of the Green Bay Packers in 1965. He played alongside Bart Starr and Unitas, and he had seen every NFL quarterback up close. But he hadn't seen anyone, he thought, who had a better drop-back than Broadway Joe or got rid of the ball quicker. Curry thought Namath was a kind of poetry in motion. Those beautiful, nimble feet carrying him back, Curry thought, plus a wonderfully quick release, and hard to beat.

Baltimore continued to blitz, but Namath's rapid retreat and rapier release allowed him to get rid of the ball a split second before the Colts could get to him. "Can't Get Next To You" was a Motown hit for the Temptations in the late 1960s, and it also served as the theme song for the Colts defense in Super Bowl III.

The third quarter ended with Snell hammering to Baltimore's 6-yard line. Two plays into the final quarter, after Bill Mathis fought his way to the Colts 2, Jim Turner drilled his third field goal of the day, this from the 9, to give New York a 16–0 lead with 13:26 remaining.

Time was running out on the Colts. As Unitas came back onto the field, Sample hollered at him. "You know better, John. This just isn't the day for your team." Sample didn't expect Unitas to answer, and he didn't. He wasn't the kind of guy to respond to harassment, and Sample knew it. What Unitas did do was get back to work. He opened with a five-yard completion to Mackey, then sent Matte sweeping right for seven. Shockingly, the first down was Baltimore's first of the second half. Unitas dropped back and hit Willie Richardson for five yards. Sample followed Richardson into the Colts bench and was drilled in the back of the helmet by tight end Tom Mitchell.

Matte followed guard Dan Sullivan off the left side for a gain of 19 yards. The Colts were in Jets territory for the first time since the first half.

> Gowdy: *"The Colts are moving now, they're surging. Unitas is moving the club, he's inspired them."*

Namath thought the Jets defense was bending. From the Jets 37-yard line, Jerry Hill bucked for 12 yards off right tackle and another first down for Baltimore. Two plays later, Unitas sent Orr on a deep post pattern. As he approached the end zone, Orr was a step ahead of cornerback Randy Beverly. A good throw would give the Colts a touchdown, but as Unitas launched his pass, a shiver of pain ran up his arm and the old master cringed.

Merle Harmon called the play on Jets radio:

> *"Unitas goes back to pass, he's in the pocket... Unitas throwing for the end zone... It is intercepted in the end zone by Randy Beverly! He downs the ball..."*
> Gowdy: *"That's the fourth interception by the Jets."*

The Colts promising drive had ended in another frustrating turnover. Still, Unitas had proved he could move the ball against the Jets. But New York's defense was no longer the only obstacle or even the most important. Time was an enemy, as well. Namath, who would not throw another pass in the game, was content to keep the ball on the ground. He directed another time-consuming drive, and Snell, Emerson Boozer, and Bill Mathis took turns grinding out yards and grinding down the clock. The Jets march carried from their 20 to the Baltimore 35 and took five minutes off the scoreboard clock. Turner attempted a 42-yard field goal, but it was no good.

There was 6:34 left, and Baltimore was still three scores down. The fourth quarter was dying. So, too, were the hopes of the Colts and the NFL. Unitas threw three straight incompletions. The king, Namath thought, was struggling. Fourth-and-10 and it appeared as if Johnny U's magic had vanished for good. There would be no miracles, it seemed, from the Colts Miracle Man.

But with the game, the season, Baltimore's championship hopes and the NFL's reputation all riding on fourth down, the old master reached back and reclaimed his youth. Unitas found Orr for a 17-yard completion and suddenly it was 1958 again. The Orange Bowl buzzed with excitement. Unitas hit Mackey for 11 yards and the Colts gained 15 more on a personal foul penalty. Dropping, wheeling, faking, Unitas stirred images of the young maestro who had orchestrated the Colts comeback victory against New York's other championship team, the Giants, a decade earlier. Everything about him—the blue-and-white Colts jersey, the famous No. 19, the white helmet with blue horseshoe logo, the black hightop cleats—seemed classic and familiar and struck a responsive chord with the crowd.

Pearson thought Unitas was reaching deep into himself, back to his glory days. Unitas threw to Richardson for 21 yards and then to Orr for 11. "He was moving the ball," Sample said, "hitting his receivers for good gains." It's not over yet, thought Namath.

The Colts were at the Jets 2-yard line, but it took three more plays before Hill burrowed into the end zone behind Ressler and left tackle Bob Vogel.

> Gowdy: "*They give it to Hill and he goes over. Baltimore finally gets on the scoreboard with 3:19 to play... Can the Jets hold?*"

Unitas had driven the Colts 80 yards in 14 plays, and had done so by coolly converting twice on third down and once on fourth. Given new life, Baltimore still believed in a comeback. So, too, did New York. "Watch the kick," several Jets shouted from the sideline. "Watch for the ball."

Lou Michaels squibbed the ensuing kickoff and the ball squirted out of Sauer's hands and was recovered by Tom Mitchell of the Colts at the Jets 44. Namath exploded in frustration. "Damn!" he shouted. More than three minutes remained, and the ball would once again be in the hands of Johnny U. The Jets were shaken. The Colts have the ball, Sample thought, and the momentum. They also had the crowd behind them. Unitas had recaptured the fans that had gone over to Namath earlier in the game. Joe Willie listened to the crowd thundering as Unitas came back onto the field. A touchdown and a field goal, Namath realized, would win it for Baltimore.

> Gowdy: "As long as Unitas is in there, this isn't over... He just took Baltimore 80 yards."

"I thought, 'Okay, here we go,'" Pearson said. "Johnny couldn't throw the ball with any real steam, but he had a presence."

On first down, Unitas found Richardson for six yards. He hit Orr for 14 more. The Colts were at the Jets 24, poised to score again.

> Gowdy: "It's amazing how many plays you can get off if you work those sidelines..."
>
> DeRogatis: "Here, Curt, is where John Unitas is absolutely brilliant. He has no fear when it comes to the two- and three-minutes to go in the game. The down-and-outs, the look-ins... He's just brilliant."

Pandemonium reigned inside the stadium. The Orange Bowl had replaced Baltimore's Memorial Stadium as the world's largest outdoor insane asylum. Unitas seemed least affected by the craziness. Sportswriter Jimmy Cannon wrote that the football field becomes a "quiet lawn" when Unitas walks on it:

"The screams of the buffs don't seem to reach him. The excitement subsides around him as he strolls toward the center's rump. The great quarterback acts as if he is in some private place.... It is as though he can establish a personal solitude in a congested stadium."

Johnny U's celebrated calm amazed his teammates, as well. Curry would look at him—"that ol' humpacked, bowleggedy guy," he called him—and it didn't seem from a physical standpoint as if Unitas could do anything great. But there was something in his personal makeup that was inspiring. The great defensive linemen of the era—Merlin Olsen, Deacon Jones, Alan Page, Willie Davis, Bob Lilly—would be clawing at the Colts quarterback as he stood in the pocket and prepared to pass, but Curry never saw Unitas flinch. Olsen had a thunderous voice and would be two feet away from Unitas when he'd shout in an effort to distract him.

"John! John!"

Olsen's voice was so strong it rattled the ears of the Colts linemen.

"John! John!"

Unitas was unmoved. "I just can't understand it," Olsen would say after games. "Unitas will not flinch. Nothing fazes that man."

Robert Liston interviewed Unitas and other NFL players in the mid-1960s for his book, *The Pros*, and found that while most men doubt themselves, question their abilities, worry about their mistakes, Unitas seemed to bypass the process. Liston found him to be totally self-confident. Liston was certain that if it was third-and-long with time for only one play in a championship game, Unitas would have no doubt nor hesitation about which play to call.

Johnny U had no doubt which were the right plays to call late in Super Bowl III. Continuing to work the sidelines to save time, he connected with Richardson for a gain of five and the Colts were at the Jets 19.

> Gowdy: "Unitas is really getting hot. Unitas, in dramatic fashion, after being injured all year, coming off the bench and trying to save the Colts from one of sports history's biggest upsets."

The social significance of the moment could not be missed. Conservatives who had sat mostly silent through a game dominated by a shaggy-haired symbol of the counterculture suddenly erupted in cheers for their hero—the crewcut quarterback.

Is it possible, Hawkins wondered, for a proud old man like Unitas to reach down in that bag of tricks and come up with some miracles to bail out this one?

Unitas had succeeded in turning Super Bowl III into a romantic classic—Namath, the young rebel, had proved his worth, but the old master was rallying against all odds.

> Gowdy: *"Unitas is now 10 out of 19 (passing)...If he pulls this one out, what a story it's going to be."*

The dramatic impact that writers and historians would see in a Colts comeback wasn't lost on the Jets. They saw the game's final moments as a showdown between the young gun who had led the AFL to victory's doorstep and the aging legend who was trying to save the NFL from defeat.

Some of the Colts looked across the field and thought the AFL champions appeared thunderstruck. Pearson, a student of sports history, felt the Jets looked as if they suddenly expected to play Ralph Branca to Baltimore's Bobby Thomson. Herman doesn't deny it. "I thought, 'Here we go,'" he said. "Here comes the legend."

Even Namath seemed awed by the moment. He would later say he thought it was beautiful the way his boyhood idol, Unitas, could work a defense, keep it off-balance, and move the ball down the field.

Super Bowl III was no longer Jets versus Colts; AFL versus NFL. On some level, it was two sons of western Pennsylvania mill towns locked in a personal duel. Namath felt it, felt the game had become a showdown between New School and Old School. No one, he thought, could have asked for a better story.

Unitas, still reaching back for more of the old magic, fired a pass to Richardson on second down. Sample batted it away. On third down from New York's 19, Unitas underthrew Orr.

Fourth down and five yards to go.

Shula had a choice. He could call on Michaels for a field goal that could cut the Colts deficit to 16-10, and then hope to regain another onside kickoff and go for the winning touchdown. But Michaels was not a sure thing. He had misfired from the same distance on Baltimore's opening drive of the game. The salty crosswind in the Orange Bowl was still tricky; Michaels and Turner both missed two field goals on the day.

If the Colts could score a touchdown on this drive, they would still need to recover an onside kick. If they did, a field goal could win it for them.

Baltimore had momentum on its side, as well as Unitas. Shula decided to go for it all on this drive.

> Gowdy: "This will be it for Baltimore if they don't hit this one."

As Johnny U approached the line of scrimmage, the Orange Bowl was in an uproar. He scanned the Jets defense, shouted signals, then took the snap.

> Gowdy: "Unitas back..."

Fading to pass, Unitas read the movements of New York's defenders. He looked in the direction of Orr. He set up in the pocket as the Jets' front line strained to reach him.

> Gowdy: "His pass..."

Unitas fired a spiral to Orr.

> Gowdy: "Incomplete! ... The Jets take over."

Finally, it had ended. Unitas had ignored pain and injury to take the Colts as far as he could. "Give Johnny Unitas a lot of credit," Gowdy told his audience, "for rallying Baltimore."

The rally, heroic as it was, had fallen short. And now, for the first time, the NFL champions realized they were going to lose.

Jets fans in the Orange Bowl chanted "A-F-L! A-F-L!" Grantham took off his helmet and flung it high into the night air in celebration.

New York's offense took over with 2:21 to go, and Namath engineered one final drive that exhausted all but eight seconds off the clock. When Baltimore finally got the ball back, NFL referee Tommy Bell paid a quick visit to their huddle.

"Now men, you're champions," Bell said. "Let's finish this game like champions and leave the field with your heads held high."

Harmon counted down the final seconds:

"Two seconds, one second... Unitas throwing to Richardson. He has the ball on the 49, brought down by Sample... The clock has run out, and the ball game is over! There is the gun, and the Jets are champions of the football world!"

Super Bowl III had been a historic battle between champions, and no two players had exemplified that more than Broadway Joe and Johnny U. Namath because of his skill; Unitas because of his will.

They were two champions on a Sunday afternoon, vying for a trophy only one could win.

16

The AFL Comes of Age

At 5:40 PM (EST), the final gun sounded, ending Super Bowl III. Covered in grass stains and glory, the Jets literally leapt with joy as they ran across the darkened field of the Miami Orange Bowl.

Jets coach Weeb Ewbank met his Colts counterpart, Don Shula, at midfield.

"We got all the breaks," Ewbank said.

"Your team played well," Shula responded.

"Nice of you to say that," Ewbank said.

The Colts walked slowly off the field, their horseshoed helmets hung in stunned defeat. Baltimore special teams star Alex Hawkins had to convince himself that the seemingly impossible had indeed happened. Before he left the field, he stopped, turned around, and stared once more at the scoreboard:

Jets 16, Colts 7.

Behind the Jets bench, AFL players stood with pride. San Diego Chargers star receiver Lance Alworth, who would become the first AFL player to be inducted into the Pro Football Hall of Fame, had jumped from his seat late in the game when he realized the Jets were on the verge of winning. "They're doing it!" he shouted with a mix of joy and wonderment. "They're doing it!"

Kansas City Chiefs quarterback Len Dawson, who was a year away from engineering his own Super Bowl upset of an NFL favorite, sat quietly for three quarters while fans around him degraded the American Football League. When the final Colts rally had failed, Dawson stood and confronted his hecklers. "How do we look now against the great NFL?" he asked.

Weaving his way through the crowd pouring onto the field, Joe Namath bowed his helmet and raised his right arm and index finger high into the night air. The Jets were No. 1. Broadway Joe felt a surge of inner joy so strong it literally tingled.

The AFL had come of age, and because it had, the Super Bowl was now on its way to becoming the nation's premier sporting event.

On NBC Radio, sportscaster Charlie Jones told listeners that New York's victory answered "all the questions about the future of the Super Bowl."

The mood inside the winner's locker room was a mix of elation and relief. "If this win means anything," guard Bob Talamini said, "it's that the AFL and NFL are equal and can be mentioned in the same breath."

Linebacker Ralph Baker waited for reporters to enter New York's boisterous locker room, then called out to his teammates. "Hey, you guys hear the latest? We've just been made 14-point underdogs to the College All-Stars."

Namath, named Most Valuable Player and awarded a Dodge Charger by *Sport* magazine, refused at first to talk with NFL writers. Finally, he relented. When he met with reporters, his face was still covered with grime from the field and his famous knees were being freed from yards of protective tape and wrappings.

"I told you so," Namath said, and NFL writers like Jerry Green of the *Detroit News* thought Broadway Joe had earned the right to gloat. "We beat 'em in every phase of the game. I never thought there was any question about our moving against their 'great' defense."

"Joe was fabulous," Ewbank said. "He called a great game. The running game was going good, so we stuck with that."

The prime mover in the running game, fullback Matt Snell, could have been named MVP. Rather than talk himself up, he paid tribute to Talamini, Winston Hill, John Schmitt, Randy Rasmussen, and Dave Herman.

"Our offensive line won the game with its straight-ahead blocking," Snell said. "Their defensive line likes to hit and slide off the tackle. They have great pursuit, so we didn't want to try to run anything that would delay hitting the hole.

"We were hitting to the right side of their defensive line. I've been telling reporters for a long time that Winston Hill is a great offensive tackle, and today he proved it. I mean, when he blocks he doesn't just get a stalemate with the guy he's on. He blows him out."

Hill returned the compliment when he told reporters that Snell was a great runner who didn't ask for much room. Mediocre running backs, Hill said, always came back to the huddle and cried if they didn't get a hole big enough to back a truck through. Not Snell.

Was he surprised, Hill was asked, that the Jets ran so effectively against a Baltimore defense that had dominated the NFL?

Hill shook his head. "We ran against the best teams in our league," he said. "What's so special about the Colts?"

Backfield mate Emerson Boozer credited Al Atkinson, Larry Grantham, Verlon Biggs, Randy Beverly, et al. "It was our defense," Boozer said, "that broke their back."

Jets cornerback Johnny Sample took a yellowed newspaper clipping from his wallet, unfolded it and showed it to reporters:

KC Not in Class With NFL's Best—Lombardi.

Sample had carried the clipping since January 16, 1967, the day after Vince Lombardi's Green Bay Packers had beaten Kansas City by 25 points in Super Bowl I. Now it was Sample's turn to hold court about the relative merits of the AFL and NFL.

"It'll take the NFL 20 years to catch us," he said. "Kansas City and Oakland are better than the Colts.... They panicked. They were so shaken up they forgot the game plan.... We're the greatest team ever."

Jim Turner, whose three field goals provided the margin of victory, was struck by the emotion of the moment. It was something, Turner said, to see AFL players like Kansas City's huge defensive tackle Buck Buchanan breaking down and crying tears of joy.

When NBC-TV analyst Kyle Rote asked Gerry Philbin if anything about the game surprised him, the defensive end nodded.

"The fact that Baltimore scored at all," Philbin said.

Philbin would stay in his grass-stained white uniform for some time after the game. "I'm waiting for Tex Maule," Philbin said, referring to *Sports Illustrated*'s NFL writer. "When is Maule coming in here?"

Maule never showed. Later, he would say that the outcome of Super Bowl III "made me sick."

He began his cover story for *Sports Illustrated* praising Namath:

"Broadway Joe Namath is the folk hero of the new generation. He is long hair, a Fu Manchu mustache worth $10,000 to shave off, swinging nights at the live spots of the big city, the dream lover of the stewardi—all that spells insouciant youth in the Jet age.

"Besides all that, Namath is a superb quarterback who in the Super Bowl last week proved that his talent is as big as his mouth—which makes it a very big talent, indeed. He went from Broadway Joe to Super Joe on a cloud-covered afternoon in Miami, whipping the Baltimore Colts, champions of the National Football League, 16-7 in the process."

Maule said later he had to "lean over backward" to give New York full credit for the victory. So he emphasized Namath's passing and his ability to beat Baltimore's blitz. Covering Broadway Joe for the first time, he saw in him many of the same qualities he saw in John Unitas. "They are so different," Maule wrote at the close of his Super Bowl story, "yet so very much alike."

Maule also emphasized George Sauer's receptions and Snell's hard running. "What I did not point out," he said later, "was that the Colts, given a little more luck, might have put the ball game out of reach in the first half."

The *New York Daily News* played up the Namath angle as well. The banner headline for its Monday edition read "SUPERDUPER!" and featured a full-page photo of a smiling Namath savoring victory. "B-way Joe Jolts Colts by 16-7" served as the drop headline.

In his story, *Daily News* writer Larry Fox stated:

"They challenged Joe Namath to put up or shut up today and Broadway Joe hadn't stopped talking yet. In one of pro football's greatest upsets, the Jets scored the AFL's first Super Bowl victory in three tries by beating the Colts."

When NFL commissioner Pete Rozelle walked into the Jets locker room to present the Tiffany Super Bowl trophy, he was greeted with shouts from several players:

"Welcome to the AFL!"

Namath said later he didn't realize the impact the victory had on AFL players and coaches until they arrived at New York's hotel later that night and thanked the Jets for proving their league had come of age.

"That's what made our victory more special," Namath said. "We won it for the old Houston Oilers and Kansas City Chiefs and all those AFL teams that hung in there the first five years when things were bleak. When I saw those guys from the Chiefs and Raiders with tears in their eyes, that's when I felt proud."

The Colts were feeling anything but proud. Their locker room had all the life of a morgue. Coach Don Shula likened the defeat to a death knell. "We were the first NFL team to lose a Super Bowl to the upstart AFL," he said. "Nobody will ever forget that."

Shula told his players that despite their disappointment, they would have to take this loss like men.

No one had to tell Unitas, who was his usual stoic self. "How good is Namath?" someone asked. Johnny U shrugged.

"Sixteen-seven," he said.

Unitas always believed that if he had started the game or at least the second half, he would have beaten the Jets. "Things would have ended up differently," he would say.

Shula understood Unitas' thoughts on Super Bowl III. Johnny U, he said, had great belief in his own ability, belief that sooner or later, things would fall into place for him. "And," Shula added, "they did."

One of the Jets concerns was that Unitas would enter the game at some point. When he finally did, Namath nudged Sauer on the sideline. "Johnny U," Broadway Joe said.

"Come on clock," Sauer responded.

Why didn't Shula replace Morrall with Unitas earlier? Everything that happened in the first half, Shula said, all the crazy plays, the tipped passes, were not all Morrall's fault. Shula had decided at half-time to give Morrall one more series to put some points on the board and told Johnny U, "Be ready." But halfback Tom Matte's fumble short-circuited the first series, and by the time Unitas did take the field, Namath had exhausted much of the third-quarter clock with time-consuming marches.

Afterward, Morrall stood by his locker and answered a line of questioning that would have done justice to the Inquisition. Most of the queries had to do with the failed flea-flicker pass. Ewbank knew Baltimore might use it; it had been in Cleveland's playbook when he and Shula were on Paul Brown's squad. Brown called it the "triple pass."

"I should have seen him," Morrall said of Jimmy Orr. "Countless people have told me he was wide open. But I had to turn to the right to take the pass from Matte and when I looked up, Jimmy wasn't in my line of vision. Jerry Hill was, and I went to him."

Some of the Colts thought their team was unprepared to play the game. Some felt the squad was overconfident; others disagreed. At the time, flanker Willie Richardson called the 1968 Colts the "hungriest team I've ever seen." Matte said Baltimore was motivated by a fear of losing. The Colts knew that the AFL was eventually going to win a Super Bowl. "You damn sure don't want to be on the first NFL team to lose to them," Matte said. The Colts were up for the game because they were representing more than themselves, he said, they were representing an entire league.

"We have had a great year," Matte said. "But if we blow it Sunday, no one will remember that we lost only one game during the regular season. They'll remember that we were the NFL team that lost for the first time in a Super Bowl."

One Colts player who preferred anonymity said that when the NFL champs did find themselves losing, they lost their poise, just as Sample said they did. "We should have had points on the board with the way we moved the ball, and we were behind 7–0," he said. "We should have stuck with the game plan, but we began to panic. That's what they were supposed to do, but they played with great poise. We didn't."

Stung by the upset, some Colts were less than complimentary toward the AFL champions in the locker room.

Center Bill Curry: "It seems stupid to say, but we played 10 or 12 teams better than the Jets."

Middle linebacker Dennis Gaubatz: "They still don't impress me. The breaks didn't come our way. We're still a better ballclub."

Tight end John Mackey: "We beat ourselves."

Outside linebacker Don Shinnick lamented his lost chance at a drive-killing interception of Namath on the Jets lone touchdown march. "I was a little off-balance, and I had to make sure I knocked it down. I should have had it."

Frustrated with his team's missed opportunities, Shula still sought to be gracious toward the Jets.

"Namath beat our blitz more than it beat him," Shula said. "We didn't do it, and they did. We had all the opportunities, especially in the first half. We didn't make the big plays we have all season. They deserved it."

No one deserved it more so than Ewbank. Today, Colts players give more credit to the Jets elfin coach for beating them than they give to Namath, Snell, the Jets offensive line, Sauer, Don Maynard, or New York's defense.

"Namath did an excellent job of reading our coverages and getting the ball to the open spot," Colts defensive captain Bobby Boyd said. "But Weeb knew our strong-side zone, our weak-side zone, all of our coverages. And he knew our personnel because he had coached a lot of us."

"Snell was a good running back, and they had a good offensive line," said safety Rick Volk, who went into convulsions after the game and had to be rushed to the hospital. "Weeb, though, knew everything about the Colts. He knew our weak points on offense and defense."

Despite the fact that he will forever be the only man to win championships in the NFL and AFL, and despite being 4-1 in the post-season—4-0 in title games—and developing two of the game's greatest quarterbacks in Unitas and Namath, Ewbank is rarely mentioned when talk turns to the NFL's greatest coaches. His legacy, however, suggests he should be. It was Ewbank, after all, who was the winning coach in the two most important games in pro football history—the 1958 NFL championship and Super Bowl III.

Hill, so instrumental in New York's success that day, said no one foresaw the lasting impact Super Bowl III would have on American sports and society.

"The long-range effect of that game, the historical aspect of the impact it had on the game of football, we didn't realize any of that at the time," Hill said.

The Colts soon did. Star linebacker Mike Curtis and some of his Baltimore teammates caught flak from NFL players at the Pro Bowl game that followed Super Bowl III. "They were looking at us like we were traitors, losing to those clowns," he said.

Green Bay middle linebacker Ray Nitschke was among those who thought the Colts had let the NFL down. "Having any AFL team win would have been bad enough, but I hated to have it done by Namath," Nitschke said. "No question about it, as a player he's outstanding. But I didn't feel he used good judgment in the things he did and said off the field.

"I'll guarantee that if it had been the Packers playing the Jets in that third Super Bowl, we wouldn't have laid an egg like the Colts."

Nitschke's teammate, Bart Starr, was named MVP of the first two Super Bowls for his masterful performances against the two preceding AFL champions. He watched Super Bowl III with mixed emotions. As an NFL man, he was naturally disappointed, he said, to see the mighty Baltimore Colts beaten. But Starr was personally pleased for Namath, a fellow University of Alabama alumnus. "What Namath and the Jets accomplished," Starr said, "was an eye-opener for most of the NFL."

Yet not an eye-opener to the degree many believe. Popular pro football history states that the Jets victory allowed the 9-year-old AFL to achieve parity with the 49-year-old NFL. The truth is, many pro football experts looked at the game as a fluke. If the AFL had truly achieved parity in Super Bowl III, its league champion in 1969, the Kansas City Chiefs, would not have been established by Vegas oddsmakers as 14-point underdogs to the NFL champion Minnesota Vikings in Super Bowl IV.

"They're doing it again," Oakland Raiders star George Blanda said. "They haven't learned a thing since last year. They're underestimating the AFL all over again."

Green was among the members of the media who stayed true to his NFL bloodlines. He figured the Vikings would handle the Chiefs and win big. "By two touchdowns," he said.

AFL writer Larry Felser of the *Buffalo Evening News*, staying true to his bloodlines, thought the point spread "absurd."

It wasn't until the massive Chiefs manhandled the physical Vikings 23-7 in New Orleans on January 11, 1970, that the AFL-NFL playing field was finally and truly level. NFL Films president Steve Sabol said that while the Jets had secured a beachhead in the AFL's charge to respectability, it was the Chiefs who broke down the final barriers.

Curry, while still contending that the '68 Colts were better than the '68 Jets, didn't share that same thought about the Vikings and Chiefs. Kansas City's Super Bowl IV squad, he opined, was much better than the Jets' Super Bowl III team. Interestingly, the two quarterbacks from Super Bowl IV, the Vikings Joe Kapp and Chiefs Len Dawson underwent a role reversal from Namath and Morrall/Unitas in Super Bowl III. This time, the NFL had the swashbuckling leader in Injun' Joe; the AFL had the older, more conservative veteran in Dawson.

New York Giants quarterback Fran Tarkenton thought after Super Bowl IV that the AFL had not only achieved parity with the NFL but had maybe even surpassed it. Kansas City, Oakland, and New York, he said, would have excelled in the NFL. "Our league," he said, "isn't as good as it used to be."

The AFL, personified by the Jets and Chiefs, evened the score with the NFL in Super Bowl victories at 2-2. It will remain that way for infinity. Under the terms of the merger, the American Football League was absorbed into the NFL prior to the 1970 season and renamed the American Football Conference. In one of the many twists to the Super Bowl III tale, the Baltimore Colts were one of three old-line NFL teams, along with Cleveland and Pittsburgh, to leave the NFC in 1970 to join the AFC.

For the Colts, the effects of their loss in Super Bowl III proved far reaching. They played without their customary swagger and confidence in 1969 and struggled to an 8-5-1 finish that left them out of the NFL playoffs. Relations between Shula and team owner Carroll Rosenbloom became strained, and Shula left Baltimore following the '69 campaign to take over as head coach in, of all places, Miami, the site of his most bitter coaching defeat.

Don McCafferty, Shula's offensive lieutenant in Super Bowl III, took over as Colts head coach in 1970 and the man affectionately called "Easy Rider" by his players for his laid-back style guided the team back to Super Bowl V. The site of the game was again the Orange Bowl, but the Colts this time managed to win 16–13 over Dallas due, in part, to the heroics of their own long-haired free spirit, kicker Jim O'Brien.

Unitas and Morrall were in different roles in 1970; Unitas was the starter, Morrall the reliever. Ironically, they reversed their roles from Super Bowl III during the game, as well. Morrall came on to replace Unitas in Super Bowl V—Johnny U was injured—and he led Baltimore to a world championship. Still, most of the Colts who played in 1968 and 1970 believe there was little comparison between the two title teams.

"The 1968 Colts were the best team I ever played on, and we lost the Super Bowl," Curtis said. "The 1970 Colts were the worst team I ever played on, and we won the Super Bowl."

The '68 Colts not only remain the best Baltimore team of their era, but also one of the best teams to lose a Super Bowl. The undefeated 2007 New England Patriots share that legacy. The Patriots, like the Colts, lost their chance to gain immortality when they suffered a Super Bowl upset to another underdog team from New York, the Giants.

After leaving Baltimore following the dismal 1969 campaign, Shula took the Dolphins to the Super Bowl three consecutive seasons (1971–73), and in 1972 he finally won the NFL championship that had eluded him for so long. His backup quarterback that season was Morrall, who subbed for starter Bob Griese and helped Miami fashion a 17–0 record, the only undefeated season in modern history. For a quarterback who had endured a series of mistakes in the Orange Bowl in Super Bowl III, returning to Miami and being a big part of a perfect season was extraordinary.

Shula and Morrall added another Super Bowl title to their records in 1973, and remain forever linked on a Dolphins squad whose 32–2 record in 1972–73 and back-to-back Super Bowl titles makes them arguably the greatest team over a two-year period in the game's modern history.

Shula's Dolphins dynasty was replaced in 1974 by the ascension of Pittsburgh's Steel Curtain, headed by another Colts coach from Super Bowl III, defensive backfield boss Chuck Noll. Between them, McCafferty, Shula, and Noll combined to dominate the AFC from 1970–75, winning six straight AFC titles and five Super Bowls.

The Jets followed their victory over Baltimore in Super Bowl III with a win over the crosstown rival New York Giants in the Yale Bowl in 1969. The highly publicized, highly charged preseason matchup marked the first meeting between New York's two pro football teams and proved as emotional for the Jets as the Super Bowl against Baltimore had been.

Cornerback John Dockery, who was entering his second season with the Jets in the summer of '69, said his teammates took their game against the Giants in the Yale Bowl as seriously as the Super Bowl.

"Oh my God, that was a huge game," Dave Herman said. "To play the Giants in the Yale Bowl.... The first play from scrimmage, I hit the guy playing against me as hard as I've ever hit anyone."

Namath threw three touchdown passes, and the Jets blew out the Giants, 37–14.

New York repeated as Eastern Division champions in 1969, the final year of the AFL. But for the first time in its history, the league had a new playoff format that allowed the second-place team from the Eastern and Western Divisions to make the playoffs as a wild-card entrant. The expanded playoffs had come at the prompting of Rozelle, and it cost the Jets a possible return trip to the Super Bowl. Rather than heading to Oakland for a title game rematch, the Jets hosted Kansas City in the first round of the playoffs in wind-swept Shea Stadium. The Chiefs surrendered just two Turner field goals and won 13–6, ending the Jets reign as Super Bowl champions.

The Namath-led Jets never returned to the playoffs after 1969. Injuries and advancing age caught up with the team, and they fell into a string of sub-par seasons. They would even lose their next four encounters with the Colts after Baltimore joined the Jets in the AFC East following the AFL-NFL merger in 1970. The Colts took out their frustration on Broadway Joe in their first meeting since Super Bowl III when they went to Shea Stadium in Week Five of the 1970 season Namath was sidelined with a broken wrist after hitting his hand on defensive tackle Fred Miller's helmet. Baltimore went on to win, 29–22.

On September 24, 1972, Namath and Unitas hooked up in one final, memorable matchup. Broadway Joe firebombed the Baltimore defense for 496 yards and six touchdowns. Unitas responded by throwing for 376 yards and two scores. New York won, 44–34, and many NFL experts cite this Namath-Unitas duel as the greatest combined display of passing in league history.

Ironically, Unitas and Namath both finished their careers on West Coast teams. Even more ironic was the fact that Johnny U retired after the 1973 season as a member of one of the AFL's original franchises, the San Diego Chargers. Broadway Joe called it a career in 1977 as a member of an NFC team, the Los Angeles Rams. The Rams would eventually migrate to St. Louis, the NFL city Namath spurned back in 1964 to sign with the AFL. Decades later, St. Louis could finally claim Joe Namath as part of its franchise's football history.

One by one, the participants of Super Bowl III left the game. But they never left it far behind. It left its mark on them physically and mentally. Today, many struggle to meet medical expenses on player pensions far too inadequate to compensate them for what they gave to the game.

"I'm 70 years old, and I have to go back to work," Matte said. "I told my kids, 'The inheritance is gone.'

"We were the creators of the game as it is today, and these modern players are the benefactors. But a lot of them don't want to give back."

"We played for the love of the game," said Herman, who like most players from the 1960s and '70s needed two jobs to survive. "I would drive into Manhattan in the morning, go to work, and then drive to Shea Stadium in the afternoon for practice. Weeb used to kid me. 'You're the only guy on the team who shows up for practice in a tie.'

"We played to win. We didn't play for paychecks."

Maynard remembers having to fight for every dollar he could get from the Jets.

"After we finished contract negotiations, Weeb would always say, 'Now don't tell anybody what you're making,'" Maynard said. "I'd say, 'Don't worry, Weeb, I won't. I'm just as ashamed of it as you are.'"

In many ways, NFL and AFL players are the NFL's forgotten war veterans, as the *Oakland Tribune* called them in a 2006 article, a band of brothers "growing old gracelessly after sacrificing life and limb not for their country but for victory on Sunday."

The players of yesteryear played through pain for their team, surrendered knees, shoulders, and other body parts for their team, and ultimately took years off their life for their team. In many cases, their reward from the guardians of the game is less than $2,000 per month. This from a league that in 2006 was projected to make $25 billion over the next eight years from TV contracts alone. That staggering figure does not include the additional billions to be made from ticket sales, memorabilia, and apparel.

And the former players who built the game are left to struggle on, through multiple surgeries and through sleepless nights. Some have trouble walking; others battle dementia. All bear the scars, physical or mental, of their Sunday battles. For some, the pain and misery is too much. They end up homeless and on the streets; some have taken their own lives.

Hall of Fame defensive end Deacon Jones became so disgusted with the league's treatment of its aging players that he boycotted the annual induction events at the Pro Football Hall of Fame in Canton, Ohio. The late Gene Upshaw, a Hall of Fame guard with the Oakland Raiders and the former NFL Players Association director, said once that the older players—many of whom were his peers—didn't hire him, couldn't fire him, and were free to complain about him all day long. His concern, he said, was focused on the active players. "That's who pays my salary," he said in 2006. And Upshaw's salary at the time was reported to be $3 million a year.

Hall of Famers Mike Ditka and Gale Sayers, among others, have taken up the battle to help their struggling brothers. In September 2007, Ditka testified before Congress on behalf of retired NFL players. Ditka has also joined with former Green Bay guard Jerry Kramer—who teamed with center Ken Bowman in the 1967 Ice Bowl to throw the most famous block in NFL history—and several Hall of Famers to start Gridiron Greats, a fundraising effort to benefit former players who were disabled and couldn't receive help from the NFL's Retirement Board.

In 2007, the NFL and NFLPA (NFL Players Association) took steps to enhance its retirement system by creating a $7 million fund to offer free joint-replacement surgery to uninsured ex-players. They also started the "88 Plan." Named after former Colts great John Mackey, who wore No. 88 and has suffered from dementia in retirement, the plan provides for up to $88,000 per year for institutional care or up to $50,000 a year for in-home care for players suffering mental illness.

In that same year, Ditka sent a letter to each of the 32 team owners requesting a donation of $100,000 each to help the former players. He received two responses—one was a check for $10,000; the other for $5,000. Disgusted, Ditka sent both back.

"If we can't help them," Ditka said, "then nobody will."

The aging warriors continue to hurt. In many cases, their monthly pensions aren't enough to pay for an adequate amount of groceries, much less medical bills or physical or mental therapies. Green Bay Hall of Fame defensive back Herb Adderley played 12 years in the NFL and reportedly draws a pension of $126.85 per month. He's unable to pay off the surgery he needs from his years in the game. In stark contrast, a major league baseball player whose career spanned the same amount of time earns $6,000 per month. Adderley's former Packer teammate, Hall of Fame safety Willie Wood, is in an assisted-living facility. Without the financial aid of Ditka and others, Wood wouldn't be able to afford the necessary care.

"The thing that's been making my heart ache," Kramer said, "is some of my teammates and warriors are having a hard time."

Like Matte and many other former players, Ditka is angry with the lack of response and aid by current players who are making millions of dollars. The players of today's game, he said, are merely the keepers of the game. The warriors from the 1950s, '60s and '70s, he remarked, are the makers of the game.

"Some guys from our era are getting $200 a month from the pension," Gaubatz said. "If we had played in the 1980s, we'd be getting $3,000 a month. To me, it doesn't make sense. It's ridiculous."

He paused. "To make matters worse," he said, "we started the damn thing."

Indeed. Ewbank hailed the Jets triumph as a "new era in pro football." He was right. The Jets victory made certain that the Super Bowl would take its place alongside the World Series, Kentucky Derby, and Indianapolis 500 as premier sporting events. Today, the Super Bowl is not only America's greatest sports spectacular, it is a global event.

It all began in January 1969. Shula's remark that no one would ever forget Super Bowl III has proven prophetic. The game and its outcome remain vibrant and relevant for many reasons. It will forever be a classic American success story.

That much is guaranteed.

"Someone should write in big, bold headlines, 'This is America,'" Maynard said. "I think a lot of people who were underdogs in their lives looked at the Jets win in Super Bowl III and thought, 'If the Jets can do it, so can I.'"

Super Bowl III remains a mirror of its tumultuous time, a reflection of life at the close of a year that changed the world—1968. It is a reflection, as the Supremes sang in their Motown classic, of the way life used to be.

Acknowledgments

This book was 19 years in the making and could not have been completed without the help of many people.

First, I would like to thank my family. My wife, Michelle, and my daughters, Patty and Katie, have provided me with the love and support necessary to complete a project as sweeping as this one. I would also like to thank my mother, Roberta, who continues to be my source of inspiration. She and my late father, John Gruver, always encouraged my late brother, Michael, and my sisters, Kathy and Patrice, to have faith and believe in ourselves.

I would also like to thank my agent, John Monteleone, for his belief in this book, and Adam Motin, my editor at Triumph Books. Researching a project such as this takes untold hours, and I would like to thank Matt Blymier and Matt Pawlikowski for their help in that process.

My intentions in this book were to shed new light where possible on a multi-layered story that had been largely flattened over time into a one-dimensional tale. Through the years, Super Bowl III has come to be remembered as the "Joe Namath game," almost to the exclusion of so many others who helped make it the most important Super Bowl ever played and one of the two most important games—along with the 1958 NFL championship—in pro football history.

Namath himself has said that the New York Jets 16–7 upset of the heavily-favored Baltimore Colts on January 12, 1969, was not the work of one man but of many. "We didn't win on passing or running or defense," he said. "We beat 'em in every phase of the game."

The intent here was to credit not only Namath for his role in the Jets win, but also his teammates and coaching staff who made New York's 1968 championship season possible. I thank the members of the 1968 Jets who were gracious enough to spend their time with me, including their great head coach Weeb Ewbank, whom I had the opportunity to speak with on a number of occasions prior to his passing in 1998.

I also wish to thank former Jets radio announcer Merle Harmon. Growing up in north Jersey in the 1960s, my older brother Mike and I spent many Sunday afternoons in the fall shooting pool and listening to Merle Harmon and Sam DeLuca broadcast Jets games on WABC radio. When New York won Super Bowl III, WABC and the *New York Daily News* put out a record album titled "Super Jets" that was narrated by Harmon and included the radio calls highlighting the Jets super season. Mike purchased that album through the *Daily News* in 1969, and it still occupies a treasured place in my collection. Having the opportunity to speak with Mr. Harmon brought back fond memories of time spent with my brother.

It was my intention as well to help readers recall the greatness of the 1968 Baltimore Colts, a team that has either been forgotten or remembered only as mere bit players on the Super Bowl III stage. The '68 Colts were one of the dominant squads of their era, and they fielded a defense that has had few peers in NFL history. They were the first NFL team to win 15 games in a season, and their greatness can best be measured, perhaps, by the fact that if they weren't as highly regarded as they were, their loss to the Jets in Super Bowl III wouldn't rank as pro football's greatest upset. I thank the members of that unforgettable Colts team for their candor in recalling their era and in particular a 1968 campaign that middle linebacker Dennis Gaubatz aptly described as a "season of glory and a day of defeat."

The story of Super Bowl III is, in a very large sense, the story of the American Football League. It is the story of an underdog that triumphs against all odds. Three men who proved instrumental in the history of the AFL—founder and Kansas City owner Lamar Hunt, San Diego Chargers coach Sid Gillman, and broadcaster Curt Gowdy—have passed, but their interviews when this project first began proved invaluable.

For their help, and for the help of everyone involved in this book, I express my thanks and gratitude.

Appendix

1968 New York Jets

Won 11 Lost 3, Finished First in AFL Eastern Division, Coach Weeb
Ewbank

Schedule and Statistics

Date	Opponent	Result	Score	Record
9/15	at Kansas City	W	20–19	1–0
9/22	vs. Boston (at Birmingham)	W	47–31	2–0
9/29	at Buffalo	L	35–37	2–1
10/5	SAN DIEGO	W	23–20	3–1
10/13	DENVER	L	13–20	3–2
10/20	at Houston	W	20–14	4–2
10/27	BOSTON	W	48–14	5–2
11/3	BUFFALO	W	25–21	6–2
11/10	HOUSTON	W	26–7	7–2
11/17	at Oakland	L	32–43	7–3
11/24	at San Diego	W	37–15	8–3
12/1	MIAMI	W	35–17	9–3
12/8	CINCINNATI	W	27–14	10–3
12/15	at Miami	W	31–7	11–3

(419–280)

Postseason

Date	Opponent	Result	Score	Record
12/29	OAKLAND	W	27–23	AFL Championship
1/12/69	vs. Baltimore (at Miami)	W	16–7	Super Bowl III

	Offense	Defense
Total Yards	5047	3363
First Downs	249	178
Passing	144	104
Rushing	80	59
By Penalty	25	15
Passing		
Completions	217	187
Attempts	436	409
Percentage	49.8	46.4
Net Yards	3439	2168
Net Yards/Attempt	7.6	4.9
Sacks/Yards Lost	18/135	43/399
Touchdowns	20	17
Interceptions	19	28
Rushing		
Attempts	467	368
Yards	1608	1195
Yards/Attempt	3.4	3.2
Touchdowns	22	9
Turnovers	28	43
Punt Returns		
Returns	36	39
Yards	286	531
Touchdowns	0	3
Yards/Return	7.9	13.6
Kickoff Returns		
Returns	46	82
Yards	995	1664
Touchdowns	0	0
Yards/Return	21.6	20.3

	Offense	Defense
Kicking		
FG Attempts	46	17
FG Made	34	9
FG Percentage	73.9	52.9
PAT	43	33
PAT Attempts	43	34
PAT Percentage	100.0	97.1
Punting		
Punts	68	98
Yardage	2977	3763
Yards Per Punt	43.8	38.5
Blocked	1	0

Individual Statistics

Rushing

	No.	Yds.	LG	Yds./Att.	TD
Snell	179	747	60	4.2	6
Boozer	143	441	33	3.1	5
Mathis	74	208	16	2.8	5
Joe	42	186	32	4.4	3
Sauer	2	21	15	10.5	0
Smolinski	12	15	5	0.9	0
Namath	5	11	4	2.2	2
Parilli	7	–2	10	–0.3	1
Johnson	2	–6	0	–3.0	0
Rademacher	1	–13	–13	–13	0

Passing

	Att.	Comp.	Pct.	Yds.	TD	Int.
Namath	380	187	49.2	3147	15	17
Parilli	55	29	52.7	401	5	2
Snell	1	1	100.0	26	0	0

Receiving

	No.	Yds.	LG	Yds./Rec.	TD
Sauer	66	1141	43	17.3	3
Maynard	57	1297	87	22.8	10
Lammons	32	400	27	12.5	3
Snell	16	105	39	6.6	1
Boozer	12	101	23	8.4	0
B. Turner	10	241	71	24.1	2
Mathis	9	149	31	16.6	1
Smolinski	6	40	19	6.7	0
Johnson	5	78	18	15.6	0
Rademacher	2	11	6	5.5	0
Joe	2	11	11	5.5	0

Interceptions

	No.	Yds.	LG	TD
Sample	7	88	39	1
Hudson	5	96	45	0
Beverly	4	127	68	1
Baird	4	74	36	0
Baker	3	31	20	0
Gordon	2	0	0	0
Atkinson	2	24	22	0
Christy	1	16	16	0

Punting

	No.	Yds.	Avg.	LG	Blk.
Johnson	68	2977	43.8	65	1

Punt Returns

	No.	Yds.	Yds./Ret.	LG	TD
Baird	18	111	6.2	20	0
Christy	13	116	8.9	39	0
Richards	4	27	14.3	37	0

Kickoff Returns

	No.	Yds.	Yds./Ret.	LG	TD
Christy	25	599	24.0	87	0
B. Turner	14	319	22.8	36	0
Snell	3	28	9.3	15	0
D'Amato	1	32	32.0	32	0
Smolinski	1	27	27.0	27	0
Neidert	1	0	0.0	0	0
Rademacher	1	0	0.0	0	0

Kicking

	FGA	FGM	PCT.	PAT ATT.	PAT	PCT.	Points
J. Turner	46	34	73.9	43	43	100.0	145

1968 Baltimore Colts

Won 13 Lost 1, Finished First in NFL Coastal Division, Coach Don Shula

Schedule and Statistics

Date	Opponent	Result	Score	Record
9/15	SAN FRANCISCO	W	27–10	1–0
9/22	at Atlanta	W	28–20	2–0
9/29	at Pittsburgh	W	41–7	3–0
10/6	CHICAGO	W	28–7	4–0
10/13	at San Francisco	W	42–14	5–0
10/20	CLEVELAND	L	20–30	5–1
10/27	LOS ANGELES	W	27–10	6–1
11/3	at New York	W	26–0	7–1
11/10	at Detroit	W	27–10	8–1
11/17	ST. LOUIS	W	27–0	9–1
11/24	MINNESOTA	W	21–9	10–1
12/1	ATLANTA	W	44–0	11–1
12/7	at Green Bay	W	16–3	12–1
12/15	at Los Angeles	W	28–24	13–1
			(402–144)	

Postseason

Date	Opponent	Result	Score	Record
12/22	MINNESOTA	W	24–14	Divisional Playoff
12/29	at Cleveland	W	34–0	NFL Championship
1/12/69	vs. New York Jets (at Miami)	L	7–16	Super Bowl III

	Offense	Defense
Total Yards	4681	3377
First Downs	258	207
Passing	131	119
Rushing	110	71
By Penalty	17	17
Passing		
Completions	196	224
Attempts	359	432
Percentage	54.6	51.9
Net Yards	2872	2038
Net Yards/Attempt	7.4	4.3
Sacks/Yards Lost	29/222	45/367
Touchdowns	28	9
Interceptions	22	29
Rushing		
Attempts	463	375
Yards	1809	1339
Yards/Attempt	3.9	3.6
Touchdowns	16	6
Turnovers	34	41
Punt Returns		
Returns	42	19
Yards	350	62
Touchdowns	0	0
Yards/Return	8.3	3.3
Kickoff Returns		
Returns	38	71
Yards	1003	1391
Touchdowns	2	0
Yards/Return	26.4	19.6

	Offense	Defense
Kicking		
FG Attempts	28	19
FG Made	18	11
FG Percentage	64.3	57.9
PAT	48	15
PAT Attempts	50	16
PAT Percentage	96.0	93.8
Punting		
Punts	49	78
Yardage	1935	3182
Yards Per Punt	39.5	40.8
Blocked	1	0

Individual Statistics

Rushing

	No.	**Yds.**	**LG**	**Yds./Att.**	**TD**
Matte	183	662	23	3.6	9
Cole	104	418	21	4.0	3
Hill	91	360	21	4.0	1
Brown	39	159	10	4.1	2
Mackey	10	103	33	10.3	0
Pearson	19	78	13	4.1	0
Morrall	11	18	11	1.6	1
Lee	3	12	21	4.0	0

Passing

	Att.	Comp.	Pct.	Yds.	TD	Int.
Morrall	317	182	57.4	2909	26	17
Unitas	32	11	34.4	139	2	4
Ward	3	9	33.3	46	0	1
Matte	1	0	0.0	0	0	0

Receiving

	No.	Yds.	LG	Yds./Rec.	TD
Mackey	45	644	45	14.3	5
Richardson	37	698	79	18.9	8
Orr	29	743	84	25.6	6
Matte	25	275	50	11.0	1
Hill	18	161	19	8.9	1
Perkins	15	227	29	15.1	1
Cole	13	75	18	5.8	0
Mitchell	6	117	41	19.5	4
Brown	4	53	18	13.3	0
Pearson	2	70	61	35.0	2

Interceptions

	No.	Yds.	LG	TD
Boyd	8	160	49	1
Volk	6	154	90	0
Lyles	5	32	11	0
Logan	3	9	9	0
Gaubatz	2	15	13	0
Curtis	2	38	38	1
Stukes	1	60	60	1
Hilton	1	13	13	1
Shinnick	1	2	2	0

Punting

	No.	Yds.	Avg.	LG	Blk.
Lee	49	1935	39.5	59	1

Punt Returns

	No.	Yds.	Yds./Ret.	LG	TD
Volk	25	198	7.9	24	0
Brown	16	125	7.8	25	0
Logan	1	27	27.0	27	0

Kickoff Returns

	No.	Yds.	Yds./Ret.	LG	TD
Pearson	15	527	35.1	102	2
Brown	15	298	19.9	29	0
Cole	5	123	24.6	34	0
Matte	1	22	22.0	22	0
Porter	1	19	19.0	19	0
Logan	1	14	14.0	14	0

Kicking

	FGA	FGM	PCT.	PAT ATT.	PAT	PCT.	Points
Michaels	28	18	64.3	50	48	96.0	102

Super Bowl III Play-by-Play
Orange Bowl

Miami, Florida

January 12, 1969

Attendance: 75,389

MVP: Joe Namath, QB, New York

New York won the coin toss and elected to receive.

FIRST QUARTER

New York (15:00)

Michaels kick 2 yards into end zone, Christy 25 return (Hawkins).

NY 23 1-10 Snell 3 run left tackle (Shinnick).

NY 26 2-7 Snell 9 run left tackle (Volk).

NY 35 1-10 Boozer run right end, loss of 4 (Shinnick).

NY 31 2-14 Namath 9 pass to Snell (Boyd).

NY 40 3-5 Snell draw middle, loss of 2 (Miller).

NY 38 4-7 Johnson 44 punt to B 18. Play nullified and Baltimore penalized 5 for offsides.

NY 43 4-2 Johnson 39 punt, Brown 9 return (McAdams).

Baltimore (10:55)

B 27 1-10 Morrall 19 pass to Mackey (Elliott).

B 46 1-10 Matte 10 sweep right (Baker).

NY 44 1-10 J. Hill 7 sweep left (Hudson).

NY 37 2-3 Matte 1 run left (Elliott).

NY 36 3-2 J. Hill 5 run right tackle (Baird).

NY 31 1-10 J. Hill run right, loss of 3 (Philbin).

NY 34 2-13 Morrall pass to Orr underthrown, incomplete.

NY 34 3-13 Morrall 15 pass to Mitchell (Baird).

NY 19 1-10 Morrall pass to Richardson dropped.

NY 19 2-10 Morrall pass to Mitchell overthrown, incomplete.

NY 19 3-10 Morrall run evading rush, no gain (Atkinson).

NY 19 4-10 Michaels's 27-yard field-goal attempt was wide right, no good.

New York (5:33)

NY 20 1-10 Namath pass to Snell dropped.

NY 20 2-10 Namath 2 pass to Lammons (Lyles).

NY 22 3-8 Namath 13 pass to Mathis (Gaubatz).

NY 35 1-10 Namath pass to Maynard overthrown, incomplete.

NY 35 2-10 Namath 6 pass to Sauer (Lyles).

NY 41 3-4 Namath pass to Sauer overthrown, incomplete.

NY 41 4-4 Johnson 38 punt, Brown 21 return (Snell).

Baltimore (3:05)

B 42 1-10 Morrall pass to Mackey dropped, incomplete.

B 42 2-10 J. Hill 3 run middle (Elliott).

B 45 3-7 Morrall pass to Richardson broken up (Sample).

B 45 4-7 Lee 51 punt downed at NY 4.

New York (1:58)

NY 4 1-10 Snell 4 run right tackle (Shinnick).

NY 8 2-6 Snell 5 draw right (Gaubatz).

NY 13 3-1 Namath 3 pass to Sauer left (Lyles), fumbled, Porter recovered for Baltimore at NY 12.

Baltimore (:14)

NY 12 1-10 J. Hill run left tackle, loss of 1 (Philbin).

END OF FIRST QUARTER:
Baltimore 0, New York 0

SECOND QUARTER

NY 13 2-11 Matte 7 sweep left (Beverly).

NY 6 3-4 Morrall pass to Mitchell off his shoulder pad and intercepted in end zone, Beverly no return, touchback.

New York (14:09)

NY 20 1-10 Snell 1 run left tackle (Braase).

NY 21 2-9 Snell 7 run left tackle (Shinnick).

NY 28 3-2 Snell 6 run left end (Lyles).

NY 34 1-10 Snell 12 draw left end (Lyles).

NY 46 1-10 Namath pass to Sauer broken up (Shinnick), incomplete.

NY 46 2-10 Namath 6 pass to Mathis (Bubba Smith).

B 48 3-4 Namath 14 pass to Sauer (Lyles).

B 34 1-10 Namath 11 pass to Sauer (Volk).

B 23 1-10 Boozer 2 run right (Shinnick).

B 21 2-8 Namath 12 pass to Snell (Gaubatz).

B 9 1-goal Snell 5 run right tackle (B.R. Smith).

B 4 2-goal Snell 4 run over left tackle, touchdown (9:03). J. Turner kicked extra point.

New York scoring drive: 80 yards, 12 plays, 5:06.

New York 7, Baltimore 0

Baltimore (9:03)

Johnson kick to B 2, Pearson 26 return (Richards).

B 28 1-10 Morrall pass to Richardson overthrown, incomplete.

B 28 2-10 Morrall 30 pass to Matte (Hudson).

NY 42 1-10 J. Hill 4 run right tackle (Atkinson).

NY 38 2-6 Matte run right, no gain (Biggs).

NY 38 3-6 Morrall pass to Mackey broken up (Sample), incomplete.

NY 38 4-6 Michaels's 46-yard field-goal attempt was no good.

New York (6:37)

NY 20 1-10 Boozer 1 run right (Logan).

NY 21 2-9 Namath 35 pass to Sauer (Lyles).

B 44 1-10 Snell 9 run left (Gaubatz).

B 35 2-1 Snell 3 run middle (Shinnick).

B 32 1-10 Namath pass to Maynard overthrown, incomplete.

B 32 2-10 Namath pass to B. Turner underthrown, incomplete.

B 32 3-10 Namath sacked, loss of 2 (Gaubatz).

B 34 4-12 J. Turner's 41-yard field-goal attempt was no good.

Baltimore (4:13)

B 20 1-10 Morrall 6 pass to Richardson (Sample).

B 26 2-4 Matte 58 run around right end (Baird).

NY 16 1-10 J. Hill 1 run left tackle (Atkinson, Hudson).

NY 15 2-9 Morrall pass to Richardson intercepted at NY 2, Sample no return. Two-Minute Warning.

New York (2:00)

NY 2 1-10 Snell 2 run left (Shinnick).

NY 4 2-8 Snell 3 run left tackle (Miller).

NY 7 3-5 Snell draw left, no gain (Bubba Smith).

NY 7 4-5 Johnson 32 punt, Brown fair catch. Play nullified by off-setting penalties, illegal procedure against New York and roughing the kicker against Baltimore.

NY 7 4-5 Johnson 39 punt, Brown 4 return (Neidert).

Baltimore (:43)

NY 42 1-10 Morrall 1 pass to J. Hill (Crane).

NY 41 2-9 Matte lateraled back to Morrall, Morrall pass to J. Hill middle intercepted at NY 12, Hudson 9 return to NY 21 as time expired.

END OF SECOND QUARTER:
New York 7, Baltimore 0

THIRD QUARTER

Johnson kick to goal line, Brown 25 return (Smolinski).

B 25 1-10 Matte 8 run, fumbled, Baker recovered for New York at B 33.

New York (14:25)

B 33 1-10 Boozer 8 run left (Volk).

B 25 2-2 Snell 4 run right (Bubba Smith).

B 21 1-10 Boozer 2 run left (Curtis).

B 19 2-8 Namath 5 pass to Snell (Curtis).

B 14 3-3 Snell 3 run right (Gaubatz).

B 11 1-10 Boozer run left end, loss of 5 (Lyles).

B 16 2-15 Namath sacked, loss of 9 (Bubba Smith).

B 25 3-24 Namath pass to Lammons broken up (Logan), incomplete.

B 25 4-24 J. Turner, 32-yard field goal (10:08).

New York scoring drive: 8 yards, 8 plays, 4:17.

New York 10, Baltimore 0.

Baltimore (10:08)

Johnson kick to B 5, Brown 21 return (D'Amato).

B 26 1-10 Morralll pass to Mackey overthrown, incomplete.

B 26 2-10 Morrall pass to J. Hill, no gain (Grantham).

B 26 3-10 Morrall run evading rush, loss of 2 (McAdams).

B 24 4-12 Lee 44 punt, Baird no return (S. Williams).

New York (8:04)

NY 32 1-10 Namath 1 pass to Mathis (Curtis).

NY 33 2-9 Namath 14 pass to Sauer (Volk).

NY 47 1-10 Namath pass to Maynard overthrown, incomplete.

NY 47 2-10 Boozer 4 run left (B.R. Smith).

B 49 3-6 Namath 11 pass to Lammons (Logan).

B 38 1-10 Namath pass to Maynard overthrown, incomplete.

B 38 2-10 Namath 14 pass to Snell (Curtis).

B 24 1-10 Mathis 1 draw middle (Shinnick).

B 23 2-9 Namath pass to Maynard incomplete. Namath hurt.

B 23 3-9 Parilli pass to Sauer underthrown, incomplete.

B 23 4-9 J. Turner, 30-yard field goal (3:58).

New York scoring drive: 45 yards, 10 plays, 4:06.

New York 13, Baltimore 0

Baltimore (3:58)

Johnson kick hit goal post, touchback.

B 20 1-10 Matte 5 sweep right (Baker).

B 25 2-5 Unitas pass to Matte, no gain (Grantham).

B 25 3-5 Unitas pass to Orr dropped, incomplete.

B 25 4-5 Lee 38 punt, Baird fair catch.

New York (2:24)

NY 37 1-10 Snell 3 run left (B.R. Smith).

NY 40 2-7 Namath pass to Sauer overthrown, incomplete.

NY 40 3-7 Namath 11 pass to Sauer (Lyles).

B 49 1-10 Namath 39 pass to Sauer (Lyles).

B 10 1-goal Snell 4 run right tackle (Gaubatz).

END OF THIRD QUARTER:
New York 13, Baltimore 0

FOURTH QUARTER

B 6 2-goal Snell 3 run left tackle. Play nullified and Baltimore penalized 3 (half the distance) for offsides.

B 3 2-goal Snell run left, no gain (Volk).

B 3 3-goal Mathis 1 run left (Gaubatz).

B 2 4-goal J. Turner, 9-yard field goal (13:26).

New York scoring drive: 61 yards, 7 plays, 3:58.

New York 16, Baltimore 0

Baltimore (13:26)

Johnson kick 6 yards into end zone, Pearson 33 return (Richards).

B 27 1-10 Unitas 5 pass to Mackey (Grantham).

B 32 2-5 Matte 7 sweep right (Baker).

B 39 1-10 Unitas 5 pass to Richardson (Sample).

B 44 2-5 Matte 19 run left (Hudson).

NY 37 1-10 J. Hill 12 run right tackle (Baird).

NY 25 1-10 Unitas pass to Richardson overthrown, incomplete.

NY 25 2-10 Unitas pass to Orr deep intercepted in end zone, Beverly no return, touchback.

New York (11:06)

NY 20 1-10 Boozer 2 draw middle (Miller).

NY 22 2-8 Snell 2 run left (Porter).

NY 24 3-6 Boozer 7 sweep left (Gaubatz).

NY 31 1-10 Snell 10 run left (Curtis). Baltimore penalized 15 for personal foul.

B 44 1-10 Snell 7 run middle (Bubba Smith).

B 37 2-3 Boozer 2 run right tackle (B.R. Smith).

B 35 3-1 Mathis run left tackle, no gain (Michaels).

B 35 4-1 J. Turner's 42-yard field-goal attempt was no good.

Baltimore (6:34)

B 20 1-10 Unitas pass to Mackey broken up (Grantham), incomplete.

B 20 2-10 Unitas pass to Richardson overthrown, incomplete.

B 20 3-10 Unitas pass to Mackey overthrown, incomplete.

B 20 4-10 Unitas 17 pass to Orr (Beverly).

B 37 1-10 Unitas pass to Richardson overthrown, incomplete.

B 37 2-10 Unitas pass to J. Hill underthrown, incomplete.

B 37 3-10 Unitas 11 pass to Mackey (Baird). New York penalized 15 for personal foul.

NY 37 1-10 Matte 1 run left (Biggs).

NY 36 2-9 Unitas 21 pass to Richardson (Sample).

NY 15 1-10 Unitas pass to Matte overthrown, incomplete.

NY 15 2-10 Unitas 11 pass to Orr (Beverly).

NY 4 1-goal NY penalized 2 (half the distance) for offsides.

NY 2 1-goal Matte run left, no gain. Play nullified and New York penalized 1 (half the distance) for offsides.

NY 1 1-goal Unitas keeper middle, no gain (Biggs).

NY 1 2-goal Matte run right, no gain (Atkinson).

NY 1 3-goal Hill 1 run over left tackle, touchdown (3:19). Michaels kicked extra point.

Baltimore scoring drive: 80 yards, 14 plays, 3:15.

New York 16, Baltimore 7

New York (3:19)

Michaels onside kick, Mitchell recovered for Baltimore at NY 44.

Baltimore (3:14)

NY 44 1-10 Unitas 6 pass to Richardson (Sample).

NY 38 2-4 Unitas 14 pass to Orr (Beverly).

NY 24 1-10 Unitas 5 pass to Richarson (out of bounds).

NY 19 2-5 Unitas pass to Richardson broken up (Sample), incomplete.

NY 19 3-5 Unitas pass to Orr underthrown, incomplete.

NY 19 4-5 Unitas pass to Orr overthrown, incomplete.

New York (2:21)

NY 20 1-10 Snell 1 run right (Bubba Smith). Baltimore-first time out.

NY 21 2-9 Snell 6 run right (Logan). Two-Minute Warning.

NY 27 3-3 Snell 4 run right (Gaubatz). Baltimore-second time out (1:54).

NY 31 1-10 Snell 2 run right tackle (Boyd).

NY 33 2-8 New York penalized 5 for delay of game.

NY 28 2-13 Snell 1 run right (B.R. Smith).

NY 29 3-12 New York penalized 5 for delay of game.

NY 24 3-17 Snell 3 sweep left (Austin). Baltimore-third time out (:15)

NY 27 4-14 Johnson 39 punt, Brown no return, out of bounds.

Baltimore (:08)

B 34 1-10 Unitas pass to Richardson incomplete.

B 34 2-10 Unitas 15 pass to Richardson (Sample).

FINAL SCORE:
New York 16, Baltimore 7

FINAL RECORDS:
New York 13-3, Baltimore 15-2

Super Bowl III Box Score

New York (AFL)	0	7	6	3	-16
Baltimore (NFL)	0	0	0	7	-7

NYJ- Snell 4 run (J. Turner kick)	5:57	2nd
NYJ- FG J. Turner 32	4:52	3rd
NYJ- FG J. Turner 30	11:02	3rd
NYJ- FG J. Turner 9	1:34	4th
BAL- Hill 1 run (Michaels kick)	11:41	4th

TEAM STATISTICS

	NYJ	Baltimore
Total First Downs	21	18
Rushing	10	7
Passing	10	9
Penalty	1	2
Total Net Yardage	337	324
Total Offensive Plays	74	64
Average Gain per Offensive Play	4.6	5.1
Rushes	43	23
Yards Gained Rushing (Net)	142	143
Average Yards per Rush	3.3	6.2
Passes Attempted	29	41
Passes Completed	17	17
Had Intercepted	0	4
Tackled Attempting to Pass	2	0
Yards Lost Attempting to Pass	11	0
Yards Gained Passing (Net)	195	181
Punts	4	3
Average Distance	38.8	44.3

	NYJ	**Baltimore**
Punt Returns	1	4
Punt Return Yardage	0	34
Kickoff Returns	1	4
Kickoff Return Yardage	25	105
Interception Return Yardage	9	0
Fumbles	1	1
Own Fumbles Recovered	0	0
Opponent Fumbles Recovered	1	1
Penalties	5	3
Yards Penalized	28	23
Total Points Scored	16	7
Touchdowns	1	1
Rushing	1	1
Passing	0	0
Returns	0	0
Extra Points	1	1
Field Goals	3	0
Field Goals Attempted	5	2
Safeties	0	0
Third-Down Efficiency	8/18	4/12
Fourth-Down Efficiency	0/0	1/2
Time of Possession	36:10	23:50

INDIVIDUAL STATISTICS

Rushing

New York (AFL)	No.	Yds.	LG	TD
Snell	30	121	12	1
Boozer	10	19	8	0
Mathis	3	2	1	0

Baltimore (NFL)	No.	Yds.	LG	TD
Matte	11	116	58	0
Hill	9	29	12	1
Unitas	1	0	0	0
Morrall	2	-2	0	0

Passing

New York (AFL)	Att.	Comp.	Yds.	TD	Int.
Namath	28	17	206	0	0
Parilli	1	0	0	0	0

Baltimore (NFL)	Att.	Comp.	Yds.	TD	Int.
Unitas	24	11	110	0	1
Morrall	17	6	71	0	3

Receiving

New York (AFL)	No.	Yds.	LG	TD
Sauer	8	133	39	0
Snell	4	40	14	0
Mathis	3	20	13	0
Lammons	2	13	11	0

Baltimore (NFL)	No.	Yds.	L	TD
Richardson	6	58	21	0
Orr	3	42	17	0
Mackey	3	35	19	0
Matte	2	30	30	0
Hill	2	1	1	0
Mitchell	1	15	15	0

Interceptions

New York (AFL)	No.	Yds.	LG	TD
Beverly	2	0	0	0
Hudson	1	9	9	0
Sample	1	0	0	0

Baltimore (NFL)	No.	Yds.	LG	TD
None	~	~	~	~

Punting

New York (AFL)	No.	Avg.	LG	Blk.
Johnson	4	38.8	39	0

Baltimore (NFL)	No.	Avg.	LG	Blk.
Lee	3	44.3	51	0

Punt Returns

New York (AFL)	No.	FC	Yds.	LG	TD
Baird	1	1	0	0	0

Baltimore (NFL)	No.	FC	Yds.	LG	TD
Brown	4	0	34	21	0

Kickoff Returns

New York (AFL)	No.	Yds.	LG	TD
Christy	1	25	25	0

Baltimore (NFL)	No.	Yds.	LG	TD
Pearson	2	59	33	0
Brown	2	46	25	0

New York Jets		Baltimore Colts	
Offense			
Schmitt, John	C	Curry, Bill	C
Rasmussen, Randy	G	Ressler, Glenn	G
Talamini, Bob	G	Sullivan, Dan	G
Herman, Dave	T	Ball, Sam	T
Hill, Winston	T	Vogel, Bob	T
Lammons, Pete	TE	Mackey, John	TE
Maynard, Don	WR	Orr, Jimmy	WR
Sauer, George Jr.	WR	Richardson, Willie	WR
Boozer, Emerson	RB	Hill, Jerry	RB
Snell, Matt	RB	Matte, Tom	RB
Namath, Joe	QB	Morrall, Earl	QB
Defense			
Elliott, D. John	DT	Miller, Fred D.	DT
Rochester, Paul	DT	Smith, Billy Ray Sr.	DT

New York Jets		Baltimore Colts	
Biggs, Verlon	DE	Braase, Ordell	DE
Philbin, Gerry	DE	Smith, Bubba	DE
Baker, Ralph	OLB	Curtis, Mike	OLB
Grantham, Larry	OLB	Shinnick, Don	OLB
Atkinson, Al	MLB	Gaubatz, Dennis	MLB
Beverly, Randy	CB	Boyd, Bobby	CB
Sample, Johnny	CB	Lyles, Lenny	CB
Baird, Bill	FS	Volk, Rick	FS
Hudson, Jim	SS	Logan, Jerry	SS

Substitute

Christy, Earl	Austin, Ocie
Crane, Paul	Brown, Timmy
D'Amato, Mike	Cole, Terry
Dockery, John	Hawkins, Alex
Gordon, Cornell	Hilton, Roy
Johnson, Curley	Johnson, Cornelius
Mathis, Bill	Lee, David
McAdams, Carl	Michaels, Lou
Neidert, John	Mitchell, Tom
Parilli, Babe	Pearson, Preston
Rademacher, Bill	Perkins, Ray
Richards, Jim	Porter, Ron
Richardson, Jeff	Stukes, Charles
Smolinski, Mark	Szymanski, Dick
Thompson, Stephen	Unitas, Johnny
Turner, Jim B.	Williams, John M.
Turner, Bake	Williams, Sidney
Walton, Sam	

Did Not Play

Ward, Jim

Index